Magic

Genre Fiction and Film Companions

Series Editor: Simon Bacon

MAGIC

A Companion

Edited by Katharina Rein

PETER LANG

Oxford • Bern • Berlin • Bruxelles • New York • Wien

Bibliographic information published by Die Deutsche Nationalbibliothek. Die Deutsche Nationalbibliothek lists this publication in the Deutsche Nationalbibliografie; detailed bibliographic data is available on the Internet at http://dnb.d-nb.de.

A catalogue record for this book is available from the British Library.

Library of Congress Cataloging-in-Publication Data

Names: Rein, Katharina, 1986– editor.
Title: Magic : a companion / Katharina Rein.
Description: Oxford ; New York : Peter Lang, [2022] | Series: Genre fiction and film companions ; vol. 9 | Includes bibliographical references and index.
Identifiers: LCCN 2021016746 (print) | LCCN 2021016747 (ebook) | ISBN 9781800793255 (paperback) | ISBN 9781800793262 (ebook) | ISBN 9781800793279 (epub)
Subjects: LCSH: Magic in literature. | Magic in motion pictures.
Classification: LCC PN56.M23 M34 2022 (print) | LCC PN56.M23 (ebook) | DDC 791.43/677—dc23
LC record available at https://lccn.loc.gov/2021016746
LC ebook record available at https://lccn.loc.gov/2021016747

Cover photograph by Philipp Rein

Cover design by Brian Melville for Peter Lang.

ISSN 2631-8725
ISBN 978-1-80079-325-5 (print)
ISBN 978-1-80079-326-2 (ePDF)
ISBN 978-1-80079-327-9 (ePUB)

© Peter Lang Group AG 2022
Published by Peter Lang Ltd, International Academic Publishers,
Oxford, United Kingdom
oxford@peterlang.com, www.peterlang.com

This publication has been peer reviewed.

Contents

Roger Luckhurst

Foreword
Magical Thinking/Thinking the Magical

The shadow of developmental thought hangs heavy over the field (or fields?) of magic. Magical thinking was something to eliminate, a survival of an earlier, primitive mode of thought to Edward Tylor, Oxford University's first anthropologist, in his *Primitive Culture* (1871). In nineteenth-century developmental thought ontogeny recapitulates phylogeny; that is, the individual restages the passage of the species from earliest to latest, from simple to complex and so from primitive magical to modern rational thought. This idea underpins everything from J. G. Frazer's *The Golden Bough* (1890–1902), that vast synthesis of the place of magic in primitive culture, to Sigmund Freud's new-fangled psychoanalysis, where the child's fantasy of omnipotence and control over the world is a form of magical thinking to which the rational adult might fall back at any moment. In 'The Uncanny' Freud wrote: 'All supposedly educated people have ceased to believe that the dead can become visible as spirits', yet it took only one uncanny moment to slide back aeons and find 'almost all of us think as savages do on this topic'.[1]

The developmental disparagement of magic continues long into the twentieth century. It haunts Weber's disenchantment thesis in 'Science as a Vocation'. It is critical to Jean Piaget's model in *The Child's Conception of the World* (1929), which sees magical misconceptions of cause and effect universally ironed out by the age of 9 or 10, leaving belief in magic as intrinsically childish. Some of Theodor Adorno's funniest explosions of bad-temper are about 'the metaphysic of dunces' he ascribes for all modes of occult theory and practice.[2] The logic

1 Sigmund Freud, 'The Uncanny', Penguin Freud Library 14 (Harmondsworth: Penguin, 1985), 335–76, 365.
2 Theodor Adorno, 'Theses against Occultism', in *Minima Moralia: Reflections on a Damaged Life* (London: Verso, 2005), 238–44, 241.

of ideological demystification in this mode of Marxian critique shares much with the spirit of Weber's *Entzauberung der Welt,* which Thibaut Rioult early on in this books suggests is best translated as 'the demagification of the world'. Modernity is meant to steadily erase magical thinking, and academia has long aligned with this project.

One of the pleasures of this collection is the ambition to reassess the compacted negative associations of magical thinking, and instead reanimate different ways of apprehending magic: to rethink the magical. This is done with gloriously eclectic verve in chapters that move fast from Byzantine amulets to Indian rope tricks, the Harry Potter franchise, Thai cinema, or the memoirs of Robert-Houdin. Katharina Rein's collection is thus part of a wider project to interrogate the limits of the disenchantment thesis to explore instead a more complex rhythm in modernity where disenchantment is always accompanied by a symbiotic counter-effect of *re*-enchantment. Sources here might range from Charles Taylor's interrogation of secularization in his magnum opus, *A Secular Age* to Alex Owen's resituating of occult thought not as a retreat or evasion of modernity, but as thoroughly entangled with it in her *Place of Enchantment*.[3] This has been central to cultural and literary scholars such as Marina Warner, from her *Inner Eye* catalogue to her recent works, *Stranger Magic* and *Forms of Enchantment*, or the work of Gauri Viswanathan or Joshua Landy and Michael Saler.[4] And an equivalent body of work has come out of the academic network The European Society for the Study of Western Esotericism, which emerges from the study of the occult and hermetic traditions, syncretic theology and New Religious Movements.[5] The attempt to rethink the revival

---

3   Charles Taylor, *A Secular Age* (Boston, MA: Harvard University Press, 2007); Alex Owen, *The Place of Enchantment: British Occultism and the Culture of the Modern* (Chicago: Chicago University Press, 2007).

4   Marina Warner, *The Inner Eye: Art Beyond the Visible* (London: Hayward Gallery, 1999), *Stranger Magic: Charmed States and the* Arabian Nights (London: Chatto, 2011) and *Forms of Enchantment: Writings on Art and Artists* (London: Thames and Hudson, 2018). For Gauri Viswanthan, see her essay 'In Search of Madame Blavatsky: Reading the Exoteric, Retrieving the Esoteric', *Representations* 141 (2018), 67–94. Joshua Landy, and Michael Saler, *The Re-Enchantment of the World: Secular Magic in a Rational Age* (Stanford, CA: Stanford University Press, 2009).

5   See, for instance, the work of one of the central figures of this network, Wouter J. Hanegraaf, *Esotericism and the Academy: Rejected Knowledge in Western Culture*

of the supernatural and the occult in the nineteenth century has long abandoned the urge to decode or demystify spiritualism or psychical research as
the result of mistake, illusion or self-delusion and instead to explore them in
more sympathetic frameworks derived from the history of science, whether
as 'fringe sciences', or (in Michel Foucault's term) 'subjugated knowledges'
that have been edged out of orthodoxy but still have historical value in evi-
dencing the modalities by which institutional discourses police legitimacy.
The work of Pamela Thurschwell or Christine Ferguson or Richard Noakes
are exemplary here.[6]

In the same vein, the history of technology or media archaeology has taken
its steer from Arthur C. Clarke's famous 'Third Law' that 'any sufficiently advanced technology is indistinguishable from magic'.[7] In the early years of the
Second Industrial Revolution, the electronic one, nineteenth-century men of
science and engineers produced a stream of seemingly magical devices that
collapsed space and time. They were intrinsically intertwined with magical
thinking, not just in popular wonderment, but by the engineers themselves.
One of the earliest spiritualist newspapers was called the *Spiritual Telegraph*;
Alexander Graham Bell's assistant Thomas Watson, who received the first
telephone call, was also a psychic medium, who listened to the crackles on the
line for messages from the dead; the gramophone was built to capture and
preserve the voice after death; the eminent physicist Oliver Lodge detected
invisible 'ethereal' waves (soon after named for Heinrich Hertz) in the midst
of experiments to determine the physics underpinning telepathy, making radio
waves intrinsically uncanny. A host of studies over the last twenty years have
examined 'haunted media', and both Simon During and Simone Natale have

---

(Cambridge: Cambridge University Press, 2012) or Jeffrey Kripal, *Authors of the
Impossible: The Paranormal and the Sacred* (Chicago: Chicago University Press, 2010).

6   Pamela Thurschwell, *Literature, Technology and Magical Thinking 1880–1920*
(Cambridge: Cambridge University Press, 2001); Christine Ferguson, *Determined
Spirits: Eugenics, Heredity and Racial Regeneration in Anglo-American Spiritualist
Writing 1848–1930* (Edinburgh: Edinburgh University Press, 2012); Richard
Noakes, *Physics and Psychics: The Occult and the Sciences in Modern Britain*
(Cambridge: Cambridge University Press, 2019).

7   Arthur C. Clarke, *Profiles of the Future: An Inquiry into the Limits of the Possible*
(London: Gollancz, 1974), 39.

sought to explicate the media technologies intertwined with the golden age of performance magic in the late nineteenth and early twentieth century.[8]

There is also a lot of recent work on the pan-European modernist movement and its entanglements with the occult. Christopher Partridge's two-volume study, *The Re-Enchantment of the West* has brought this almost up to date.[9] Partridge introduced the expansive concept of 'occulture' to attest to the blurring of many cultural arenas in this hybrid and multi-disciplinary field.

It's also important to acknowledge that psychologists have explicitly tackled the negative conceptualization of magical thinking as a mode solely of cognitive error. In several studies at the turn of the millennium, magical thinking was reconceived more sympathetically as a potentially highly adaptive mode, a useful cognitive frame that can order the world meaningfully in times of change or stress. Freud and Piaget's developmental models were displaced here for much more complex and nuanced conceptions.[10]

8   See, for instance, Jeffrey Sconce, *Haunted Media: Electronic Presence from Telegraphy to Television* (Durham, NC, London: Duke University Press, 2000). Friedrich Kittler's formulations on 'Discourse Network 1900' also imbricated electronic technologies with magical and occult thinking, in *Gramophone Film Typewriter*, trans. Geoffrey Winthrop-Young and Michael Wutz (Stanford, CA: Stanford University Press, 1999). See also Simon During, *Modern Enchantments: The Cultural Power of Secular Magic* (Cambridge, MA: Harvard University Press, 2004) and Simone Natale, *Supernatural Entertainments: Victorian Spiritualism and the Rise of Modern Media Culture* (Philadelphia, PA: Penn State University Press, 2016).

9   See, for instance, James Mansell, Sarah V. Turner, and Christopher Scheer, eds, *Enchanted Modernities: Theosophy, The Arts and the American West* (Lopen: Fulgur Press, 2019) or John Bramble, *Modernism and the Occult* (Basingstoke: Palgrave, 2015). Christopher Partridge, *The Re-Enchantment of the West*, 2 vols (London: Continuum, 2004).

10   See, for instance, Carol Nemeroff, and Paul Rozin, 'The Makings of the Magical Mind: The Nature and Function of Sympathetic Magical Thinking', in Karl S. Rosengen, Carl N. Johnson, and Paul L. Harris, eds, *Imagining the Impossible: Magical, Scientific and Religious Thinking in Children* (Cambridge: Cambridge University Press, 2000), 1–34 or Goira Keinan, 'Magical Thinking as a Way of Coping with Stress', in Rebecca Jacoby and Giora Keinan, eds, *Between Stress and Hope: From a Disease-Centred to a Health-Centred Perspective* (Westport, CT: Praegar, 2003), 123–38. I have explored these psychological models at more length in my essay, 'Reflections on Joan Didion's *The Year of Magical Thinking*', *New Formations* 67 (2009), 91–100.

I want to evoke these ever-widening frameworks, multiplying far beyond my merely indicative footnotes, to situate the work undertaken by this collection. Rethinking the magical requires not only an expansive conception of 'magic' in the supernatural or secular senses invoked by Simon During, but also a dynamic grasp of interlocking fields of study, from philosophy, psychology and theology to film and performance studies to literary and cultural history. 'Magic', as Jessica Gossling says in her essay here on Arthur Machen, 'is a liminal practice', and it requires hovering on the edges of many magic circles.

However, being on the scuffed edge of a magic circle, as any apprentice magus or mere consumer of modern horror films could tell you, is not always the safest place to be. Demonic forces swirl there. I think it is quite right to insist that the blurred space of magic in modernity falls into the curious realm of *disavowal* – that conflicted position that both knows magic is trick or illusion yet harbours that hesitancy in which a little voice whispers ... *but what if, all the same, it was true*? Disavowal explains how we can believe and disbelieve simultaneously, that 'half-belief' invoked by the sociologist Colin Campbell.[11] This allows a form of enchantment to survive within a routinized and disenchanted world; indeed, it allows us to explain how a fervent desire of dogged materialists to stamp on superstition or religious belief as 'false' actively *produces* whole cultures of belief in a symbiotic counter-reaction and imbues them with the glamour of refusal or resistance.

In the recent Wellcome Trust exhibition in London, *The Spectacle of Illusion,* the thrust was to expose the psychological conditions that create 'magical' (mis)perceptions, but there was also a sympathetic understanding of the power of illusion that holds us enchanted nevertheless.[12] To navigate these tricky tides requires sophisticated models for rethinking the magical that neither debunk with a cruel materialist pleasure nor effectively erase the distinction between true and false in the rush to gloss subjugated knowledge as inherently subversive. Both tactics seem important to avoid in the twenty-first century, where magical thinking is at its most intense in political conspiracy theories fostered by new digital technologies that see occulted forces everywhere,

11   Colin Campbell, 'Half-Belief and the Paradox of Ritual Instrumental Activism: A Theory of Modern Superstition', *British Journal of Sociology* 47/1 (1996), 151–66.

12   The catalogue for the exhibition is Matthew L. Tompkins, *The Spectacle of Illusion: Magic, the Paranormal and the Complicity of the Mind* (London: Thames and Hudson, 2019).

conjure up Satanic enemies, render all systems of thought equivalent and do their damnedest to undercut rational democratic discourse. Re-thinking the magical does not have to contribute to this collapse. Instead, as the contributions to this collection display across a bewildering array of cultural locations suggest, there are many productive ways to unpick the knot that continues to bind modernity and magic together.

Katharina Rein

Introduction

For the longest time, magic has been devalued as both a belief and an art form. 'In the pantheon of pursuits', Lawrence Hass writes, 'magic would seem to rank somewhere between mime and balloon folding. The very mention of magic brings to mind cute tricks, birthday parties for little kids, and Uncle Bob with his cards.'[1] In the last two decades, however, conjuring, magic and witchcraft have been persistently invading popular culture and gaining academic attention.

Not least inspired by J. K. Rowling's extremely successful *Harry Potter* series (1997–2007, film adaptations 2001–11), magic and magicians have been appearing increasingly in cultural artefacts from Hollywood blockbusters to TV series, literature, games and the arts over the last two decades. Lev Grossman's *The Magicians* (2009–14, adapted for television in 2015–20) equally addresses an audience of young adults. In 2006, two Hollywood blockbusters released within a short time of one another focused on stage magic around 1900. Christopher Nolan's *The Prestige*, based on Christopher Priest's novel of the same title and starring Christian Bale and Hugh Jackman; and Neil Burger's *The Illusionist*, loosely based on a short story by Steven Millhauser, with Edward Norton playing the eponymous magician. Like these two films, the BBC's adaptation (2015) of Susanna Clarke's award-winning novel *Jonathan Strange & Mr. Norrell* (2004) as a miniseries, starring Bertie Carvel and Eddie Marsan in the title roles, also presented a blend of period piece and fantasy, unfolding around (male) magicians. Further, several shows and films were dedicated to the most famous magician of the early twentieth century: from the biopic *Death Defying Acts* (2007),

---

1   Lawrence Hass, 'Life Magic and Staged Magic. A Hidden Intertwining', in Francesca Coppa, Lawrence Hass, and James Peck, eds, *Performing Magic on the Western Stage. From the Eighteenth Century to the Present* (New York: Palgrave Macmillan, 2008), 13–31, 14.

starring Guy Pearce and Catherine Zeta-Jones, to the biographical miniseries *Houdini* (2014) in which the eponymous escapist is played by Adrien Brody, to the entirely fictitious miniseries *Houdini & Doyle* (2016) which shows the pair as hobby detectives solving crimes bordering the supernatural in London. More recently than the aforementioned blockbusters, three films were released that centred on performance magic: *Oz the Great and Powerful* (2013), a prequel to *The Wizard of Oz* (1939), in which James Franco plays a young magician who becomes 'the wizard'. In *Now You See Me* (2013) which was followed by a sequel three years later, an impressive cast, including Michael Caine, Morgan Freeman, Isla Fisher, Woody Harrelson, Jesse Eisenberg and others, plays characters involved in producing, keeping and attempting to solve magical secrets. An adaptation of David Fisher's *The War Magician* (1983), a novel based on Jasper Maskelyne's autobiography, in which he describes his illusionistic services for the War Office during the Second World War, is currently scheduled for a 2022 release, with Benedict Cumberbatch in the leading role. These examples attest to the demand for magic-related topics in popular culture. They represent, however, merely a small portion of magic-related films and television series of the last two decades. The list would grow exorbitantly if we looked beyond performance magic and included topics such as ritual magic, occultism or witchcraft – not to mention other art forms and media.

Historically, the Western philosophical tradition has conceived of magic as being in opposition to the search of truth and to enlightenment: Plato, Heidegger, Nietzsche, Hegel and Marx considered magic a dangerous deception, which barred the way of understanding. Among the performing arts, especially performance magic has been under-researched for a long time, being associated with children's birthday parties and deemed 'beyond the pale of academic attention and serious consideration'.[2] Slowly but steadily, however, it has recently made its way into the visual field of scholars and became the topic of a number of research projects. For instance, since 2013, the Magic Research Group, founded by Nik Taylor, has been publishing the annual *Journal of Performance Magic*, and from 2015 to 2018, the francophone, international research project *Les Arts Trompeurs. Machines, Magie, Médias*, directed by Giusy Pisano and Jean-Marc Larrue, brought together interdisciplinary researchers,

---

2   Ibid.

artists and curators who work in or on magic and illusionism. The long-forgotten performance magic has received academic attention by scholars from various disciplines: most publications were penned by film scholars such as Tom Gunning, Matthew Solomon, Dan North or Colin Williamson.[3] James Cook's *The Arts of Deception*[4] contextualizes modern performance magic within an illusionistic nineteenth-century entertainment culture that also encompasses Wolfgang von Kempelen's chess playing pseudo-automaton (respectively its re-emergence facilitated by Johann Nepomuk Maelzel) and that was greatly influenced by P. T. Barnum and his economic exploitation of so-called 'freaks' and 'monsters'. Other studies explore modern conjuring's connection to and interrelation with early cinema, the sciences[5] or related entertainments such as the phantasmagoria and optical illusions[6] or modern spiritualism.[7]

3   See, for instance, Tom Gunning, 'An Aesthetic of Astonishment: Early Film and the (In)Credulous Spectator', in Linda Williams, ed., *Viewing Positions: Ways of Seeing Film* (New Brunswick, NJ: Rutgers University Press, 1995), 114–33; Rachel O. Moore, *Savage Theory: Cinema as Modern Magic* (Durham, NC: Duke University Press, 2000); Dan North, *Performing Illusions: Cinema, Special Effects and the Virtual Actor* (London, New York: Wallflower Press, 2008); Matthew Solomon, *Disappearing Tricks: Silent Film, Houdini, and the New Magic of the Twentieth Century* (Urbana: University of Illinois Press, 2010); Colin Williamson, *Hidden in Plain Sight: An Archaeology of Magic and the Cinema* (New Brunswick, NJ: Rutgers University Press, 2015). See also Simone Natale, 'The Cinema of Exposure: Spiritualist Exposés, Technology and the Dispositif of Early Cinema', *Recherches Semiotiuse/Semiotic Inquiry* 31/1 (2011), 101–17.

4   James W. Cook, *The Arts of Deception: Playing with Fraud in the Age of Barnum* (Cambridge, MA: Harvard University Press, 2001).

5   See, for instance, Sofie Lachapelle, *Conjuring Science: A History of Scientific Entertainment and Stage Magic in Modern France* (New York: Palgrave Macmillan, 2015).

6   See, for instance, Laurent Mannoni's seminal book *The Great Art of Light and Shadow: Archaeology of the Cinema*, trans. Richard Crangle (Exeter, Devon: University of Exeter Press, 2000 [1995]).

7   On modern Spiritualism, see, for instance, Peter Lamont, *The First Psychic: The Peculiar Mystery of a Notorious Victorian Wizard* (London: Little, Brown, 2005); Peter Lamont, 'Magician as Conjuror: A Frame Analysis of Victorian Mediums', *Early Popular Visual Culture* 4/1 (2006), 21–33; Simone Natale, *Supernatural Entertainments: Victorian Spiritualism and the Rise of Modern Media Culture* (University Park: The Pennsylvania State University Press, 2016). See also Jeffrey Sconce's seminal *Haunted Media: Electronic Presence from Telegraphy to Television* (Durham, NC: Duke University Press, 2000) on the supernatural connotations of technical media.

Contributing to this emerging field of interest, this collection of essays aims to explore a variety of concepts in magic by providing a historical overview as well as investigating representations and translations across various media. It covers a broad selection of topics related to performance magic and beliefs in the supernatural such as witchcraft, folklore and spiritualism throughout history and today. Their sum provides an insight into the various guises of magic in past and present cultures. The chapters collected here explore representations of conjuring and magic in television, literature, the arts and in digital media. Particular attention is paid to non-Western artefacts and issues of gender, body and identity politics. Among the questions addressed are: does magic influence our perception of reality and subjectivity? In what ways do magic and its representations broach issues of different bodies, abilities, ethnicities and sexualities? How was magic construed as opposing reason, and is this distinction even tenable? How can magic be understood as producing new ways of viewing the world instead of as something blinding us to reality? How does it function as a political instrument for dominant cultures or minority groups? How do concepts and practices of magic change with enlightenment, industrialization and digitization, from the early modern period to modernity to the twenty-first century?

This book is divided into six parts. Each gathers essays by a particular interest in their topics that focus on different aspects or functions of magic. The first part covers examples of magic beliefs from the early Middle Ages to the twentieth century. As Immanuel Kant has already observed,[8] a curious trait of illusions is that they are neither ended nor diminished by the knowledge that we are faced with illusions. For this reason, magical thinking has not been replaced by rationalism and scientification. Psychoanalyst and anthropologist Octave Mannoni has famously summarized this kind of rationalized, modern magical thinking in his formula, 'I know well, but all the same …' ('je sais bien mais … quand même').[9] We may know well, on a rational level, that a piece of

---

8   Immanuel Kant, *Anthropology from a Pragmatic Point of View*, trans. Victor Lyle Dowdell, rev. and ed. Hans H. Rudnick (Carbondale: Southern Illinois University Press, 1996 [1796/1797]), 35–6.

9   Octave Mannoni, '"I Know Well, but All the Same …". Perversion and the Social Relation', trans. G. M. Goshgarian, in Molly Anne Rothenberg, Dennis A. Foster, and Slavoj Žižek, eds, *sic IV* (New York: Duke University Press, 2003), 68–92; respectively

metal does not change the course of our lives, but we may nevertheless carry a lucky charm or an amulet. Such tokens are discussed in the two chapters framing the first section of this volume: it opens with Antje Bosselmann-Ruickbie's examination of magical amulets in the Byzantine period. Analysing material evidence from the Christian Middle Ages, this chapter shows that during that time, while non-Christian beliefs were oppressed, people still turned to 'pagan' magic for protection. Byzantine folk magic often incorporated Christian elements, thus merging conflicting belief systems, for instance, when 'pagan' amulets were lettered with Christian inscriptions.

Alternative, 'pagan' religions existed alongside Christianity throughout the Middle Ages and the early modern period when followers of other beliefs were persecuted and punished. The witch-hunts reached a peak in Europe from about 1550 to 1650, following the Reformation and being heavily intertwined with the Counter-Reformation and the Thirty Years' War. In this time, in 1584, Reginald Scot published his authoritative *Discoverie of Witchcraft*, considered the first book on magic tricks in English. Thibaut Rioult demonstrates that it is much more than that: Scot's *Discoverie* is also a complex theological treatise, providing an insight into the multifaceted conceptualization of magic during the Renaissance. Rioult further argues that it casts a critical glance at Catholicism and Christian demonology, comes up with its own blend of natural philosophy and empiricism with Calvinism and is in fact a contribution to the 'demagification' of the Western world. The latter term is Rioult's suggestion for a translation of Max Weber's 'Entzauberung der Welt'. How effective this 'demagification' was is a question that runs through this volume like a thread – be it addressed explicitly or implicitly.

Through the centuries, magic has been transforming, adapting and updating itself, and re-emerging at different times in different contexts and in different shapes. A form of magic belief that persisted throughout and gained relevance in a secular, industrialized world at a time of crisis stands at the centre of the following chapter: Leo Ruickbie explores tokens of luck that were widely used during the First World War. Associations with luck have been attached to various objects, ranging from flowers and leaves to coins to

---

the French original: Octave Mannoni, 'Je sais bien, mais quand même ...', in *Clefs pour l'imaginaire ou l'autre scène* (Paris: Édition du Seuil, 1969), 9–33.

mass-produced charms. Ruickbie's discussion of concrete examples in view of their materiality reveals how, during the First World War, new types of lucky charms emerged that were suitable for the twentieth century. These examples show that industrialization did not come into conflict with magical beliefs but in fact worked in their favour and helped them adapt to the conditions of an industrialized, modern mass society.

Another belief in the supernatural that peaked in the wake and the aftermath of the First World War is addressed by Murray Leeder. This last chapter of the first section analyses spiritualism as it presents itself through the lens of 1920s melodramatic film, specifically *Unseen Forces* (1920), which undermines the modern concept of secular magic. Having emerged in 1848, as the Fox sisters started communicating with spirits via raps and knocks in Hydesville, New York, modern spiritualism developed into a religious movement in the following decades. Its peaks of popularity are related to major wars that lead to heavy casualties: while spiritualism's first prime was a response to the American Civil War, the second one reacted to the First World War, in which millions of soldiers left for the front and never returned. Spiritualist mediums who contacted the other world could be offering peace in a time of grief. However, others regarded them as shameless frauds that exploited their customers' emotional vulnerability for their own financial gain. This public discourse found its way into the film industry. While cinema's role as an anti-spiritualist medium has been well studied, Leeder presents an analysis of an example of pro-spiritualist film.

Both spiritualism and cinema share a history of mutual interaction with each other as well as with magic. Taking us deeper into the field of cinematic magic, the chapters gathered in Part II examine more recent examples across different continents and cultures. In his analysis of *Veneno para las hadas*, Gothic scholar Enrique Ajuria Ibarra explores the uncanny side of magic in Mexican cinema. Combining the eerie with the innocent by focusing on a girl who identifies as a witch, this 1984 film highlights magic as a source of power. It is nourished by the manipulation of others and, in turn, enables it. Demonstrating that magic's potency can derive from its assertion when contingent events are interpreted as magical, this uncanny film reminds us that whether or not a magical ritual has any tangible effect on our surroundings is irrelevant – as long as its efficacy is believed in, its practitioners can draw power from it.

A more straightforward understanding assumes that magic is a means to manipulate one's environment – a way of making things happen. A portrayal of this kind of magical ability is analysed by Katarzyna Ancuta who discusses representations of Khmer black magic in Thai popular cinema. Through the example of *The Art of the Devil* trilogy (2004–8), she illustrates how magic becomes a form of political power. It can serve a defamatory purpose (and has done so at least since the days of witch-hunts) by branding individuals as practitioners of 'black' magic and thus justifying their oppression and persecution. The visualization of this mechanism as well as of black magic's horrific effects can prompt extreme graphic violence, as the examples discussed in this chapter evidence. Moreover, as Thai popular films use magic as an impetus to broach political subjects such as ideology and gender, Ancuta argues, they also mirror beliefs prevalent until today, raising the question of these beliefs' interplay with fictional representations and vice versa.

While Ancuta and Ajuria Ibarra analyse sinister renderings of witchcraft and magic, the following two chapters turn to more positive depictions. Picking up the discussion of Mexican fantastic films, Álvaro Martín Sanz delves into the magical realism of Guillermo del Toro. Drawing on older films like *The Creature from the Black Lagoon* (1954), del Toro tells a love story involving magical beings in *Shape of Water* (2017). The protagonist of the film is Elisa, a cleaner at a secret government laboratory who has a speech disability due to wounds on her neck that she received as a child. She falls in love with a humanoid amphibian creature that is held captive at the lab for experimentation and eventually rescues it. Here, the openness to the supernatural and the curiosity about the Other is romantically portrayed as a driving force that enables both protagonists to liberate themselves from a repressive regime.

Continuing the examination of audiovisual representations of magic, Part II closes with a contribution by Josephine Diecke and Noemi Daugaard. Their chapter discusses the colour purple and its association with magic through the example of the Afrofuturistic fantasy blockbuster *Black Panther* (2018). Throughout film history, magic and magical creatures have not only been persistently associated with purple but also with people of colour. Especially in the USA, the stock character of the 'magical negro', a stereotypical, benevolent character helping the white protagonists by possessing supernatural abilities that they themselves do not have, appears in such films as *The Shining*

(1980), *Ghost* (1990) or *Matrix* (1999), to name only a few examples. Diecke and Daugaard show how *Black Panther* not only avoids following this pattern but also breaks down the association of magic, the colour purple and the racist character of the 'magical negro'.

Turning to a kind of magic that flourished in Europe and in the USA concurrently with colonialism and orientalism, Part III of this book focuses on what Simon During called *secular magic*. He uses this term to differentiate 'the technically produced magic of conjuring shows and special effects. [...], which stakes no serious claim to contact with the supernatural'[10] from *real* or *supernatural magic*. However, it is important to keep in mind that these two are not clearly distinguishable from one another but have always been intertwined and interrelated. Their mutual entanglement is a recurring theme throughout this book and is explicitly examined in some of the chapters. Turning to *secular magic*, the third section highlights performance magic during the Golden Age of conjuring, a period of fifty to ninety years (opinions on this periodization vary) around 1900. During this time, magicians moved their art to permanent theatre stages and strived to increase its respectability as a form of entertainment. They developed a new repertoire of large-scale illusions that could be seen from the distance of a theatre or music hall and made use of set design, stage machinery, artificial lighting, etc., taking full advantage of fixed stages. As part of the promotional campaign for their art and their newly established image as honest entertainers, magicians further started to author and publish texts. Following the example of Jean Eugène Robert-Houdin's programmatic memoirs, *Confidences d'un prestidigitateur* (1858), many magicians of the time released autobiographies. In the first chapter of Part III, Beatrice Ashton-Lelliott analyses this influential publication and Antonio Blitz's *Fifty Years in the Magic Circle* (1871) as examples of magicians' autobiographies. She examines these as a text form that was used to construct narratives around magicians' stage personas, thereby primarily aiming to entertain and to promote their careers rather than to accurately recount factual events.

---

10   Simon During, *Modern Enchantments. The Cultural Power of Secular Magic* (Cambridge, MA: Harvard University Press, 2002), 1.

Focusing on specific performances of magic and their intertwining with politics, in the following chapter, Christopher Pittard focuses on a popular magic trick of that time, the Bullet Catch. He argues that it emphasizes magic's agonistic qualities as audience members are dared to shoot at the magician who withstands the shooting unharmed. On Victorian stages, this illusion gained wider political significance within the context of colonialism and wars. Through the examples of Robert-Houdin and Khia Khan Kruse, Pittard examines how the Bullet Catch was used as a political presentation to stage conflicts between the colonized and the colonizers, as well as to demonstrate political dominance in different ways and contexts.

Another discourse that interlaces magic with the establishment and continuation of power is Victorian magicians' interaction with spiritualist mediums. Here, we can observe a combination of public debunking and tacit appropriation: while the most successful magicians of the Golden Age were exposing the methods of spiritualist mediums, their repertoires consisted to a considerable extent of illusions informed by séances. Because the most visible campaigners against spiritualism were male magicians and the majority of mediums was female, we are also looking at a matter of gender inequality. The chapter by Katharina Rein turns to women in the magicians' own trade at that time. Using three examples, it illustrates how women took on the roles of magiciennes and assistants during the Golden Age of conjuring. While few exceptions enjoyed very successful solo careers as conjuresses, the majority of magiciennes at that time may have been highly accomplished but undercredited and objectified. Moreover, magicians' assistants' labour and skills were systematically eliminated in the performances, while they were presented as passive bodies, submitted to the (male) magicians' power. This is one of the reasons why even much vaunted female assistants failed to establish careers of their own, especially at a time when women were usually reduced to the role of men's companions.

An illusion that literally presents the assistant's body as bending under the magician's touch, is 'The Suspension Ethéréenne', which is at the centre of the last chapter of Part III, by Frédéric Tabet and Pierre Taillefer. Performed in variations up to the present day, this illusion was popularized in Europe by Jean Eugène Robert-Houdin who first presented it in his Parisian magic theatre in 1847. In his version, his son Émile was put in a trance and lifted up to float horizontally in the air, being supported only by a stick under his elbow. In later variations, this feat was usually performed with women – so was the version examined by Tabet and Taillefer. Bridging the history of stage magic and the history of photography, the authors examine a series of photographs taken at the Parisian Théâtre de la Gaîté in 1873 that show the performer Lily Edith presenting 'The Suspension Ethéréenne'. Through this example, Tabet and Taillefer examine the transformation of dynamic, narrated stage effects into static photographs as well as the conflict between the inherently illusory character of performance magic and photography's association with objectivity (which would later fall victim to a whole catalogue of photographic effects that proved this medium's proneness to manipulation).

This chapter shows how a stage illusion was adapted to the specificity of another, then new medium – a flexibility that made a more sweeping impact several decades later, when magicians began transforming stage effects into cinematic ones. The transition from stage to screen is at the forefront of the following two chapters that analyse it from different angles. In the first chapter of Part IV Frank Kessler explores the *féerie*, a largely forgotten genre that was popular in French theatres in the nineteenth century. Among others, it was presented at the Théâtre de la Gaîté, where the photographs examined in the previous chapter were taken and where, under the directorship of Jacques Offenbach, the *féerie* was crossed with the opera. Kessler shows that while the *féerie*, on the one hand, was closely related to magic by its supernatural themes and use of elaborate stage effects, on the other hand, it differed from magic in that it did not incite an interest in how the effects were achieved but aimed primarily to enchant and produce a sense of wonder.

Today, this genre is mostly known to us via its representation in early cinema, most famously in the work of Georges Méliès, whose oeuvre is examined in the following chapter by Matthew Solomon. Méliès is the most prominent example of what Solomon has called 'magician-filmmakers' in his book *Disappearing Tricks* (2010). As the new medium emerged, the professional magician and director of one of Europe's most renowned magic theatres, the Théâtre Robert-Houdin, Méliès soon became a cinematographer himself. Other magicians did the same: some started to construct and market cinematic apparatus; others founded film production companies, distributed films as agents or contributed to the spreading of the new medium around the world by taking film projectors along on their tours.[11] Solomon analyses the transition of magic from stage to screen at the close of the nineteenth century through the example of Méliès' first trick film, *Escamotage d'une dame chez Robert-Houdin* (1896). Tracing the transformation of the stage effect known as 'The Vanishing Lady' or 'Escamotage d'une dame', invented by magician Buatier de Kolta in 1886, as it migrated to celluloid and the cinema screen, Solomon's analysis concentrates on its material foundation and the materiality of early film as a medium.

Continuing the discussion of magic as it transitioned between media or conflated characteristic features of several media in one, the following two chapters turn to the defining medium of the second half of the twentieth century: television. If around 1900, performance magic, in part, migrated to cinema, then in the mid-1950s, it began to invade television. Here, magicians found a new area of activity after the big live shows of the Golden Age had declined and eventually disappeared in the wake of the two World Wars. In the following chapter, Jamy Ian Swiss shows how, in an attempt to revive the popularity of the past and to reach a wider public, magicians pushed into a medium decidedly unsuited for their art. Magic, he argues, relies heavily on the direction of attention but the camera is not susceptible to misdirection in the same manner as human perception is. Moreover, transmissions via television raise the suspicion of their contents already having been visually manipulated – which is why magicians in TV shows go to great lengths to demonstrate that their illusions are not achieved by camera tricks. This effort to establish credibility culminates in the twenty-first century, when magicians like David Blaine introduce a new kind of magic show that borrows its authentication methods from reality TV. Swiss traces the discourses and practices surrounding authenticity despite mediation to the current situation in which

11   On the interrelation between stage magic and early cinema see Matthew Solomon, *Disappearing Tricks: Silent Film, Houdini, and the New Magic of the Twentieth Century* (Urbana: University of Illinois Press, 2010); Erik Barnouw, *The Magician and the Cinema* (New York, Oxford: Oxford University Press, 1981); Katharina Rein, 'Magicians and Early Cinema', in Diego Cavallotti, Simone Dotto, and Leonardo Quaresima, eds, *A History of Cinema Without Names/2* (Milan: Mimesis, 2017), 169–78.

prevention measures related to the Covid-19 pandemic make magicians turn to online shows.

Through audiovisual media, magic has also penetrated into popular culture in the course of the twentieth century. In the following chapter, Roswitha Schuller analyses a television appearance by David Seville, presenting his number one hit song 'Witch Doctor' on the *The Ed Sullivan Show* (which also regularly featured professional magicians in the 1960s). This performance, titled 'My Friend the Witch Doctor' and broadcast on CBS in 1958, exemplary illustrates how magic works as a popular-cultural trope. It combines elements loosely associated with magic with cheerful comedy and a narrative about unrequited love that gets resolved with the help of a 'witch doctor'. A problematic appearance for a number of reasons from today's perspective, this performance presents voodoo magic as a colonial trope of popular culture. Schuller's chapter demonstrates how 'magic' here is visualized by a combination of media-specific image manipulation effects with gestures. The latter are not only reminiscent of magicians' body language as an indication of their influence on the surrounding world but also, Schuller observes, of gestures we perform in our everyday lives today to manipulate touchscreen-based electronic devices.

While this example uses experimental sound and video manipulation, the following chapter analyses a different way of conflating sound and visual effects to represent magic. Five decades later, we encounter magic in state-of-the-art high-budget blockbuster films. Michael Wedel analyses *Harry Potter and the Deathly Hallows, Pt. 1* (2010) as exemplary of a new, characteristic style of surround sound aesthetics that is deeply influenced by digital sound design. He demonstrates how the fantasy blockbuster of the last two decades employs sound to generate a synesthetic, three-dimensional experience in which the theatre space, imbued by film sound, appears as an immersive extension of the two-dimensional image on the screen. This effect creates a paradox in perception which Wedel identifies as belonging to a long tradition of magical thinking.

Another paradox that emerges in the depiction of magic is examined in the last chapter of this part. Sarah Faber analyses twenty-first-century videogames that prominently feature magic within their narrative as well as on the level of game mechanics. The popularity of magic in videogames may not be surprising in view of the prevalence of fantasy-themed games. But because videogames are highly rule-based, Faber argues that there is some tension between common game mechanisms and magic, at least when it is conceptualized as an elemental power that transcends rational regulation. While natural magic is often considered imprecise and, to some degree, unpredictable, videogame magic reliably produces the exact same effect every time it is executed. This contradiction and the question how magic is nonetheless included in videogames is discussed in this chapter through the example of the *Dragon Age* series (2009–14).

The last two parts of this book turn more explicitly to political topics in relation to magic and its representations. While Part V has a stronger focus on individuals and identities, tackling issues such as gender, sexuality and body politics, Part VI opens the field for broader societal issues, approaching ways in which magic has been instrumentalized to represent and oppose political regimes. Beginning with the most notorious example of magic as a socio-political means, the witch-hunt, Hannah Segrave analyses the exceptional painting *La Strega* (1647–50). In it, Neapolitan artist Salvator Rosa depicts the witch as a naked, ferocious old woman. She is recognizable as a representative of what Mary J. Russo called 'the female grotesque', an abject human body. Segrave argues that, while it is an unusual depiction for its time, this paradigmatic, misogynous rendering served as a canvas for the artist's display of skill and originality. This chapter demonstrates how, at the time of the historical witch-hunt and at the height of visual representations of witches, depictions of the female body became a screen for male fantasies of the demonic as well as a way to reinforce their own superiority.

Turning to a different discourse revolving around bodies, in the following chapter Anna Grebe looks at magic from the perspective of Disability Studies. While the Golden Age of conjuring was also the time of the so-called 'freak shows', with P. T. Barnum highly successively combining the two forms of entertainment, Grebe moves away from this most famous dispositive of disability in entertainment culture. She identifies three dominant narratives of disability with regard to magicians: adaptation, overcoming and inspiration. Her examination of these through historical and contemporary examples such as René Lavand, Matthias Buchinger, The Amazing Jeffo and Mahdi Gilbert investigates both the self- and the external perception of performing magicians with disabilities.

Taking yet a different perspective on magical bodies and their capacities, Jasmin Kathöfer and Jens Schröter discuss instances in which magic is used to avoid physical labour, focusing primarily on Disney's animated feature films. While in *Fantasia* (1940), the magical automation of work ends in a disaster for Mickey Mouse (as the Sorcerer's Apprentice), twenty-three years later, in *The Sword in the Stone*, it fails not because the magician loses control but because others intervene. Both examples imply a moral judgement about delegating labour to magical processes – instead of the desired effect, it leads to chaos, destruction and punishment. Through the analyses of these examples as well as a cursory glance at a more recent film that conflates magic with technology, Christopher Nolan's *The Prestige* (2006), the authors identify an ambiguity that contrasts 'honest labour' with its evasion via magic.

In the last two chapters of Part V, the linkage of magic, the body and in-dividual identity come to the fore. Stephanie Weber examines the ascription of magical powers to tattoos in Ray Bradbury's short story 'The Illustrated Man' (1950). While tattooing is traditionally rejected by Christianity, Judaism and most of the Muslim tradition as a sinful modification of the human body that was created by and belongs to God, other cultures view the practice posi-tively and have a long history of ritual tattooing. For instance, in Buddhism and Hinduism tattoos are attributed with protective powers, while the Maori *tāmoko* employ a complex visual language to signify individual history, iden-tity and social status. In Bradbury's fiction, this chapter demonstrates, tattoos gain prophetic powers and an agency of their own, while the tattooed person's body becomes a site of their magic.

A more comprehensive transformation of the body is analysed in the last chapter of this part. Through the example of Charles Foster's novel *Being a Beast* (2016), Dunja Haufe examines shapeshifting in shamanistic cultures as a way of bridging the differentiation between human and non-human ani-mals. In it, the shapeshifter's identity is transformative and liminal, putting the shapeshifter in a mediatory role not only between the human and the non-human but also between the rational and the irrational, between science and magic. Foster's work, Haufe demonstrates, offers a new understanding of shapeshifting as a means of breaking down the boundaries that establish and reinforce these categories.

The sixth and last part of this book continues the examination of magic as a force that shapes societies and politics. The chapters gathered here investigate how magic becomes a tool of self-expression, self-liberation, empowerment and resistance for oppressed groups in various contexts and across media. In parallel with the preceding part, this one opens with an investigation of a pictorial representation of a witch. While Segrave's analysis at the beginning of Part V considered a painting that was created at the time of the persecution of witches in the early modern period and that depicts the witch's body as grotesque and abject, the examination at the beginning of Part VI reveals an entirely different rendering of the witch. Here, Marie Barras analyses a Victorian painting, John William Waterhouse's *The Magic Circle* (1886), which depicts the witch as a young, independent woman who performs a ritual inside a magic circle that she draws on the ground with her wand. Representative of the late nineteenth-century romantic reimagining of the figure of the witch, this painting also stands at the dawn of a period of about two decades during which women gained unprecedented socio-political visibility. It was also created at a time that saw the peaks of stage illusionism, modern spiritualism and occultism. Barras' in-depth analysis of the painting and its historico-cultural context discusses it as a representation of untamed, subversive female power as seen through the lens of witchcraft.

The Victorian spiritual revival was also reflected in the literature of the time, in particular as decadent writes cultivated a fascination for occultism, rituals and non-Western cultures. In the following chapter, Jessica Gossling analyses Arthur Machen's novel *The Hill of Dreams* (1907) as an example of the decadent literary movement's involvement with magic. Imbued with ideas of Romanticism, the writer explores the concept of a sensitive, solitary poet who is in search of arcane knowledge and refined, mind-broadening sensual experiences. Magic, Gossling demonstrates, is an integral part of this quest, in which it becomes a form of artistic rebellion and decadent self-expression.

Machen's novel appeared a decade after it had been written because its proximity to the decadent and aesthetic movement had rendered it unpublishable directly after the highly publicized trials of Oscar Wilde in 1895. Wilde's conviction on the grounds of his romantic and sexual relationships with men ruined his career and health, possibly even leading to his premature death of what may have been the result of an injury that he sustained in prison. While homosexuality has now been decriminalized in large parts of the world, homophobia persists until today. As Hayes Hampton demonstrates in the following chapter, magic is among the means sometimes invoked to fight it. In 1984, at the height of the HIV craze, the experimental music group Coil released its provocative album *Scatology*, a milestone of queer culture. Deeply influenced by esotericism and occultism, it invokes transgressive issues and conjures up modes of thinking and acting outside of social norms as well as non-conforming bodies and sexualities. Hampton shows that *Scatology* follows the traditional structure of a grimoire, while invoking pagan gods and occultist methods to dispel reactionary and homophobic attitudes of traditional Christianity and to enable listeners to liberate themselves from an oppressive power.

This album appeared during another heyday of esotericism and occultism in the 1970s and 1980s – decades that also saw an unprecedented rise of neo-paganism and Wicca. Since then, the witch has been a symbol of self-empowerment, transgression and resistance against the patriarchal society, in particular in queer-feminist culture. As Luce deLire demonstrates, this image, while empowering to many, is also a problematic one: not only is it grounded in an ahistorical fantasy of the witch as a self-determined and insubordinate woman, it is also often riddled with questionable elements such as a fascination for other cultures that is reminiscent of colonial exoticism and often accompanied by cultural appropriation. DeLire critically examines magical practices of the present day as acts of political empowerment in the context of queer feminism. Advocating the Spinozean concept of Embodied Reason, she proposes an understanding of magical practices as a way to reclaim and re-shape reason for the purposes of the oppressed rather than ascribing it to the dominant power of the disciplining force.

An increasingly powerful political tool as well as an essential ingredient of our daily lives is social media. While cult leaders and radical organizations use social media and chat groups to widely disseminate their worldviews and to indoctrinate rising numbers of followers, the internet also offers spaces of resistance in which the liberal and the oppressed can be heard and seen. In the last chapter of this book, Daniela Lazoroska analyses contemporary, politically motivated magical practices online. In particular, she examines rituals against Donald Trump that were performed on site, filmed and distributed via social media under the hashtags #MagicResistance and #BindTrump during his presidency. Carried out by politically left-oriented groups that are often rooted in activist contexts and identifying as queer, these rituals were intended to disempower Trump. In this example, Lazoroska argues, a new kind of magic, underpinned by technology and suitable for the digitized society of the twenty-first century, becomes an instrument of collective, political activism that takes place outside of the system of party politics.

In order to do justice to an extremely multifaceted topic, this book brings together a variety of perspectives on diverse representations of conjuring and magic in different media and throughout history and fiction. In this manner, it offers an overview of the broad spectrum of shapes and variations of magic, while at the same time presenting close readings and in-depth specialist analyses of selected cultural products. The chapters gathered here shed light on magic as a political act, a means of personal and collective empowerment, a capitalist metaphor, a form of entertainment, an explanatory belief system structuring worldviews, and an instrument of oppression and liberation alike. Its practitioners have been demonized, oppressed, persecuted, objectified, sexualized, romanticized, or used as a symbol of empowerment and self-determination. Magic itself has been intertwined with other performing and visual arts, with religion and ritual, with gender and body politics, and with colonial and capitalist dynamics. Having proved equally constant and mutable, magic has appeared in many guises throughout history. Today, we encounter new kinds of magical thinking and practices in a highly technical, digitized world of social media and video platforms. This book's selection of themes and examples strives to reflect a section of the spectrum of discourses revolving around magic and their permeation into different aspects of our culture, thus contributing to a wide and multifaceted field of interest which has only begun to unfold.

Part I

Magic Beliefs in History and Today

Antje Bosselmann-Ruickbie

Demon Amulets and Christian Crosses

Magic and the Christian Middle Ages seems like a contradiction in terms. However, there is much evidence that magical beliefs persisted after 'pagan' Antiquity. Throughout history, beliefs, rituals and thinking existed that can be called magical, although we are far from a clear definition. Church Fathers and legislators as well as academic researchers have tried to define the semantic categories concerning magic and religion, but borders remain fluid. To shed light on the co-existence of different belief systems in the Middle Ages, we will consider the evidence of material culture in the form of amulets from Byzantium.[1] Together with written sources, they prove that although Christianity was the state religion since the fourth century, and Church and State fervently fought deviations from the prescribed path, a need to seek protection and help beyond Christianity was a persistent concept.[2]

---

1   For an overview of types and geneses see Antje Bosselmann-Ruickbie, 'Protection against Evil in Byzantium: Magical Amulets from the Early to the Late Byzantine Period', in Judith Noble and Daniel Zamani, eds, *Visions of Enchantment. Occultism, Spirituality and Visual Culture* (London: Fulgur, 2018), 36–57.

2   See on magic, sorcery and the occult in Byzantium: Ilse Rochow, 'Zu "heidnischen" Bräuchen bei der Bevölkerung des Byzantinischen Reiches im 7. Jahrhundert, vor allem aufgrund der Bestimmungen des Trullanum', *Klio* 60 (1970), 483–97. Carolina Cupane, 'La magia a Bisanzio nel secolo XIV: azione e reazione. Dal Registro del Patriarcato costantinopolitano (1315–1402)', *Jahrbuch der Österreichischen Byzantinistik* 29 (1980), 237–62. Richard P. H. Greenfield, *Traditions of Belief in Late Byzantine Demonology* (Amsterdam: Adolf M. Hakkert, 1988). Henry Maguire, ed., *Byzantine Magic* (Washington, DC: Dumbarton Oaks Research Library and Collection, 1995). Spyros Troianos, 'Zauberei und Giftmischerei in mittelbyzantinischer Zeit', in Günter Prinzing and Dieter Simon, eds, *Fest und Alltag in Byzanz* (Munich: Beck, 1990),

Figure 1. Byzantine casting mould, Museum Schnütgen, Cologne. © Rheinisches Bildarchiv, Cologne.

Figure 2. Byzantine casting mould, detail of the cavity for the hystera (womb) amulet, Museum Schnütgen, Cologne. © Rheinisches Bildarchiv, Cologne.

37–51. Paul Magdalino, and Maria Mavroudi, eds, *The Occult Sciences in Byzantium* (Geneva: La Pomme d'Or, 2006). Marco Frenschkowski, 'Magie', *Reallexikon für Antike und Christentum* 23 (2010), cols 857–957. Jean-Michel Spieser, 'Christianisme et magie du IIIe au VIIe siècle', in Veronique Dasen and Jean-Michel Spieser, eds, *Les savoirs magiques et leur transmission de l'Antiquité à la Renaissance. Magie, Savoirs et Religion dans le Monde Byzantin* 3 = Micrologus' Library 60 (Florence: Sismel, 2014), 333–51. Alicia Walker, 'Magic in Medieval Byzantium', in David Collins, ed., *The Cambridge History of Magic and Witchcraft in the West* (Cambridge: Cambridge University Press, 2015), 209–34. Maria K. Papathanassiou, 'The Occult Sciences in Byzantium', in Stavros Lazaris, ed., *A Companion to Byzantine Science*, vol. 6 (Leiden: Brill, 2019), 464–95.

Case Study: A Demon Amulet and a Christian Cross Combined

This can be demonstrated through an interesting object in the Schnütgen Museum in Cologne (Figures 1 and 2)[3]: one half of a Byzantine casting mould made of stone, dated to the twelfth to fourteenth centuries by the style of its ornaments. The two largest of the eight cavities were in the shape of a cross and round with the stylized head of a demon. The 'antennae' surrounding the head remind one of the ancient Medusa, and amulets of this type were in former times thought to depict the Gorgon. However, comparison with some of the over seventy surviving amulets of this type (Figures 3 and 4) prove that this was a demon representing the *hystera*, Greek for the womb, protecting fertility and pregnancy.[4] It was widely believed until the nineteenth century that the womb would roam in the female body and make women 'hysterical'. This is reflected in the magical formula used on many of these amulets, in different variations:

ΥСΤΕΡΑ ΜΕΛΑΝΗ ΜΕΛΑΝΟΜΕΝΗ ωС ΟΦΙС ΕΙΛΥΕСΑΙ ΚΑΙ ωС ΔΡΑΚΟΝ ΣΥΡΙΖΗСΕ ΚΑΙ ωС ΛΕωΝ ΒΡΥΧΑСΑΙ ΚΑΙ ωС ΑΡΝΙΟΝ ΚΟΙΜΟΥ

'Womb, black, blackening, as a snake you coil and as a serpent you hiss and as a lion you roar, and as a lamb, lie down!'[5]

---

3   Antje Bosselmann-Ruickbie, 'A Byzantine Casting Mould for a Hystera (Womb) Amulet and a Cross in the Museum Schnütgen, Cologne: A Contribution to the Cultural and Religious History of Byzantium and the Material Culture of Byzantine Magic', in Jörg Drauschke et al., eds, *Lebenswelten zwischen Archäologie und Geschichte. Festschrift für Falko Daim* (Mainz: Verlag des Römisch-Germanischen Zentralmuseums, 2018), 629–44.

4   On these amulets see Jeffrey Spier, 'Medieval Byzantine Magical Amulets and Their Tradition', *Journal of the Warburg and Courtauld Institute* 56 (1993), 25–62. Katharina Schoneveld, 'Ein Bronzeamulett des 4.–7. Jahrhunderts als Bindeglied in der Genese der mittelbyzantinischen Hystera-Amulette', *Jahrbuch des RGZM* 61 (2015, published 2018), 267–306. Bosselmann-Ruickbie, 'Casting Mould'. Bosselmann-Ruickbie, 'Magical Amulets', 23–4. Eirini Panou, 'Between Condemnation and Use: Byzantine Amulets of Pregnancy', in Antje Bosselmann-Ruickbie and Leo Ruickbie, eds, *The Material Culture of Magic* (forthcoming).

5   Spier, 'Magical Amulets', 29–31. See also the analysis of the inscriptions by Schoneveld, 'Bronzeamulett', 279–82.

Figure 3. Lead amulet with womb demon on the one side and Christ Pantokrator on the other, Ashmolean Museum, Oxford. Photo by Antje Bosselmann-Ruickbie.

These formulas are directed towards the organ itself, hoping it would fulfil its duty and stay calm – very important in times in which procreation and fertility were determining factors in life. The amuletic pendants were mostly made of lead or bronze, with only a few known examples made of gold, silver or enamel (Figures 3 and 4).[6]

Figure 4. Hystera amulet with Greek inscription, made in enamel, Musée du Louvre, Paris, inv. OA6276, © RMN-Grand Palais, D. Aranudet

6   For the materials and descriptions, see Spier, 'Magical Amulets', 27–9.

An exception is one of the few silver rings, a simple band with a round, flat bezel from medieval Corinth (not later than the tenth century), which simply states on its shank that it is an (Υ)CTEPHKѠN ΦΥΛΑΚΤΗΡΙΟΝ, a '*phylakterion* for the womb', a protective amulet.[7] While the pendants around the neck could have been worn hidden under the clothes, this ring would have been openly worn on the finger, although any Christian reference is missing here. The use of magic to provide help in procreation is testified for all social strata, including imperial circles. In the eighth century, the usurper Philippikos Bardanes (711–13), for example, apparently believed in the power of amulets.[8] In the eleventh century, Michael Psellos (1018–c.76) described in his *Chronographia* that the 50-year-old Byzantine Empress Zoe (c. 978–1050, r. 1042), otherwise very pious, used amulets and incantations to conceive the desired heir – although to be read *cum grano salis* in light of Psellos' not always flattering representation of the empress, this source is still interesting.[9]

The Greek inscription on the Schnütgen mould differs from the widespread magical formula to calm the womb. The partly damaged writing – mirror-inverted on the cast amulet[10] – begins with a cross (typical for Christian inscriptions): PHTHOPO(Υ?) … … OC … … IOCKCC. Two reconstructions can be suggested, both mentioning K[YRIO]C C[ABAOΘ], Lord Sabaoth, the most frequent attribute of god in the Old Testament, expressing god's power and majesty.[11]

In addition to wording, Christian iconography could also be combined with the womb demon: several of the *hystera* amulets represent the 'Holy Rider',

---

7   Antje Bosselmann-Ruickbie, *Byzantinischer Schmuck des 9. bis frühen 13. Jahrhunderts* (Wiesbaden: Reichert Verlag, 2011), no. 141.

8   Rochow, 'Heidnische Bräuche', 491. To keep the text brief, all written sources referred to will be found through the secondary literature quoted here.

9   Michael E. R. A. Sewter, *Fourteen Byzantine Rulers: The 'Chronographia' of Michael Psellus* (London: Penguin, 1979), 65, 188. Walker, 'Magic', 221–2. See also John Duffy, 'Reactions of Two Byzantine Intellectuals to the Theory and Practice of Magic: Michael Psellos and Michael Italikos', in Henry Maguire, ed., *Byzantine Magic* (Washington, DC: Dumbarton Oaks Research Library and Collection, 1995), 88–9.

10   Mirror-inverted writing is found on other magical objects and *hystera* amulets in particular, see, for example, Spier, 'Magical Amulets', no. 9.

11   Reconstruction of the inscription: Bosselmann-Ruickbie, 'Casting Mould', 634–5.

an ancient motif of a rider killing a (female) demon lying on the ground,[12] other examples show Christ Pantokrator (see Figure 3), the Mother of God, Saints, the Archangel Michael, the woman with the issue of blood, the Seven Sleepers of Ephesos, as well as biblical texts.[13]

The Byzantine group of *hystera* amulets had been dated to the tenth to twelfth centuries based on only a few objects from excavations or with datable iconography. However, the casting mould today in Cologne proves ongoing use into the later Byzantine era. Magic and magical thinking was a persistent element in Christian Byzantium, and sorcerers and clairvoyants were approached in times of need, and practices, such as spells, charms and potions, were widespread.[14] Also in the later period, we learn about incidents and court cases reported in the written sources, also concerning monks and the clergy, such as wearing amulets, the use of witchcraft for career purposes amongst the clergy, the possession of magic books, lecanomantic rituals (divination with a bowl of water) and prayers of vengeance in the name of Christ.[15] Also in medieval Russia, the tradition of *hystera* amulets was continued, testified to by at least 300 examples dating to the twelfth to fifteenth centuries.[16]

12   See Bosselmann-Ruickbie, 'Magical Amulets', 22–3, with bibliography.

13   Schoneveld, 'Bronzeamulett', 281. Bosselmann-Ruickbie 'Casting Mould', 632.

14   Troianos, 'Zauberei und Giftmischerei', 43. Dorothy Abrahamse, 'Magic and Sorcery in the Hagiography of the Middle Byzantine Period', *Byzantinische Forschungen* 8 (1982), 3–17, esp. 4–5, 6, 12.

15   For the sources regarding these examples and generally on different forms of unorthodox beliefs, rituals and activities, see Rochow, 'Heidnische Bräuche'. Troianos, 'Zauberei und Giftmischerei'. Spyros Troianos, 'Der Teufel im orthodoxen Kirchenrecht', in *Byzantinische Zeitschrift* 90 (1997), 97–111, 109. Maria Mavroudi, 'Occult Science and Society in Byzantium: Considerations for Future Research', in Paul Magdalino and Maria Mavroudi, eds, *The Occult Sciences in Byzantium* (Geneva: La Pomme d'Or, 2006), 39–95, 39; Walker, 'Magic in Medieval Byzantium', 211, 216–21.

16   Andrej Stanjukovič and Vasilij E. Koršun, *Neizvestin'ie pamjatniki russkoj plastiki. Oberei-zmeeviki XI–XIX vekov* (Moscow: Gruppa Iskatell, 2014).

Canon and Civil Law on Magic and Amulets

The *hystera* amulets are most interesting since they are 'hybrid' *apotropaia*, representing two different belief systems. This is the key to understanding how it was possible that a 'pagan', magical thought, materialized in the *hystera* amulets, could be tolerated in the Christian Empire of Byzantium. Looking at the legal history, it would otherwise have been strictly forbidden to wear objects such as these. In general, magic and amulets were fervently suppressed and the practitioners and wearers were persecuted, as a look at the development of attitudes of State and Church show.

Emperor Constantine I 'the Great' (r. 306–37) was the first Roman Emperor to adopt Christianity, and he financially supported this monotheistic religion with at least two dozen large church buildings. Civil and canon law increasingly dealt with the issue of magic beliefs and rituals during his reign and after. Roughly half a century after Constantine's death, Christianity became the state religion under Emperor Theodososius I (379–95) and after the fall of the Western Roman Empire (476) continued to be so in the Eastern Roman/Byzantine Empire with its capital at Constantinople. Seven oecumenical Church Councils from 312 to 787 had shaped Christianity, debating issues such as the nature of Christ and the status of his mother Mary.

Church and State tried to exclude magic right from the beginning and persecuted everything that deviated from the official religious cult, which led to a rise in trials against supposed 'magicians'.[17] In the Early Christian Period, the Church Fathers consistently condemned amulets, differentiating between licit and illicit (magical) forms.[18] In the late fourth century, the Archbishop of Constantinople and Church Father, John Chrysostom, saw the use of amulets as idolatry, even if the user was a Christian believer, and only allowed the use of the Holy Cross as a 'weapon' against and cure for disease,[19] leading to an

---

17 Almuth Lotz, *Der Magiekonflikt in der Spätantike* (Bonn: Habelt, 2005), 3, 5. See also Marie Theres Fögen, *Die Enteignung der Wahrsager. Studien zum kaiserlichen Wissensmonopol in der Spätantike* (Frankfurt on the Main: Suhrkamp, 1993).

18 Spieser, 'Christianisme et magie', 351. See also Troianos, 'Zauberei und Giftmischerei', 43.

19 Troianos, 'Zauberei und Giftmischerei', 43.

enormous increase of cross-shaped pendants, reflected in the archaeological material.[20]

Church Councils also discussed the issue of amulets, with a peak in the fourth century, when the newly established Church went on the offensive against religious activities outside the sanctioned institution. At the Council of Laodikeia, 363/364,[21] it was decided that wearers of amulets (φυλακτήρια, *phylactēria*) were to be excommunicated. In 380, the Apostolic Constitutions disapproved of many manifestations of sorcery, such as amulets (here called περιάμματα, *periammata*).[22] Emperor Justinian I (r. 527–65) was responsible for a first collection of canon laws according to which amulets were seen as sorcery and thus manifestations of apostasy.[23] A synod at the end of the seventh century, the 'Trullanum', concluded that producers of amulets (again called φυλακτήρια, *phylactēria*) should be punished with a six-year penance; recidivists should be entirely excommunicated from the Church.[24]

Civil law also condemned magic and amulets, being influenced by Church teachings from the fourth century onwards.[25] Theodosius I under whose reign Christianity became state religion tried fervently to control magical rituals outside the church, but rather than disappearing, magical rituals were replaced by Christian methods, such as praying, which were, however, redolent of the old magical formulae.[26] Earlier in the fourth century, Constantine had introduced in his legislation a distinction between good and evil magic, protective and damaging magic, or 'white magic' and 'black magic'.[27] That the line between good and evil magic is thin was acknowledged almost 600 years later by Emperor Leo VI (886–912), who ordered that sorcerers, even if they claimed that they were trying to heal somebody or help avert threats to the

---

20   Brigitte Pitarakis, *Les croix-reliquaires pectorals byzantines en bronze* (Paris: Picard, 2006).

21   Lotz, *Magiekonflikt*, 244 and note 822 (with sources).

22   Troianos, 'Zauberei und Giftmischerei', 41.

23   Ibid., 44–5.

24   Lotz, *Magiekonflikt*, 245.

25   For a concise overview of the legal situation on magic see Frenschkowski, 'Magie', 947–55.

26   Troianos, 'Der Teufel', 108–9.

27   Lotz, *Magiekonflikt*, 137–43.

harvest, should suffer capital punishment.[28] The *Ecloga* of Emperor Leo III in 741, which was influenced by the teachings of the Church, forbade amulet making by secular law. Amulet makers (ποιοῦντες φυλακτά) would see their property confiscated and themselves banned from their homelands.[29] The early ninth-century *Eclogadion*, the legislation edited under the Macedonian Dynasty, determined corporal punishment for amulet makers.[30] Thus, civil law dealt with the 'fraudulent' amulet makers, while dealing with the religious digression of the wearers was left to canon law.

Conclusion

The casting mould in Cologne is a vivid proof of Byzantine 'folk magic' in combination with Christian 'remedies'. And it was not the only one: a twelfth to thirteenth-century example, this time complete (Figure 5), was found in Turkey,[31] proving that this testimony of two 'parallel' belief systems was not unique. It was obviously common in the later Byzantine period to simultaneously offer customers either a Christian cross and/or a demon amulet to protect the womb. This is comparable to similar moulds from the Viking period, in which a cross and Thor's Hammer could be cast.[32]

28   Spyros Troianos, 'Die kirchenrechtlichen Novellen Leons VI. und ihre Quellen', in Jan H. A. Lokin et al., eds, *Novella Constitutio. Studies in Honour of Nicolaas van der Wal*. Subseciva Groningana, Studies in Roman and Byzantine Law, vol. 4 (Groningen: University of Groningen Press, 1990), 233–47, 240–1. Troianos, 'Der Teufel', 108.

29   Ludwig Burgmann, *Ecloga. Das Gesetzbuch Leons III. und Konstantinos' V*. Forschungen zur byzantinischen Rechtsgeschichte 10 (Frankfurt on the Main: Löwenklau-Gesellschaft, 1983), 241, chapter 17.44.

30   Troianos, 'Zauberei und Giftmischerei', 48. Dieter Simon and Spyros Troianos, 'Eklogadion und Ecloga privata aucta', in Dieter Simon, ed., *Fontes Minores II*. Forschungen zur byzantinischen Rechtsgeschichte, vol. 2 (Frankfurt on the Main: V. Klostermann, 1977), 45–86, 72 (17.23).

31   Ayla Ödekan, *The Remnants: Twelfth and Thirteenth Centuries Byzantine Objects in Turkey* (Istanbul: Cegbi Koç Vakfi Foundation, 2007), 257.

32   *Wikinger, Waräger und Normannen*, exhibition catalogue Berlin, Museum für Vor- und Frühgeschichte (Berlin: Staatliche Museen zu Berlin – Preußischer Kulturbesitz, 1992),

Magic in Byzantium

Figure 5. Casting mould with hystera amulet and cross, made from basalt, probably twelfth-thirteenth centuries. In Ayla Ödekan, *The Remnants: Twelfth and
Thirteenth Centuries Byzantine Objects in Turkey* (Istanbul: Cegbi Koç Vakfı Foundation,
2007), 257.

This womb amulet was apparently not considered illegal, although amulet
making in general would not have been conformable to law. It was the Christian
inscriptions and the Christian iconography, which would have made such
objects acceptable in a Christian environment. In general, Byzantine people
apparently had little issue with folk magic, which was 'an accepted part of
Byzantine life'.[33]

Most other amulet types, such as a hollow tubular amulet container that
could be filled with magical writings, bones or other materials, went out of
fashion at the end of the Early Byzantine period, while the cross-shaped pendants prevailed. Only the *hystera* pendants seem to have persisted and the
Schnütgen mould, with its date of twelfth to fourteenth centuries, represents

---

no. 195 (H. Lyngstrøm), illustration on p. 191, fig. 3: mould for two crosses and a Thor's
Hammer, second half of the tenth century.

33   Abrahamse, 'Magic and Sorcery', 3–17, 12.

the latest evidence, proving that the type was current in the later Byzantine period. It helps to explore and understand the supposed area of conflict of beliefs systems in Byzantium, which exists until today. For example, blue glass beads with an eye – supposedly warding off the 'evil eye' – are often worn by Muslims and Christians alike in several countries, such as Turkey and Greece.

Magic in Byzantium

Thibaut Rioult

Reginald Scot's *The Discoverie of Witchcraft* (1584)

Renaissance Magic

A Candle in the Dark

In Western Europe, the Renaissance period was the last hegemonic moment for magic. Through multiple forms, magic played a central role in intellectual life, deeply structuring people's mindsets (or rather, in Foucauldian terms, the Renaissance *episteme*). In 1438, the introduction of Platonism, Neoplatonism and Hermeticism in Italy by Gemistus Pletho led to a strong revival of 'scholarly magic'. Thanks to the translations of Ficino, the ideas of magic forces, imaginary powers and 'sympathy'[1] spread in Europe. The most prominent scholars, like Pico della Mirandola, Paracelsus, Cardano, Della Porta, or even later Newton, were all fascinated by magic. The boundaries between magic and natural science or philosophy became quite blurred.[2]

At the same time (c. 1440), a few clerics and theologians created the modern concept of witchcraft and the Witches' Sabbath.[3] It culminated a few years later, in 1486, in the publication of the *Hammer of Witches* (*Malleus Maleficarum*), the most (in)famous book on witchcraft written by Jacob

---

1   Ann Moyer, 'Sympathy in the Renaissance', in Eric Schliesser, ed., *Sympathy: A History* (New York: Oxford University Press, 2015), 70–101.

2   Lynn Thorndyke, *A History of Magic and Experimental Science*, 8 vols (New York: Macmillan, 1923–58); Frances Yates, *Giordano Bruno and the Hermetic Tradition* (Chicago: University of Chicago Press, 1964).

3   Martine Ostorero, Agostino Paravicini Bagliani, and Kathrin Utz Tremp, *L'imaginaire du sabbat: Édition critique des textes les plus anciens (c. 1430–c. 1440)* (Lausanne: University of Lausanne, 2000).

Sprenger and Heinrich Institoris, two Dominicans. In this context, the first wave of persecution resulted in the killing of thousands of witches until the 1520s. Then, a second 'witchcraze' thundered throughout Europe, from the 1550s until the middle of the seventeenth century.[4] The defenders of the social order, whether Catholic or Protestant, furiously attacked all potential practitioners of magic and persecuted so-called 'witches' as scapegoats for all inexplicable events.

Thirty years before Scot, Johann Weyer[5] published his pivotal treatise *On the Illusions of the Demons, on Enchantments and Poisons* (*De Praestigiis Daemonum et Incantationibus ac Venificiis*, Basel, 1563). Questioning the validity of witch trials, the book triggered a fierce controversy throughout Europe and probably led to the proliferation of demonological literature during the second part of the sixteenth century. Considered by Freud[6] as one of the most critical thinkers of all time, especially in the psychological field, Weyer argued that witches are nothing else but crazy old women who should not be pursued and condemned but, on the contrary, helped and cured. However, Weyer did not question the reality of diabolical feats but did vigorously condemn witchcraft and vicious magicians. Indeed, despite intense controversies about the nature of magic and demonic power, the existence of the supernatural was not disputed by scholars prior to the writings of Reginald Scot (c. 1538–99), who was the first to clearly propose a radical scepticism about and cast systematic doubt on these 'wonders'.

Scot was a Protestant country gentleman from Kent and a Member of Parliament.[7] In 1584, he published *The Discoverie of*

---

4   Brian P. Levack, *The Witch-Hunt in Early Modern Europe* (London: Pearson, 2006).

5   Michaela Valente, *Johann Wier agli albori della critica razionale dell'occulto e del demoniaco nell'europa del cinquecento* (Florence: Olschki, 2003). Vera Hoorens, 'Why Did Johann Weyer Write *De praestigiis daemonum*?', *BMGN – Low Countries Historical Review* 129/1 (2014), 3–24.

6   Sigmund Freud, 'Contribution to a Questionnaire on Reading (1907)', in *The Standard Edition of the Complete Psychological Works of Sigmund Freud, Volume IX (1906–1908)* (London: The Hogarth Press, 1959), 245.

7   Among others, see Philip C. Almond, *England's First Demonologist. Reginald Scot & 'The Discoverie of Witchcraft'* (London: Tauris, 2014); S. F. Davies, 'The Reception of Reginald Scot's *Discovery of Witchcraft*', *Journal of the History of Ideas* 74/3 (2013), 381–401; R. Littlewood, 'Strange, Incredible and Impossible Things: The Early Anthropology of Reginald Scot', *Transcultural Psychiatry* 46/2 (2009), 348–64.

Witchcraft.[8] This 600-page treatise can be seen as a perfect prism through which to view magic in the Early Modern period, whilst also revealing the shadows of its ambiguities. Probably written as a response to the increase in witch trials, which occurred in England from 1579, the book challenged all of those who supported the witch-hunt, labelling them as 'witchmongers'. Later, James VI, King of Scotland (and future King of England) wrote a *Dæmonologie* (1597) to confirm the necessity of the trials and identified Scot as one of his main opponents.[9] One can always judge a man by the quality of his enemies.

As Max Weber points out, during the Renaissance period, a long-lasting movement of 'demagification of the world' (*Entzauberung der Welt*) took place, mainly driven by the Protestant Reformation. Often translated with the generic term of 'disenchantment', *Entzauberung* should be understood literally as 'elimination of magic from the world'.[10] Indeed, for the Protestant ascetic tradition, all the intermediaries between humans and God must be wiped out. Scot's *The Discoverie of Witchcraft* clearly played a role in this movement. It aimed to refute supernatural beliefs, mixing magical and Catholic ones, considered both as superstitious and unchristian.

---

8   Reginald Scot, *The Discouerie of Witchcraft, wherein the lewde dealing of witches and witchmongers is notablie detected, the knauerie of coniurors, the impietie of inchantors, the follie of soothsaiers, the impudent falshood of cousenors, the infidelitie of atheists, the pestilent practises of Pythonists, the curiositie of figure casters, the vanitie of dreamers, the beggerlie art of Alcumystrie, the abhomination of idolatrie, the horrible art of poisoning, the vertue and power of naturall magike, and all the conueiances of Legierdemaine and iuggling are deciphered and many other things opened which have long lien hidden, how-beit verie necessarie to be knowne. Heerevnto is added a treatise vpon the nature and substance of spirits and diuels &c.* (London: Broome, 1584).

9   James VI, *Dæmonologie, in forme of a dialogue, divided into three Bookes* (Edinburgh: Robert Waldegrave, 1597), f°2v°.

10   Max Weber, *The Protestant Ethic and the Spirit of Capitalism* (London: Routledge, 2001), 61; Max Weber, *Die protestantische Ethik und der 'Geist' des Kapitalismus. Neuausgabe der ersten Fassung von 1904–05 mit einem Verzeichnis der wichtigsten Zusätze und Veränderungen aus der zweiten Fassung von 1920* (Wiesbaden: Springer/Verlag für Sozialwissenschaften, 2016), 208. See also Ioan Petru Couliano, *Eros and Magic in the Renaissance* (Chicago: The University of Chicago Press, 1987), 193.

A Sceptical Encyclopaedia of Witchcraft

In *The Discoverie of Witchcraft*, Scot produced a sceptical synthesis between critical demonology, Calvinism, natural philosophy and empirical science, directed against traditional demonology and Catholicism. Indeed, an index analysis[11] allows us to see that the most cited authors were two prominent demonologists: the physician Johann Weyer (*pro*) and the jurist Jean Bodin (*contra*). They were followed by Cardano and Della Porta, two natural philosophers and compilers of secrets; then by demonologists like Lavater, Daneau, Sprenger and Institoris and, of course, by the theologian and reformer Calvin.

Following Weyer, Scot based his study of magic on the Bible. Like any fervent Protestant, he believed that the Scriptures contained the only and undisputed truth. Consequently, the majority of his treatise (books VI to XIII) was dedicated to a laborious analysis of the various Hebraic terms used to describe the figure of the magician, namely the witch (*Chasaph*), the oracle (*Ob*), the diviner or soothsayer (*Kasam*), the interpreter of dreams (*Onen*), the augur (*Nahas*), the natural magician (*Hartumim*) and the enchanter (*Habar*) which included the Catholic priest! Scot also added two important personas who do not appear in the Bible: the alchemist and the conjurer who make use of magic circles (books XIV and XV). The ease with which Scot was able to reuse the biblical framework of magic, illustrates the perennial and stable nature of the magical traditions in the Western world. From ancient Hebrew to Early Modern England (and right up until today), we find evidence of the same archetypal practices.

This return to biblical fundamentals allowed Scot to fight demonologists on their own theological ground. Thanks to a powerful sceptical hermeneutic, he attacked their common misunderstanding. Significantly he started to discuss the term *Chasaph*, since the main authority cited to prosecute and sentence to death witches relied on the biblical verse '*Thou shalt not suffer a Witch* [Chasaph] *to live*' (Exod. 22:18). Arguing that the Latin equivalent term

11 'Index', in Reginald Scot, *La Sorcellerie démystifiée* (Grenoble: Jérôme Millon, 2015), 665–73.

was *veneficas* and the Greek, *pharmakos*, Scot demonstrated that the correct translation should be 'poisoner'.[12] Thus, the crime of magic is plainly rationalized and the old women excluded from the scope of this commandment.

The disclosure or not of precise information was one of the most debated topics of Renaissance demonology. Scot considered magic and witchcraft to be true mystifications and was not afraid to reveal their secrets and procedures. On the other hand, his main adversary, the French jurist and political theorist Jean Bodin constantly repeated in his book *On Demonomania of Warlocks* (*De la Démonomanie des sorciers*, 1580) that formulas or recipes should not be written down, so as to prevent his treatise being used as a grimoire.[13] Arguing with Weyer, Bodin accused him of teaching devilish witchcraft and overall 'putting the words and invocations'.[14] In his book X dedicated to dreams, like Weyer, Scot provided the dreadful description of 'sundrie receipts and ointments, made and used for the transportation of witches', copying the whole '*Lamiarum unguenta*' given by Della Porta.[15] In this horrific recipe, the witches were supposed to take 'the fat of yoong children, and seeth it with water in a brasen vessell [...] They put hereunto *Eleoselinum, Aconitum, Frondes populeas*, and Soote'.[16] This description was obviously extremely shocking and disturbing during the Renaissance. It is worth mentioning that, confronted with the same accusation made by Bodin, Della Porta explicitly answered the French jurist in the second expanded edition of the *Magiae Naturalis* (1589). The Neapolitan explained that he gave its composition precisely to 'expose the execrated frauds of devils and witches'.[17] However, it is difficult to totally exclude a certain amount of morbid fascination for occult practices by the Italian scientist. Scot seemed to share both the same goal and fascination. Two visions were fighting. Demonologists acknowledged the power of secrets and

---

12   Scot, *The Discouerie of Witchcraft*, VI 1, 111.

13   Jean Bodin, *De la Démonomanie des sorciers* (Paris: Jacques du Puys, 1580), ff° 112 r°, 129 r°, passim.

14   Ibid., ff° 218 v°–9 r°.

15   Giambattista Della Porta, *Magiae naturalis sive de miraculis rerum naturalium libri IIII* (Naples: Cancer, 1558), 101–2.

16   Scot, *The Discouerie of Witchcraft*, X 8, 184.

17   Giambattista Della Porta, *Magiae naturalis libri XX* (Naples: Horatium Saluianum, 1589), n.p. ('Ad lectores'): 'quod ego ad detestandas daemonum strigiumve fraudes attuleram'.

recipes and tried to erase witchcraft beliefs by occultation. On the contrary, anti-demonologists and natural philosophers resorted to exposure; they wanted to disclose so-called 'secrets' to show publicly their inanity.

Scot is particularly prolific and related many intriguing short stories to the reader. He also provided complex magic formulas and signs (like the magic circle to enclose a spirit in crystal, see Figure 6), which were certainly amazing for the common reader. Consequently, *The Discoverie of Witchcraft* became a source of inspiration for Elizabethan and Jacobean dramatists. Such famous names as William Shakespeare, John Lyly, William Percy, Thomas Middleton, Thomas Shadwell and Ben Johnson, amongst others, used it to build their magical plots and characters.[18]

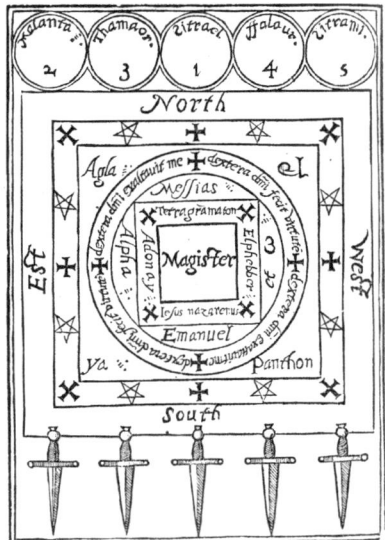

Figure 6. Magic circle for conjuration in *The Discouerie of Witchcraft* (London: Broome, 1584), XV 12, 414. Public domain.

18   Pierre Kapitaniak, 'Introduction', in Scot, *La Sorcellerie démystifiée*, 66–70; Pierre Kapitaniak, 'Staging Devils and Witches: Had Shakespeare Read Reginald Scot's *The Discoverie of Witchcraft*?', in Sophie Chiari and Mickael Popelard, eds, *Spectacular Science, Technology and Superstition in the Age of Shakespeare* (Edinburgh: Edinburgh University Press, 2017), 43–64.

An Amateur Magician Handbook

Scot's fascination with magical practices appears clearly in book XIII dedicated to natural magic, which took place under the patronage of the biblical *Hartumim*, namely Pharaoh's magicians. But these magic practices were reconsidered from the angle of juggling (which meant: performing tricks of dexterity) or *legerdemain* (a French term anglicized by Scot, literally 'light-of-hand', which corresponded to our 'sleight of hand').[19]

Scot first exposed the tricks of jugglers 'because [...] the life of witchcraft and cousenage [was] so manifestlie delivered in the art of juggling'.[20] But it quickly becomes clear that beyond polemic use, he really liked this art, inquired about it and probably practised it as an amateur.

Scot considered illusionism as a way to debunk all forms of magic. Once the hypothesis of trickery was raised, every supernatural feat could be questioned. This criticism was not new. During the long story of religious polemics, the religion of the other was always conveniently associated with deceptive arts. Church fathers (like Hippolytus of Rome) were already denouncing pagan beliefs as trickery.[21] Outside the Christian world, Arabic scholars (like Ğawbarī) also uncovered the frauds of the false prophets.[22] The demonologists (like the authors of *Malleus Maleficarum*) were used to invoke the figure of the juggler

---

19   On illusionism during the Renaissance, see: Philip Butterworth, *Magic on the Early English Stage* (Cambridge: Cambridge University Press, 2005); Thibaut Maus de Rolley, 'Le diable à la foire: jongleurs, bateleurs et prestigiateurs dans le discours démonologique à la Renaissance', in Kirsten Dickhaut, ed., *Kunst der Täuschung – Art of Deception: Über Status und Bedeutung von ästhetischer und dämonischer Illusion in der Frühen Neuzeit (1400–1700) in Italien und Frankreich* (Wiesbaden: Harrassowitz Verlag, 2016), 173–95; Thibaut Rioult, *Illusion du surnaturel et illusionnistes à la Renaissance*, doctoral thesis (Paris: École Normale Supérieure, 2018); Thibaut Rioult, 'L'illusionnisme renaissant entre secrets et merveilles', *Arcana Naturae* I (Sarzana: Agorà & Co., 2020), 51–70.

20   Scot, *The Discouerie of Witchcraft*, XIII 22, 321.

21   Hippolytus of Rome (ps.), *Philosophumena or the Refutation of All Heresies* (London: Society for Promoting Christian Knowledge, 1921).

22   'Abd al-Raḥmān ibn 'Umar Ğawbarī, *Le Voile arraché: l'autre visage de l'Islam* [*Kitāb al-moukhtār fī al-asrār wa hatk al-asrā*], 2 vol. (Paris: Phébus, 1979–80); Manuela

as a didactic example to symbolize the illusory powers of the devil. During the sixteenth century, Protestantism had also widely portrayed the priest to juggler and sorcerer. As Calvin stated: 'The Priest, like an enchanter or a cups and balls performer, blows on bread to bewitch it.'[23]

Scot inherited all these traditions. But for him, it was not a comparison but a fact: magicians (and priests) were frauds. He overturned the traditional claim of demonologists that jugglers are diabolical magicians, demonstrating that, on the contrary, magicians are jugglers. Furthermore, he proved the powerlessness of magic, arguing that mere jugglers are superior to witches, because they 'can make a more livelie shew of working miracles than anie inchantors can doo'.[24] By every means, Scot aims to ridicule 'real' magic. He killed two birds with one stone: the supposed magicians and their ignorant opponents. Of course, he also kept his Calvinist spirit even in his explanations of tricks and did not refrain from substituting the Catholic term 'transubstantiation' with the more common 'transformation' (e.g. of a coin into another) to make fun of the Eucharist, representing it as a mere juggling trick.[25]

However, Scot went far beyond simply describing some tricks from classical books of secrets. He showed true interest in the art of juggling and was probably initiated to its subtleties by the Frenchman John Cautares, 'a matchles fellowe for legierdemaine'.[26] Finally, Scot provided a real handbook for the apprentice juggler. He even apologized to professionals for exposing the tricks of the trade! For the English sceptic,

---

Höglmeier, *Al-Ǧawbarī und sein Kašf al-asrār: ein Sittenbild des Gauners im arabisch-islamischen Mittelalter (7./13. Jahrhundert)* (Berlin: Schwarz, 2006).

23   Jean Calvin, 'Petit traité de l'homme fidèle' (1543), in *Recueil des opuscules* (Geneva: Jacob Stoer, 1611), col. 879: 'Mais le Prestre à la façon des enchanteurs ou joueurs de gobelets souffle sur le pain pour l'ensorceller.'

24   Scot, *The Discouerie of Witchcraft*, XIII 21, 320.

25   Ibid., XIII 24, 325 ('To convert or transubstantiate monie into counters, or counters into monie.'); XIII 26, 331 ('seeme to transubstantiate it'). Even if this etymology is still debated, for some late authors of the seventeenth century, the famous magic formula 'Hocus, pocus' could be also a protestant distortion of the words 'Hoc est corpus', pronounced by the priest while he changes substantially bread and wine into Body and Blood of Christ. Cf. [John Tillotson], *A Discourse against Transubstantiation* (London: Flescher, 1684), 34.

26   Scot, *The Discouerie of Witchcraft*, XIII 34, 352.

whose dooings herein are not onlie tollerable, but greatlie commendable, so they abuse not the name of God, nor make the people attribute unto them his power; but alwaies acknowledge wherein the art consisteth, so as thereby the other unlawfull and impious arts may be by them the rather detected and bewraied.[27]

Scot described around sixty magic tricks (quite impressive for the sixteenth century), mixing tricks extracted from books of secrets, professional sleight of hand techniques learned on the field, and debunking contemporary or ancient mysteries. He was one of the first authors to give some wonderful didactic engravings to help our understanding of complex technical description, like the trick table and plates for the 'decollation of John Baptist' (see Figure 7) or the counterfeit bodkins (see Figure 8).

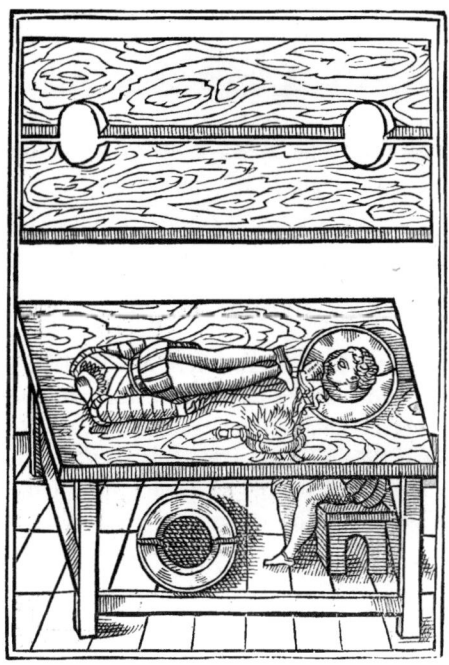

Figure 7. 'Decollation of John Baptist' in *The Discouerie of Witchcraft* (London: Broome, 1584), XIII 34, n. 352–3. Public domain.

27   Ibid., XIII 22, 321.

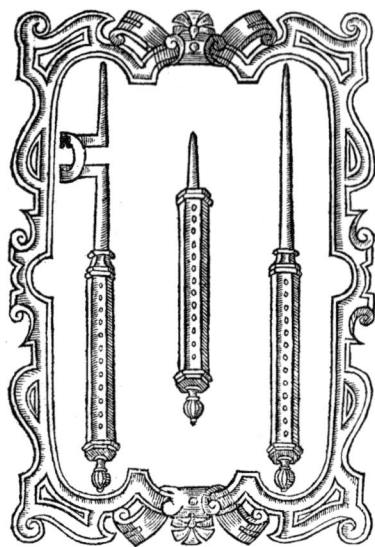

Figure 8. Counterfeit bodkins in *The Discouerie of Witchcraft* (London: Broome, 1584), XIII 34, n. 352–3. Public domain.

But he also exposed, for the first time, the principles of modern close-up with cards, balls and coins:

> The true art therefore of juggling consisteth in legierdemaine; to wit, the nimble conveiance of the hand, which is especiallie performed three waies. The first and principall consisteth in hiding and conveieng of balles, the second in the alteration of monie, the third in the shuffeling of the cards. He that is expert in these may shew much pleasure, and manie feats, and hath more cunning than all other witches or magicians. All other parts of this art are taught when they are discovered: but this part cannot be taught by any description or instruction, without great exercise and expense of time.[28]

28   Ibid.

The identification of these principles was a step change in the history of illusionism theory. Of course, in the field, these principles had been known since the dawn of time by the jugglers themselves. Ancient Greeks and Romans were already going to see the wonders of the cups and balls (pebbles) at the theatre. But with Scot, they are printed for the first time.

Schematically, the Renaissance scholarly literature of secrets[29] did not require specific manual skills and were easily performed by people who knew the trick ('taught when they are discovered'). It also relied on the equivalence between one effect and one secret trick. With Scot's strongly manual conception of legerdemain, a vast field of new possibilities opened up. Indeed, 'he that hath once atteined to the facilitie of reteining one peece of monie in his right hand, may shew a hundreth pleasant conceipts by that meanes'.[30] Henceforth, amateur illusionists could have a real handbook of the art of juggling.

But, buried in the impressive theological treatise of Scot, this decisive 'Book XIII' would have remained limited to narrow circles, if in 1612 Samuel Rid had not published, *The Art of Juggling or Legerdemain*. This pamphlet was a pure copy of Scot's juggling handbook, adding only an introduction. Then, in a slightly augmented version, there were at least sixteen editions, between 1634 and 1715, under the name *The Anatomie of Legerdemain*.[31] Through them, for at least a century, the work of Scot remained the reference book for amateur illusionists.

29   William Eamon, *Science and the Secrets of Nature: Books of Secrets in Medieval and Early Modern Culture* (Princeton, NJ: Princeton University Press, 1994); Allison Kavey, *Books of Secrets: Natural Philosophy in England, 1550–1600* (Champaign: University of Illinois Press, 2015).

30   Scot, *The Discouerie of Witchcraft*, XIII 24, 325.

31   Raymond Toole Stott, *A Bibliography of English Conjuring, 1581–1876* (Derby: Harpur, 1976), 124–31.

The Glamour of Magic

In 1687, Ann Watt, a fortune teller from London was arrested and *The Discoverie of Witchcraft* was found among her belongings. Ironically, she probably used it as a grimoire[32] and a manual to deceive her dupes![33]

Nevertheless, magic kept its inherent power and maintained its age-old logical structure. Thus, it imposed its own grammar on the performer. Blurring boundaries between natural and supernatural, illusionism created an in-between area, where magic could be legitimately practised, to an (un)certain extent. Indeed, a few times in his juggling explanations, Scot flirted with the line. He addressed the reader directly and enjoined him to 'use words of course as, *Allif, castle, zaze, hit mel meltat* [...] or such like'[34] or to say 'that you knew by your familiar'.[35] Even the greatest sceptic of his time was struggling with the glamour of magic.

Acknowledgement
I would like to thank Killian Daly and Jenny Shorten for carefully reviewing this essay.

---

32   English 'grammar', 'grimoire' and 'glamor' are all derived from Old French *gramaire*, relating to magic, witchcraft spells and power of signs.

33   James Sharpe, *Instruments of Darkness: Witchcraft in Early Modern England* (Philadelphia: University of Pennsylvania Press, 1996), 281. Almond, *England's First Demonologist*, 7.

34   Scot, *The Discouerie of Witchcraft*, XIII 25, 329.

35   Ibid., XIII 25, 330. Familiars were a specificity of English and Scottish witchcraft. In 1584, they had been at the centre of a recent (1579) witch trial studied by Scot (III 7, 51) in the pamphlet: *A Rehearsall both Straung and True, of Hainous and Horrible Actes Committed by Elizabeth Stile ...* (London: R. White, 1579). For a more global approach, see Emma Wilby, *Cunning Folk and Familiar Spirits: Shamanistic Visionary Traditions in Early Modern British Witchcraft and Magic* (Brighton: Sussex Academic Press, 2005).

Leo Ruickbie

Lucky Charms in the First World War

> Nearly every man at the front has a mascot of some sort – a rosary, a black cat, a German button, a lucky elephant, or a weird sign – which is supposed to keep him safe.[1]

From his vantage point of first-hand experience, the journalist and later politician Vernon Bartlett was moved to remark upon the range and near universality of the lucky charm during the First World War. 'Luck' could inhabit any sort of object, either through the imagined indwelling properties of the material (such as silver) or its shape (such as the horseshoe), or through association with something else (an incident, place or person). What does this near universality of the charm tell us? And what can we learn from the materiality of the charms themselves?

The First World War has often been described as industrialized warfare and charms (and superstitious practices) have been separately analysed, but what needs to be addressed is the way in which the war saw a combination of these forms to create an 'industrialized magic' fit for these times. From the many first-hand descriptions of charms, we can arrange them on a spectrum running from ad hoc found objects, to ritual objects, to mass-produced, 'industrialized' objects and to industrialized and occasionally officially sanctioned 'lucky' objects. The apparent reappearance of magic during the First World War has been seen as some sort of reversion to primitive thinking under duress, as distinctly 'unmodern',[2] but it was there all along and it continues to be there; instead, it

1   Vernon Bartlett, *Mud and Khaki: Sketches from Flanders and France* (London: Simpkin, Marshall, Hamilton, Kent & Co., 1917), 124.

2   See Jay Winter, *Sites of Memory, Sites of Mourning* (Cambridge: Cambridge University Press, 2014), 178. A 'revival' was already spoken of in 1908, see Arthur R. Wright and Edward Lovett, 'Specimens of Modern Mascots and Ancient Amulets of the British

is the overlooked process of manufacture and the official sanctioning of lucky objects that should draw our attention, for here we see that industrialization is not a counter to magic, that rationalization of production does not undermine 'irrationality' in thinking, and that industrialization does not supplant craft modes of production, but answers the specific needs of mass society.

Ad Hoc Non-industrialized Objects

Ad hoc non-industrialized objects, by which I mean simple, ordinary things, are as unique as the individual who finds meaning in them, ranging from found objects to hand-made craft items. They could be traditional symbols of good luck. The Imperial War Museum has in its collection a locket containing a four-leaf clover and a lady bird.[3] The locket is a mass-produced piece of jewellery, but the contents are not. Trooper Willis, City of London Yeomanry, was sent a piece of 'lucky' coal by his sister.[4] Another soldier, probably Irish, carried a piece of Connemara marble, hand-carved in the shape of a four-leaf clover, with a piercing so that it could be worn (probably around the neck).[5] Private Matthews, Devonshire Regiment, wore a stone with a hole bored through it – a traditional charm against witchcraft.[6]

The four-leaf clover was not the only plant valued for its supposed magical properties. The British also treasured 'lucky' white heather. For the French it was lily of the valley. Italian soldiers carried rue. German soldiers carried ferns,

---

Isles', *Folklore* 19/3 (30 September 1908), 288. See also Colin Campbell, 'Half-Belief and the Paradox of Ritual Instrumental Activism: A Theory of Modern Superstition', *British Journal of Sociology* 47/1 (March 1996), 151–66 – Campbell recognizes and embodies these problems of interpretation.

3   IWM, EPH 7459.
4   IWM, EPH 4894.
5   IWM, EPH 3464.
6   IWM, EPH 7455, dated 1917.

although the Kaiser was rumoured to keep a four-leaf clover.[7] These could be real plants picked for the purpose, or could be mass-produced trinkets.

Other objects could be much more idiosyncratic. Bartlett's soldier servant always wore an old shoe-button on a piece of string around his neck because it had been given to him by a young French girl thereby imbuing it with 'luck'. Britain's highest scoring fighter ace at the time of his death in 1917, Captain Albert Ball, VC, DSO and Two Bars, MC, carried a slice of his mother's plum pudding. Captain E. F. 'Tab' Pflaum of the Australian Flying Corps carried a stuffed baby kangaroo named 'Joey' as a lucky mascot. French flying ace, 'The Sentinel of Verdun', Jean Navarre, carried a lady's silk stocking. American Aviator John McGavock Grider, who flew with the RFC/RAF, was reported to have a considerable collection of lucky items: a piece of wreckage from his first crash; a doll given to him by the British actress Billie Carlton; a Colombian half dollar; a sixpence; as well as a stocking.[8]

Small hand-made dolls were also carried as lucky charms. The Imperial War Museum has two hand-made golliwogs, one from the First World War, the other from the Second: the First World War version is also combined with a horseshoe motif, showing that it had connotations of luck.[9] In France, cottage industry also created doll pairs called Nénette and Rintintin, and Yerri and Suzel in traditional Alsatian dress. Typically made of wool like the golliwog, Bakelite and silver varieties were also produced, and again they served as lucky charms.[10] This group is borderline, produced in quantity, but not quite mass produced, with lucky associations that, especially for the golliwog, are not clear, being neither traditional, personal nor self-evident.[11]

7   Owen Davies, *A Supernatural War: Magic, Divination and Faith During the First World War* (Oxford: Oxford University Press, 2018), 149–51.

8   Eric and Jane Lawson, *The First Air Campaign: August 1914–November 1918* (Cambridge, MA: Da Capo Press, 2002), 147–8; Mike Polston, 'John McGavock Grider (1892–1918)', *The Encyclopedia of Arkansas History and Culture*, <http://www.encyclopedi aofarkansas.net/encyclopedia/entry-detail.aspx?entryID=5277>, accessed 1 June 2018.

9   IWM, EPH 7458 and 4899.

10   Davies, *Supernatural War*, 168–9, 173.

11   Some contemporary derivations were given by Caroline Frevert, 'Nenette and Rintintin', *St Nicholas: An Illustrated Magazine for Girls and Boys* 46 (1918–19), 120.

Ad Hoc Mass-Produced Found Objects

Most people have heard the rhyme, 'Find a penny, pick it up, and all day long you'll have good luck' (although pins feature in other versions), and so coins of all shapes and descriptions were carried by soldiers, too. Coins, naturally, were often associated with good luck in gambling: soldiers were gambling with their lives.[12]

There are many documented instances of lucky coins. As he made his way to what would be the Battle of Mons, Joe Cassells, Black Watch, and a friend were given half-franc coins by an elderly Frenchman, 'saying that it would give us good luck and bring us through alive'.[13] Cassells survived the war and so did his friend: as few 'Old Comtemptibles' did, he credited their good fortune to the lucky coins.

My research also turned up what had been previously undocumented oral history. Private Shore, Machine Gun Corps, carried with him a lucky silver shilling from 1906 with the picture of King Edward VII on one side and a brooch pin soldered on to the back. He was wounded by shrapnel, but survived the war.[14]

Lucky coins came in all shapes and currencies. I have a 1916 farthing with the middle delicately cut out to highlight the King's head and pierced with a chain link so that it could be worn. Another is a Belgian five centime piece from 1914 mounted with a red stone, probably cut glass. I also have an example of a penny from 1904 shot through with a bullet, combining the belief in lucky coins with that of there being a particular bullet destined to hit the soldier.

12   For some coin superstitions, see Cora Linn Daniels, and Charles McClellan Stevens, *Encyclopaedia of Superstitions, Folklore and the Occult Sciences of the World* (Milwaukee: J. H. Yewdale & Sons, 1903); Martin Manser, *Dictionary of Proverbs* (New York: Facts on File, 2007).

13   Joe Cassells, *The Black Watch: A Record in Action* (Garden City, NY: Doubleday, Page & Co., 1918), 4–7.

14   Dave Shore, personal communication, 22 July 2014.

Figure 9. A British 1892 penny fixed onto a German brass shell case made by Krupp (stamped 'Berndorf 1895'), engraved with 'Mons 23-8-14', the name and date of the first battle between the British and German armies. According to the story, the coin was carried by a soldier of the Cheshire Regiment who survived the war. Author's collection.

The representative object examined here is a British penny from 1892 fixed onto a brass shell case, which is crudely engraved with 'Mons 23-8-14' (Figure 9), the name and date of the first battle between the British and German armies. According to the story, his name was S. (believed to be Steven) Adam, Cheshire Regiment, and he carried the coin with him through the war and survived. The shell case was manufactured by Krupp in Berndorf, Austria, in 1895, so undoubtedly would have been used early in the war, and the first Battalion, Cheshire Regiment, saw action at Mons, although his name was probably 'Samuel Adams'.[15] This artefact combines mass-produced found objects to create a unique hand-made souvenir of luck, fusing industrialization with folk modes of expression.

15   Roger Bates, personal communication, 7 January 2015. The records of the Cheshire Regiment had no S. (Steven) Adam; the closest was Private Samuel Adams, National Archives, Kew, WO 372/1/18484.

Religious Artefacts

The often morally motivated separation between religion and magic obfuscates the use of religious objects as magical charms. Crucifixes, rosaries, scapula, Agnus Dei and consecrated coins as lucky charms are all mentioned in contemporary accounts,[16] but it is the bullet-stopping Bibles that have become legendary. According to soldier Arthur Wrench, the carrying of New Testaments was widespread – an estimated 40 million Christian tracts, including Bibles, were distributed among the British military during the war – and there are some authenticated instances of their life-saving properties.[17]

Lieutenant General Sir Arthur Smith claimed to have survived the war thanks to his Bible. Already an officer in the Coldstream Guards on the outbreak of war, his father gave him a pocket Bible, with a verse from Psalms 91 on the flyleaf: 'Because thou hast made the Lord thy refuge. There shall no evil befall thee. For he shall give his angels charge over thee to keep thee in all thine ways.' His father had carried it through the Boer War and now he trusted that it would keep his son safe.[18]

In November 1914, Smith was on night reconnaissance when caught by a German bombardment. He was hit and thrown to the ground by the force: a piece of shrapnel had pierced the book before stopping at the ninety-first Psalm. He described it as 'a very significant thing and encouraged my faith'.[19]

---

16   Bartlett, *Mud and Khaki*, 124; Alex Watson, 'Self-Deception and Survival: Mental Coping Strategies on the Western Front, 1914–18', *Journal of Contemporary History* 41/ 2 (April 2006), 259.

17   For Wrench's war diaries, see Watson, 'Self-Deception and Survival', 259. For the volume of literature, see Michael Snape, *God and the British Soldier: Religion and the British Army in the First and Second World Wars* (London: Routledge, 2007), 232–3; and Alan Wilkinson, *The Church of England and the First World War* (Cambridge: Lutterworth, 2014), 153.

18   Brigadier Ian Dobbie, OBE, 'Lieutenant General Sir Arthur Smith (1890–1977)', in Michael Claydon and Philip Bray, eds, *The Fight of Faith: Lives and Testimonies from the Battlefield* (London: Panoplia, 2013).

19   Quoted in John Lewis-Stempel, *Six Weeks: The Short and Gallant Life of the British Officer in the First World War* (London: Orion, 2011), unpaginated edition.

Private Leonard Knight was also given a pocket Bible, this time from his aunt Minnie in July 1915. His edition stopped a German bullet. It has been passed down through his family and still exists today, the bullet still embedded. The Imperial War Museum has a Bible said to have belonged to Gunner John Dickinson, Royal Artillery, that took a German bullet for him in 1915.[20]

Lieutenant Colonel T. E. Lawrence, 'Lawrence of Arabia', came across something similar during his military operations in the Middle East. One of his allies, Auda abu Tayi, carried an 'amulet Koran' and, he claimed, in the thirteen years he had carried it had not once been wounded. He showed it to Lawrence after a volley of rifle fire had shot his camel from under him and torn his equipment to shreds, but otherwise left him unhurt. Auda had paid £120 for it, but Lawrence noted that it was a cheap edition printed in Glasgow: truly, magic is in the mind of the believer.[21]

Russian flying ace Alexander Alexandrovich Kazakov carried an icon of St Nicholas for good luck.[22] Crucifixes were of course widely used and mass-produced, industrialized objects, but several 'trench art' type crosses made from bone have also been documented: the Imperial War Museum has examples.[23] Combatants from both sides carried printed letters promising God's protection: the British had 'Saviour's Letters', the French *lettres du ciel* and German soldiers carried *Himmelsbriefe* and *Schutzbriefe* ('Heaven Letters' and 'Protection Letters'). Use of the Hand of Fatima, a symbol of good luck derived from Islamic tradition, is also recorded.[24] But perhaps the most unusual charm was the gift given by Maori chiefs to the Captain of HMS *New Zealand*: a *piupiu* (a skirt made of black and white flax woven together) and a *hei-tiki* (a figure carved in jade and worn around the neck as an amulet), with the instructions that these should be worn when the ship was in action.

---

20 'Pocket Bible Saved WWI Soldier's Life', *Daily Mail* (16 January 2017); IMW, EPH 2024.
21 T. E. Lawrence, *The Seven Pillars of Wisdom* (London: Jonathan Cape, 1935 [1926]), 307.
22 Lawson, *The First Air Campaign*, 147–9.
23 IWM, EPH 3476 and 7460.
24 See the French 'Porte Bonheur du Poilu' good luck postcard reproduced in Davies, *Supernatural War*, 142. For the protection letters, see Davies, *Supernatural War*, 183–92.

Industrialized Magic

The instructions were carried out and, despite being involved in the major sea battles of Heligoland, Dogger Bank and Jutland, the *New Zealand* survived.[25]

We see a mix of craft items, even art works, and mass-produced objects. The Bibles and Korans run off modern printing presses in their thousands were just as lucky as hand-painted icons. The manner of their creation was secondary to the method of their employment.

Mass-Produced Charms

As well as large numbers of charms fashioned in the shape of traditionally 'lucky' objects, such as horseshoes, four-leaf clovers, white heather, pigs and black cats, we also find more unusual objects, such as pocket mirrors advertised as being able to deflect bullets. Black cats and the number thirteen were also used in charms, although folklore did not always support their lucky associations, especially the number thirteen. Another item that appears surprising from our historical perspective was the swastika. A variety of swastika charms were manufactured and carried by British and Allied soldiers during the war. Some 'limited edition' pieces included iron crosses and swastikas made from the wreckage of a downed German Zeppelin.[26] Manufacturers also created two curious 'lucky' figurines: Touchwood (or Touchwud) and Fumsup (from 'thumbs up'), with their names reflecting their specific functions.

The practice of 'touching wood' to avert misfortune is a well-documented European custom and the Touchwood figure was designed to continually do this on the owner's behalf, or provide an easy source of wood to touch

---

25   For the numerous sources to this story, see Ruickbie, *Angels in the Trenches*, passim; the *hei-tiki* was known to Wright and Lovett, 'Specimens', 293.

26   '51. Collection of Amulets and Charms Worn by the Troops', *Medicine and Surgery in the Great War, 1914–1918: An Exhibition* (London: Wellcome Institute, 1968), 16. See also the discussion in Vanessa Chambers, 'A Shell with My Name on It: The Reliance on the Supernatural during the First World War', *Journal for the Academic Study of Magic* 2 (2004), 79–102.

when the need arose. The Irish journalist Michael MacDonagh described the Touchwood as 'a tiny imp, mainly head, made of oak, surmounted by a khaki service cap, and with odd, sparkling eyes, as if always on the alert to see and avert danger. The legs, either in silver or gold, are crossed, and the arms, of the same metal, are lifted to touch the head.'[27]

They came in several varieties and sold in huge numbers. I have a 'John Bull' type with the Union Flag painted on his wooden belly (Figure 10). A Mrs Touchwood was also produced, as well as more specifically martial models: 'Tommy Touchwud' in a peaked forage cap and 'Jack Touchwud' with a sailor's cap.[28] One distributor, Henry Brandon, reported sales of over a million Touchwoods during the war. He claimed to have received many letters from frontline soldiers attributing their survival to his charm.[29]

Figure 10. A Touchwud lucky charm, with crossed legs and both hands touching the round wooden head/body. Provenance unknown. Author's collection.

Fumsup depicted the 'thumbs up' gesture, described during the war as 'Tommy's expression which means "everything is fine with me"'.[30] As a

---

27 Michael MacDonagh, *The Irish on the Somme* (London: Hodder & Stoughton, 1917), 88.

28 Davies, *Supernatural War*, 162–3.

29 MacDonagh, *Irish on the Somme*, 89, quotes from one of these.

30 Arthur Guy Empey, *From the Fire Step: The Experiences of an American Soldier in the British Army* (London, New York: G.P. Putnam's Sons, 1917), 253.

decorative design, figures giving the thumbs up had appeared for some years prior to the war and could be combined with other symbols of luck.[31] The most important innovation was the development of a wearable figurine incorporating a wooden head, giving it the additional powers of a Touchwud. Like Touchwud, the design had its variants, including a 'Tommy' model wearing the characteristic 'tin hat'.

Not only were these charms mass produced, but they could also be mass distributed. MacDonagh witnessed a British Army publicity stunt in which over a thousand Touchwuds were given to soldiers of the sixth Battalion, City of London Rifles, in Regent's Park on 14 August 1915, with a Pathé news team present to film it all.[32] That the Army organized this shows how seriously they viewed the matter of lucky charms, at least as a moral booster if not a paranormal protective, and harnessed the machinery of mass communication to spread the message.

The Industrialization of Enchantment

Among the many contributions of the great sociologist Max Weber (1864–1920), was the sweeping characterization of the West's descent into disenchantment (*Entzauberung*). Although never fully articulating a theory of disenchantment as such,[33] Weber teased out the associated strands that formed the warp and weft of what he called the 'iron cage of rationality', including instrumentality, calculativeness, bureaucratization, intellectualization and so on. Central to all of these was the concept of the loss of magic as a means to salvation. Weber's Christian worldview imposed 'salvation' in contexts where it may not have been historically accurate, but the universally applicable idea

---

31   Davies, *Supernatural War*, 165.
32   MacDonagh, *Irish on the Somme*, 88.
33   Gilbert G. Germain, 'The Revenge of the Sacred: Technology and Re-Enchantment', in A. Horowitz and T. Maley, eds, *The Barbarism of Reason: Max Weber and the Twilight of Enlightenment* (Toronto: University of Toronto Press, 1994), 250.

of magic as a means to relieve suffering, or to bring about positive ontological transformation, lies at the root of the term 'salvation'.[34]

Weber's characterization of disenchantment emerged out of his own mental struggle in the final days of the First World War and may not be entirely inseparable from it.[35] Where Weber saw hope die under the relentless barrage of modern warfare, and it surely did at times, he also failed to notice the persistence of magic in such circumstances and especially the way in which it forged alliances with the very mechanisms of disenchantment.

A classic strategy of disenchantment, means-ends rationality,[36] is seen at work in the British Army's use of superstitious charms. Overlooking the deeper meaning of the objects and their implications, the military simply employs a strategy that it believes will help boost morale and hence fighting ability. In order to meet this requirement, other modes of disenchantment must also be employed, such as bureaucratization to source, supply and deliver the necessary number of magical items to the rank and file.

Industrialization was a highly visible mode of disenchantment, deploying 'dark Satanic mills' of soulless rationalized production across the land to entice the populace away from Weber's bucolic fantasies (his idealized 'enchanted garden').[37] Certainly, there could be no going back to Weber's historical moments of high enchantment – the ages of Ancient Greece and

---

34   The principal text is Max Weber, *Max Weber's 'Science as a Vocation'*, ed. P. Lassman and I. Velody (London: Routledge, 2015). For a thorough exploration of Weber's 'disenchantment', see L. P. Ruickbie, 'The Re-Enchanters: Theorising Re-Enchantment and Testing for Its Presence in Modern Witchcraft', unpublished PhD thesis, King's College, London, 2005.

35   Some have argued that 'disenchantment' is more a reflection of Weber's psychology at this time than it is of socio-cultural conditions, see Terry Maley, 'The Politics of Time: Subjectivity and Modernity in Max Weber', in Horowitz and Maley, *The Barbarism of Reason*, 139–66.

36   Germain, 'Revenge of the Sacred', 252.

37   On the concept of the 'enchanted' or 'magical garden', see Max Weber, *The Religion of China*, trans. and ed. H. H. Gerth (New York: The Free Press, 1951), 200, 227, and Max Weber, *The Religion of India*, trans. and ed. H. H. Gerth and D. Martindale (New York: The Free Press, 1958), 336.

the Old Testament[38] – but another form of enchantment was emerging. So twisted and tortured by the modes of modern production that it might be mistaken for disenchantment, yet enchantment it remained, albeit a hybridized, mechanized enchantment more fitted for its times. Magic as salvation was still there, but it could now be bought in every jewellery shop and mail ordered.

In addition to mass-produced magic, other mass production items could also take on magical functions. We saw this with printed editions of religious scripture, where at least positive spiritual associations were easy to elucidate, but also with other mass production items where meaning shaded off from underlying folk traditions to personal connotations, ranging from coins to shrapnel and wreckage. We see two modes of enchantment practices: the deliberate (and disenchanted) mass production of charms and the re-purposing of ordinary, unenchanted mass-produced items to create magical objects.

Some forms may have died out – we no longer find Touchwud and Fumsup on the shelves – but the mass production and mass distribution of lucky horseshoes, lucky four-leafed clover, etc., continues. This underscores the realization that industrialization is not a counter to magic and even means-end rationality can find uses for the 'irrational'. Disenchanted structures do not necessarily and always produce disenchantment because, as we saw, magic is in the mind of the believer, not as an impotent fantasy, but as a deep-seated way of thinking (pre-enchantment) that is necessarily expressed in material forms. We can go further to argue that magical thinking, purely as internal thought, is insufficient on its own, or else it would not require physical expression, running counter to disenchantment's intellectualizing trend. Industrialization is well suited to meet this demand. These simple 'trinkets' thus challenge and complicate one of sociology's major contributions to our understanding of the world.

---

38   Alkis Kontos, 'The World Disenchanted, and the Return of Gods and Demons', in
       Horowitz and Maley, *The Barbarism of Reason*, 229.

Conclusion

The widespread superstitiousness of military personnel has been situated within the context of broader 'coping strategies' that allowed mental survival under extreme combat conditions.[39] That is certainly true; however, as many charms were given or sent (and also kept) by relatives and loved ones at home, we must also see that they served as coping strategies for everyone affected by the war. And there was nothing new in this.

The idea of a 'revival' of magic is belied by the evidence that lucky charms were already popular, but the impression was amplified by the mechanisms of industrialized society: mass production, mass distribution and mass communication. We see a natural expansion of industrialization in progress as it transforms the charm market to meet the needs of rising demand. The industrialization of magic would never supplant the ad hoc personal item, tailored by circumstance to afford a unique sense of magical protection, but mass production enabled mass consumption, vital in an age of mass destruction.

Whatever their origin, all of these diverse objects functioned as magical amulets, offering their bearers protection through symbolic associations that activated non-logical 'magical thinking'. Their widespread use demonstrates an enduring capacity to turn to and rely on magical means in times of danger and uncertainty that survives (and confounds) hypothesized socio-cultural processes of 'disenchantment' as famously described by Max Weber, and underlines Claude Lévi-Strauss's observation that conceptions of 'mana' are so widespread as might constitute a 'universal form of thought'.[40] The carrying of charms might constitute a universal form of *behaviour* reflecting a persistent underlying want – the sanction of safety in perilous places – as well as the deep enchantment of the human psyche.

39   Watson, 'Self-Deception and Survival', 249.
40   Stuart A. Vyse, *Believing in Magic: The Psychology of Superstition* (Oxford: Oxford University Press, 1997), 3; see Levi-Strauss's 'Introduction' to Marcel Mauss, *A General Theory of Magic*, trans. R. Brain (London: Routledge & Kegan Paul, 1972).

Murray Leeder

Unseen Forces (1920)

In 1919's *The Case Against Spiritualism*, author Jane T. Stoddart notes that twenty years earlier spiritualism's opponents had basically declared victory, having seen spiritualism dwindle from the powerful social movement it was earlier in the nineteenth century to a few isolated hobbyists with little broader influence. But that turned out to be just a low ebb in the movement's popularity. Furthering her watery metaphor, she adds, 'Can we wonder that a tidal wave should have followed the late war?'[1] A decade later, in his anti-spiritualist pamphlet *The Abomination in Our Midst*, Owen Francis Dudley attributed the renewed attention to spiritualism to a number of factors. These include the decline of traditional Protestant churches leaving many former congregants looking for alternatives, certain prominent and respectable advocates for spiritualism like Oliver Lodge and Arthur Conan Doyle, and perhaps most importantly of all, the Great War and the mass climate of loss and mourning.[2] The concern about the exploitation of grief by unscrupulous frauds was not limited to anti-spiritualists but was also an important concern within the movement: even a writer sympathetic to spiritualism condemned those who 'grow fat on the easy credence of the mob of curiosity-hunters, and on the broken hearts of those who have lost their dear ones in the war and since' as 'worse than murderers.'[3] There was

---

1   Jane T. Stoddart, *The Case against Spiritualism* (New York: George H. Doran Company, 1919), 12.

2   Owen Francis Dudley, *The Abomination in Our Midst: An Exposure of Spiritualism* (London: Burns, Oates & Co., 1928), 12.

3   E. Ebrard Rees, *Spiritualism: A Criticism and Suggested Solution* (Poole: The Wessex Press, 1920), 72.

a flurry of both pro- and anti-spiritualist rhetoric after the war. It therefore seems unsurprising that filmmakers on both sides of the Atlantic saw spiritualism as attractive subject matter – operating, more often than not, with an anti-spiritualist sensibility.

This was not especially anything new; the early embrace of cinema as an anti-spiritualist medium has been well documented, notably by Matthew Solomon.[4] Georges Méliès, George Albert Smith, J. Stuart Blackton and Walter R. Booth all made trick films mocking fraudulent mediums and the credulity of their audiences. In certain respects, these depictions continue traditions of exposures by stage magicians. In 1913, a British film bore the self-explanatory title *Fraudulent Spiritualism Exposed*; another British film would be called *Fake Spiritualism Exposed* (1926). American anti-spiritualist films include two-reeler *Is Conan Doyle Right?* from 1926, naming probably the most influential spiritualist in the world, and a fairly large body of plotted dramas, including Tod Browning's *The Mystic* (1925). Phony mediums, clairvoyants and seers of various ilk are stock characters in the 1920s and would remain so for decades. Some are outright villains, working either alone or for criminal syndicates and some, like Paul Bavian (Alan Dinehart) in 1933s *Supernatural,* are even murderers. Others are more trivial, comical figures; some are even redeemable. But the most consistent characteristic is that they are motivated principally by greed.

However, the overriding concept that film's magic should be of the modern secular kind – 'illusion understood as illusion'[5] – did not entirely preclude the production of pro-spiritualist films, especially in the grief-stricken post-war. Labelling a film 'pro-spiritualist' could mean several things. D. W. Griffith's *The Greatest Question* (1919) might be regarded this way since it presents contact from beyond the grave that is mystical and positive. In publicity for this film, Griffith framed the titular question of the hereafter as an especially important one 'in this day and time when the grief of thousands of mothers have not yet healed from the lust of a War God'.[6] And indeed *The Greatest Question* features

---

4   Matthew Solomon, *Disappearing Tricks: Silent Film, Houdini, and the New Magic of the Twentieth Century* (Urbana: University of Illinois Press, 2010), esp. 11–27.

5   Simon During, *Modern Enchantments: The Cultural Power of Secular Magic* (Cambridge, MA: Harvard University Press, 2002).

6   Qtd. in John T. Soister, and Henry Nicolella, *American Silent Horror, Science Fiction and Fantasy Feature Films, 1913–1929* (Jefferson, NC: McFarland, 2012), 246.

the ghostly return of a son who died in the war. Yet the film features no mediumship, no séances, no use of automatic writing or spirit photography or similar methods of spirit contact, and though it might be broadly consistent with spiritualist ideals, it is less overtly pro-spiritualist than some other films of its period. Films that seem designed specifically to appeal to a pro-spiritualist audience mostly come from small, non-Hollywood film companies.

The best example known to me is sadly lost; this is 1923's *The Bishop of the Ozarks*. Starring, written and produced by Milford W. Howard, a reformist politician from Alabama, it was the lone film produced by the Cosmopolitan Film Company. *The Bishop of the Ozarks*'s press agent, a spiritualist named Dr Guy Bogart, tried to promote it specifically to spiritualist viewers. Among his claims was that the ghost of Abraham Lincoln was observed on the set – Lincoln being a very significant figure for spiritualism – and that W. T. Stead and James Martin Peebles, both prominent deceased spiritualists, also 'aided in the making of the picture [...] from the spirit world'[7] (see Figure 11). The publicity of *Bishop of the Ozarks* demonstrates that there was at least thought to be an audience to whom pro-spiritualist portrayals could be marketed.

Figure 11. 'Lincoln's New Job.' *The Kansas City Kansan* (9 July 1922), 16.

7   'Lincoln's New Job', *The Kansas City Kansan* (9 July 1922), 16.

Surviving films with overt pro-spiritualist messages include *Unseen Forces* (1920), *Whispering Shadows* (1921), and *Flesh and Spirit* (1922). Each of these films has a familiar suffrage-era film heroine at its centre. She is a variation on the 'serial queen' archetype[8] – active, intelligent, capable, investigative, but also vulnerable – and also in each case more spiritually advanced and in touch with the spirit world than the men around them. I will here discuss *Unseen Forces*, which was adapted from Robert W. Chambers' novel *Athalie* (1915) and produced by the short-lived Mayflower Photoplay Corporation. As with *The Bishop of the Ozarks*, publicity emphasized spiritualist sympathies by the filmmakers, claiming that its star, Australian actress Sylvia Breamer, was 'a staunch supporter of Sir Oliver Lodge', the prominent scientist who, since the war death of son Raymond, had become one spiritualism's de facto leaders, and claim[ed] that 'she herself communicated with her dead father, the late Commander Breamer of the British Navy'.[9] Breamer plays a woman named Miriam, and the film begins with her mother's death in childbirth during a thunderstorm. Emerging from this lightning-framed tragedy, Miriam is understood as a special, spiritually advanced person, referred to in intertitles as 'A STRANGELY POTENT SOUL'. By the age of 8, coming to age in a New York State hunting camp, she displays powers of precognition, and is nicknamed 'THE GIRL WHO SEES AROUND CORNERS'. The intertitles emphasize that she is not only talented but also 'HAD A PASSION FOR PROTECTING EVERYTHING – FOR GIVING HERSELF TO THE SERVICE OF OTHERS'. When she is about 18, Miriam's father (Harry Garrity) dies and she hears him whisper 'Goodbye' and witnesses a manifestation of his spirit, a so-called 'crisis apparition'[10] (See Figure 12). This and other ghostly appearances in the film are visualized with double exposures, the stock aesthetic for depicting the supernatural in the silent era and well beyond. Its gauzy, half-present images were ideal for visualizing the concept of multiple worlds intersecting on screen.[11]

8   Ben Singer, *Melodrama and Modernity: Early Sensational Cinema and Its Contexts* (New York: Columbia University Press, 2001).

9   'Spiritualism Is a Feature of Unseen Forces', *Hamilton Evening Journal* (22 April 1921), 7.

10   Henry Sidgwick et al., 'Report on the Census of Hallucinations', *Proceedings of the Society for Psychical Research* 10 (1894), 25–422.

11   Murray Leeder, *The Modern Supernatural and the Beginnings of Cinema* (Houndmills, Basingstoke, Hampshire: Palgrave Macmillan, 2017).

Figure 12. Miriam (Sylvia Breamer) observes the ghost of her father
(Harry Garrity) in *Unseen Forces*, dir. Sidney Franklin (Mayflower Photoplay
Corporation, 1920).

The young man she is in love with, Clyde Branton (Conrad Nagel),
witnesses Miriam being consoled by another man over her father's death.
Thinking that she's in love with him, a distressed Clyde immediately joins an
expedition to Africa. The narrative advances to three years later and chances its
setting to New York City, where Clyde and Miriam intersect again by chance.
He is now trapped in a loveless marriage to a cold woman named Winnifred
(Rosemary Theby) who married him for money. Miriam is now a prominent
medium in New York, characterized as 'the city of skeptics'. Miriam ministers
to both the rich and poor, but she refuses payment and only does it to help
people. This makes clear that the audience is to understand her as a kind of
spiritual guide, not a performer. Miriam is also being romantically pursued
by the 'wealthy idler and friller' Arnold Crane (Robert Cain). As plot complication piles on plot complication in the fashion of silent melodramas, it
ultimately transpires that at some point in the past, Winnifred and Arnold

Spiritualism in American Cinema

had a daughter out of wedlock who died young and whose very existence was kept secret somehow.

Fearing the reassociation of Miriam and Clyde, Winnifred and Arnold Crane scheme to accuse her of fraud. She is called before a tribunal of the 'Psychical Research Committee', which reflects the estrangement between the more academic and empirical-minded field of psychical research and spiritualism. The once friendly relationship between spiritualists and the Society for Psychical Research and the American Society for Psychical Research soured in the face of S.P.R. led exposures.[12] In 1918, the president of the A.S.P.R., James H. Hyslop, accused spiritualists of '[remaining] in the limbo of dark séances and undiscriminating performances, which carry no more weight with any intelligent man'.[13] Asked to demonstrate her powers, Miriam protests that '[t]he power that moves me is from the Source of all life and all good – to command or control it is impossible', but apparently, if she fails to perform on cue, it would destroy her reputation and thus her capacity to do good work. Miriam manages to dramatically summon the ghost of Winnifred and Arnold's deceased daughter (see Figure 13). In addition to restoring Miriam's good name, this manifestation moves Winnifred to consent to a divorce from Clyde, securing a happy ending for all.

12   Pamela Thurschwell, *Literature, Technology and Magical Thinking, 1880–1920* (Cambridge: Cambridge University Press, 2001), 17–18.

13   Beth A. Robertson, *Science of the Seance: Transnational Networks and Gendered Bodies in the Study of Psychic Phenomena, 1918–40* (Vancouver, BC: UBC Press, 2016), 8.

Figure 13. Miriam (Sylvia Breamer) conjures the spirit of a deceased girl in *Unseen Forces*, dir. Sidney Franklin (Mayflower Photoplay Corporation, 1920).

There is also a clear reference to then immediate context of war, death and loss. A subplot concerns a rich New Yorker named Joe Simmons (James O. Barrows), who has sought out Miriam to help him find his children, who were lost in Belgium during the Great War. He disappears midway through the narrative but makes a timely reappearance during the tribunal scene with said children in tow, having found them thanks to Miriam's paranormal cognition. *Unseen Forces* thus embodies spiritualism's promise that the proper consultation will reconnect you with missing loved ones, here rather more literally 'missing' than usual.

Numerous sources have detailed the particular relationship between women and spiritualism[14]. Further, it is noteworthy that, by the 1920s, the

---

14   E.g. Janet Oppenheim, *The Other World: Spiritualism and the Psychical Research in England, 1850–1914* (Cambridge: Cambridge University Press, 1985); Jill Galvan, *The Sympathetic Medium: Feminine Channeling, the Occult, and Communication Technologies, 1859–1919* (Ithaca, NY: Cornell University Press, 2010).

most prominent spiritualists were men (J. Arthur Hill, William Barrett, Conan Doyle and Lodge), often doctors and scientists. The principally female medium was instrumentalized; Lodge characterized her as

> a delicate piece of apparatus, wherewith we are making an investigation [...] an instrument whose idiosyncrasies must be learnt, and to some extent humoured, just as one studies and humours the ways of some much less delicate piece of physical apparatus turned out by a skilled instrument maker.[15]

The construction of Miriam is maybe *Unseen Forces*'s most striking feature: she is figured as a decidedly special, borderline saintly individual, ill-suited to the masculine, urban world of commerce and formal investigation. The contrast between Miriam and the villainous Winnifred is almost Manichean: after Winnifred refuses Clyde's request for a divorce, he wonders, 'Is there anything as high or as low as a woman?' – shades of Freud's Madonna-whore complex. The fact that *Unseen Forces* strives to maintain Miriam's spiritual purity through her refusal to professionalize her talents reflects a then-current drive by spiritualist organizations to distance themselves the commercial aspects of mediumship, and thus slough off the legacy of exposures.[16] As Stoddart notes, Doyle overtly sought to distance spiritualism itself from professional mediumship and indeed the séance itself, which too often attracts gawkers even when not fraudulent.[17] It is not surprising, then, that *Unseen Forces* paints Miriam's amateurism as evidence of her spiritual purity and innocence.

    Unseen Forces ends where it began, at Miriam's father's rural estate. Enervated by her experiences, Miriam nearly faints as they walk through an orchard arm in arm with Clyde. In the final scene Clyde proposes marriage to her, using his mother's ring. Removed from the 'City of Skeptics' and her draining if noble work, the film closes by containing her within heterosexual normality and within the spaces of her childhood. It is a distinctly regressive ending, reflective of masculinized 1920s spiritualism's need to manage female mediums, seen as both a necessity to the movement and a potential liability.

---

15   Qtd. in Stoddart, *The Case against Spiritualism*, 51–2.

16   Joseph McCabe, *Is Spiritualism Based on Fraud? The Evidence of Sir A. Conan Doyle and Other Drastically Examined* (London: Watts and Co, 1920).

17   Stoddart, *The Case Against Spiritualism*, 37.

There is a temptation to identify *Unseen Forces* and other pro-spiritualist films of its era as anticipating the afterlife fantasies of the 1940s that Peter L. Valenti (1978) dubbed 'film blanc'. The film blanc was also a phenomenon of war and its aftermath, and even dealt directly with the war on occasion, as in *A Guy Named Joe* (1943), *The Canterville Ghost* (1944) and *A Matter of Life and Death* (1946). These films certainly do flirt with many ideas consistent with spiritualist doctrine – notably an afterlife conspicuously free of judgement and punishment – but rarely if ever feature spiritualism directly. In the same period, fake mediums appear in a range of comedies, horror and crime films: *Pillow of Death* (1945), *Nightmare Alley* (1947), *Heading to Heaven* (1947), *The Amazing Mr. X* (1948), *Bunco Squad* (1950) and more. For whatever reason (perhaps as simple as the lack of prominent spokespersons like Doyle and Lodge), the Second World War failed to produce a dramatic upswing in spiritualism that the Second World War and other conflicts like the US Civil War had, and spiritualists never re-emerged as a block of power and thus as consumers to be sold specifically to. So while later films might contain positive depictions of mediumship – celebrity medium James van Praagh has likened his experiences to films like *Ghost* (1990) and *The Sixth Sense* (1999)[18] – the pro-spiritualist films I have outlined from the silent era did not significantly outlast it.

---

18   James Van Praagh, *Ghosts among Us: Uncovering the Truth about the Other Side* (New York: HarperOne, 2008).

Part II

Magic across Cultures

Enrique Ajuria Ibarra

Veneno para las hadas
(Poison for Fairies, 1984)

Magic in Mexican popular culture expresses a mixture of traditions that displays practices which may be widely assimilated or feared. For wellbeing or harm, magic is used either to improve the individual's body and mind, or to cause their demise. The idea of magic is deeply embedded within religious experience – the sacred and the profane, in the Roman Catholic tradition – and the belief that these rituals are effective. For Michael D. Bailey, magic in Latin America is the result of a layering of traditions that attest to a complex, hybrid network of experiences of magic: 'After the conquest, native people themselves readily identified some of these figures with Christian demons or the devil, and hence with Christian ideas of magic, but still worshiped or at least invoked them through traditional rites.'[1] Moreover, the idea or notion of magic as power is associated with people who possess extraordinary abilities that defy religious logic and nature itself; that is, witches.

In Mexican cinema, magic has been usually represented as witchcraft, such as in *El espejo de la bruja*[2] or *La tía Alejandra*.[3] Witchcraft and satanism also feature prominently in *Alucarda, la hija de las tinieblas*[4] and *Sobrenatural*.[5] Likewise, other forms of ritual magic linked with folk healing

1   Michael D. Bailey, *Magic: The Basics* (London: Routledge, 2018), 11.
2   *El espejo de la bruja* [*The Witch's Mirror*], dir. Chano Urueta (Alameda Films, 1962).
3   *La tía Alejandra* [*Aunt Alejandra*], dir. Arturo Ripstein (Conacine, 1979).
4   *Alucarda, la hija de las tinieblas* [*Alucarda, Daughter of Darkness*], dir. Juan López Moctezuma (Films 75, 1977).
5   *Sobrenatural* [*All of Them Witches*], dir. Daniel Gruener (Televicine, 1996).

are a central theme in films like *El rebozo de Soledad*.[6] Magic in Mexican cinema deals with cultural assumptions that, if magic is real, then it becomes vital and dangerous, whether for good or for evil. In this context, *Veneno para las hadas*[7] plays along with these notions, but adds a more nuanced layer for believing in the power of magic when children are engaged in these practices.

As a horror film, it demonstrates director Carlos Enrique Taboada's eloquent knowledge of an international horror aesthetic that serves as a starting point for his own films. Even though it is usually considered a minor genre in Mexico, most films have demonstrated to be inspired and to have used 'the conventions and iconography of the horror movies made by Hollywood during its own classical period of the 1930s and 1940s' onwards.[8] Misha MacLaird points out that the horror genre in Mexico has been in constant 'competition with high-budget Hollywood' films, but that recently there have been attempts to create more internationally recognized productions.[9] Rather than considering them as blatant copies of popular international films, the Mexican horror genre re-locates 'spaces, monstrous encounters, and hauntings', in order to explore 'more regional concerns about identity, reality, and history'.[10] Even though he only directed four horror films, Taboada demonstrated the use of specific genre conventions to address issues about social class and gender in modern Mexican society. In *Veneno para las hadas*, belief in magic is what frames a frightful depiction of childhood, bullying and abuse.

6   *El rebozo de Soledad* [*Soledad's Shawl*], dir. Roberto Gavaldón (Cinematográfica Televoz, 1952).

7   *Veneno para las hadas* [*Poison for Fairies*], dir. Carlos Enrique Taboada (IMCINE, 1984).

8   Andrew Syder, and Dolores Tierney, 'Importation/Mexploitation, or, How a Crime-Fighting, Vampire-Slaying Mexican Wrestler Almost Found Himself in an Italian Sword-and-Sandals Epic', in Steven Jay Schneider and Tony Williams, eds, *Horror International* (Detroit, MI: Wayne State University Press, 2005), 33–55, 38.

9   Misha MacLaird, *Aesthetics and Politics in the Mexican Film Industry* (New York: Palgrave Macmillan, 2013), 68.

10   Enrique Ajuria Ibarra, 'Media, Shadows, and Spiritual Bindings: Tracing Mexican Gothic in Óscar Urrutia Lazo's Rito Terminal', in Sandra Casanova-Vizcaíno and Inés Ordiz, eds, *Latin American Gothic in Literature and Culture* (New York: Routledge, 2018), 189–201, 192.

The film focuses on a young girl named Verónica, who firmly believes she is a witch. She befriends Flavia, another girl from her school, and convinces her of practising dark magic to fulfil their wishes and desires. Verónica is also concocting poison for fairies to destroy the witches' greatest enemies. Unlike other Mexican horror films that share the same theme of magic and witches, Taboada's film dons away the supernatural in favour of strange coincidences between real events and the girls' imaginary practice of witchcraft. Verónica forges an identity based on fairy-tale lore, and the film suggests that magic is effective because its practitioners believe it is changing their world. Therefore, Taboada's film suggests a relationship between cultural notions of magic and the naïveté of a child. The film's title ironically questions the idea of the innocent child, and points to magic as practice that can poison a girl's perception of wrongdoing. Thus, the horror in the film is not magic or witches themselves, but the actions taken to save others from these imaginary threats.

Taboada had previously explored the subject of dark magic in his film *El libro de piedra*.[11] Here, magic is defined by a Roman Catholic tradition inherited from Western Europe. In this sense, Taboada approaches it as a demonized and repressed practice that has been condemned by the development of Christianity in Europe and in the Americas.[12] The idea of magic in *Veneno para las hadas* does not acknowledge other forms of magic in Mexico; rather, it explores the implications of a fictional representation of magic and witchcraft that challenges the perceptions of such concepts in a modern, rational world. This represented magic taps at wishes and desires that can escalate to the realm of horror. Simon During claims that 'enlightened societies bring individuals to cluster around the poles of faith and freedom by means of entertainment and fiction, centred on magic – not its rational and civil citizens, but those "subjects" (buried within citizens) who desire and fantasize'.[13] Taboada examines these contradictions of rationality and irrationality towards magic in *Veneno para las hadas*, by particularly focusing on children whose free reign

11   *El libro de piedra* [*The Book of Stone*], dir. Carlos Enrique Taboada (Producciones AGSA, 1969).

12   Simon During, *Modern Enchantments: The Cultural Power of Secular Magic* (Cambridge, MA: Harvard University Press, 2002), 8–10.

13   Ibid., 62.

for imagination has not been cut short by the restrictions of logic and sense of reality pertaining to an adult view on the world.

Instilled by a tradition of fairy tales, Verónica constructs a malignant identity that is reinforced by her own behaviour towards Flavia. Following the filmic tradition in Western culture, Taboada's young witch becomes inspired by the antagonists in these tales. Willem De Blécourt argues that 'if screen witches have any historical ancestors, they are the witches in fairy tales or other literary works'.[14] *Veneno para las hadas* acknowledges a character elaboration that is already mediated by representations of witches and evil in popular culture. Verónica's identity is essentially forged on images and ideas passed on by her nanny, who reads fairy tales to her and explains what a witch is based on her own knowledge.

In her desire to impress (and possibly control) her new friend, Verónica designates herself as a witch with magical powers. Whilst Bailey notices that 'individuals do not typically designate themselves as magicians or practitioners of magic', and that the term 'magician is generally an accusation rather than a self-appellation',[15] Verónicas self-assertion as a witch carries in itself a complex self-perception that is derived from the girl's desire for power and control. Her attitude towards Flavia, a weak and shy girl, further satisfies her own fantasy, which she takes even further in the practice of rituals they perform together in secret.

Verónica's powers gain credibility when coincidental events, such as the sudden death of Flavia's piano teacher, appear as manifestations of her powers. Bothered by the fact that she is too strict on her, Flavia asks Verónica if she knows a spell that could end her piano classes. Lighted only with candles, the girls perform a series of actions they deem magical in the basement of Verónica's house: black candles for the Devil encircle Flavia's piano exercise book – an object associated with what she dislikes. The setting is dark and sombre with only key lighting focusing entirely on the girls' faces. In order to cast the spell, Verónica requests Flavia to focus on her piano teacher with her mind while she invokes Satan. She also forces Flavia to cut her index finger

---

14   Willem De Blécourt, 'Witches on Screen', in Owen Davies, ed., *The Oxford Illustrated History of Witchcraft and Magic* (Oxford: Oxford University Press, 2017), 253–80, 257.

15   Michael D. Bailey, 'The Meanings of Magic', *Magic, Ritual, and Witchcraft* 1/1 (2006), 1–23, 9.

and offer blood in exchange for taking the piano teacher away. Immediately, she burns a couple of pages from the piano exercise book to end the spell. The scene ambiguously portrays a light-hearted childhood game. At one point, even Flavia giggles at what Verónica does, but the situation quickly turns into something more macabre, a call for a change in reality to meet Flavia's whims. A few days later, Flavia's piano teacher dies during her lesson. Afterwards, she listens to her mother and father talk about the news, but she does not hear that the teacher had a pre-existing heart condition, only her mother lamenting why do these things suddenly happen.

Flavia immediately connects her secret reunion with Verónica as the true cause of her teacher's death, thus confirming her belief that her friend possesses supernatural powers. Flavia becomes convinced of Verónica's magical abilities by the inherent nature of their reunion: a secret meeting that only the two girls know about. This follows the cultural assumption that magic refers to actions or rituals that are performed in private, 'as opposed to public and communal ceremonies'.[16] Subsequently, Flavia's own notion of magic holds on to the idea that magic is 'shadowy and tenuous',[17] a tricky affair that has to be kept from the knowledge of adults. The girl's perception of nature and the world is affected by Verónica's fantasies and her control over her.

Flavia's fear is structured around the idea of a witch. According to Barbara Creed, a witch 'is usually depicted as a monstrous figure with supernatural powers and a desire for evil'.[18] Verónica's self-affirmation as a witch draws Flavia to believe that her friend is an evil-doer. Since a witch is 'thought to be dangerous and wily, capable of drawing on her evil powers to wreak destruction on the community',[19] Flavia is witness to Verónica's apparent ability to kill living beings by means of dark ceremonies. Verónica's aim to poison all fairies is additional proof to her friend that her power is outside legal and rational boundaries. Magic in Taboada's film is thus framed by a process of double enactment. On the one hand, *Veneno para las hadas* explores the consequences of believing in dark magic. On the other hand, Verónica's character is meant to act

16   Bailey, 'The Meanings of Magic', 9.
17   Ibid.
18   Barbara Creed, *The Monstrous-Feminine: Film, Feminism, Psychoanalysis* (London: Routledge, 1993), 76.
19   Ibid.

and constantly perform her desire to be a witch. The girl's cunning allows her to connect unrelated events around her to convince Flavia that she is indeed someone who is able to control nature, life and death. She takes these instances to her advantage not only to fool her friend, but to make believe that she is in control of exceptional situations in a supernatural form.

If Bailey claims that 'magic should be understood as a set of practices intended to influence or control either mystical, spiritual forces or physical properties that exist within nature but are hidden or occult',[20] then Verónica has successfully managed to instil a sense of uncanny articulations between seemingly ritual actions and unexpected events. This causes Flavia to believe her friend is more than just girl; she gradually becomes convinced that Verónica is 'malevolent' and possesses 'special knowledge'.[21] Therefore, the narrative relies on cunning actions and carefully coded speeches that shape Verónica as someone far from being normal. Additionally, Verónica is a pampered child with no parental figure that controls her whims, fantasies and desires. Her sense of magic, or the magical, allows her to project her wishful thinking and shape her identity in terms of disobedience, power and control.

This relationship between magic and desire is laid out by Sigmund Freud, who claims that 'the motives which lead men to practise magic' are, quite straightforward, 'human wishes'.[22] In this sense, the power of magic relies on a relationship between mental will and the desire to affect the physical world. As such, magic 'reveals in the clearest and most unmistakable way an intention to impose the laws governing mental life upon real things'.[23] What is of interest to Freud is this projection of desire and its coincidental association with unexpected or unprecedented events that change the perception of external reality and the interaction with other subjects. He suggests that this could be compared with a child's own 'psychical situation' in the sense that 'they create a satisfying situation by means of centrifugal excitations of their sense organs'.[24] This comparison is ideally suggested in Taboada's film: impersonated

20   Bailey, *Magic: The Basics*, 9.
21   Ibid., 45.
22   Sigmund Freud, 'Totem and Taboo', in *The Standard Edition of the Complete Psychological Works of Sigmund Freud* (London: Vintage/The Hogarth Press and the Institute of Psycho-Analysis, 1958), XIII, 83.
23   Ibid., XIII, 91.
24   Ibid., XIII, 83–4.

in a child, Verónica's wilful mind and desires seem to be linked with reality, apparently generating harmful and horrifying consequences through magic.

The film's focus on childhood provides this different dimension to the perception of magic. Verónica's transformation from a child to an evil witch is seen from the point of view of Flavia, who is constantly harassed by her friend. The figure of the child in this Mexican film is once again a reminder that age and innocence are correlated. That the main protagonists are also white girls adds to cultural assumptions of goodness inherent with race in Mexican culture. Chuck Jackson has already asked this in terms of American culture: 'What happens when the face of evil carries with it an uncanny reminder of the face of innocence?' But more importantly, it is necessary to consider how 'are our assumptions about "innocence," "evil," and "faces" suddenly unsettled?'[25] In Taboada's film, Verónica's behaviour is at odds with her looks. The idea of innocence and purity that could be ascribed to her looks forces us to question cultural perceptions of childhood.

Gothic fiction has been concerned with the portrayal of children in horror. Steven Bruhm advocates a 'dialectic' of 'innocence and possession/corruption', rather than a 'binary opposition', which 'brings into high relief exactly what the child knows, or what the child may be suspected of knowing'.[26] In *Veneno para las hadas*, magic becomes another signifier of evilness and corruption that may distort a child's imagination and sense of identity. Without any parental restraints, Verónica gradually becomes more threatening, and Flavia perceives her as bad or corrupted. As such, the reason why Verónica turns evil is more a lack of parenting than anything else. Karen J. Renner claims that 'evil children don't really exist in the popular imagination'. Rather, narratives involving evil children are attempts to 'confirm the essential innocence of children'. Their bad actions can be the result, among other circumstances, of 'flawed parenting' and 'faulty educational practices'.[27] Likewise, Bruhm alludes to the problem of 'momism' or 'momist poison' as part of the corruption of the Gothic child.[28]

25　Chuck Jackson, 'Little, Violent, White: The Bad Seed and the Matter of Children', *Journal of Popular Film & Television* 28/2 (2000), 64–73, 66.

26　Steven Bruhm, 'Nightmare on Sesame Street: Or, The Self-Possessed Child', *Gothic Studies* 8/2 (2006), 98–113, 103.

27　Karen J. Renner, *Evil Children in the Popular Imagination* (New York: Palgrave Macmillan, 2016), 7.

28　Bruhm, 'Nightmare on Sesame Street', 101.

In Taboada's film, this idea is carried over to maternal figures who are not actively involved in the narrative or are only glimpsed once or twice on screen.
Verónica's grandmother is portrayed as a senile woman, whilst her nanny is
just too busy with other house chores to focus on grounding any rules of behaviour. The nanny only dumps information about witches on her, and she
then chooses to behave like one for the sake of power.

As such, the perception of magic in *Veneno para las hadas* is strategically
framed around the possibility of wrongdoing for the sake of power and ex-
ponentially perceived as threatening and terrifying because it is a child who
desires to possess this ability. The film is characteristically presented from the
point of view of the two girls, with little intervention from the adults, whose
faces always stay off-screen. Thus, the idea of magic as something potentially
dangerous and deadly is seen persistently from the eyes of the child. The death
of the piano teacher, a coincidence voiced by Flavia's parents, is sutured instead
with illicit acts of black magic. The final scene in the film is the pinnacle of
Flavia's fear of Verónica. Verónica tells Flavia that they will concoct poison
for the fairies at night, in the crucible they have hidden in an abandoned
barn. Once inside, Flavia silently lights some stacked hay and locks Verónica
in. Despite her friend's pleas, she stares silently at the burning building, her
eyes reflecting the flames that are consuming the witch. The only way to save
herself and others is by inflicting violence on the girl who has been violent to
her with what she perceives is magic.

Bruhm notices that, rather than acting separately, the ideas of innocence
and corruption feed on each other in the construction of the idealized image
of the child. In this sense, 'childhood innocence exists "prior" to corruption,
but corruption is the only means by which we can recognise and name that
innocence'.[29] Once Flavia has recognized corruption in Verónica, the only
way to cleanse her is by destroying that very corruption. The burning of the
witch alludes to historical popular forms of eradicating these dark magic
practitioners. At the same time, it revolves around the complex contradictory
relationship between childhood, innocence and evil suggested by Bruhm. In
the film, Flavia's act of child slaughter is what allows her to destroy what she
perceives as evil. This evilness has come to the fore by the cultural assumption

29   Ibid., 108.

of what magic is, enacted and supported by Verónica herself. Magic in this Mexican horror film portrays the fear of believing in such practices, and the consequences and actions to eradicate the magical wrongdoers to preserve innocence and life. In the hands of a child, the desire for power through magic can only bring death of fairies and humans alike.

Katarzyna Ancuta

Representations of Magic in Thai Cinema

In many Asian cultures, magic remains a common cultural practice, its beliefs and rituals co-existing with official religions. Among them, the countries of Southeast Asia have gained an unsavoury reputation for practising more sinister kinds of magic seen as a means to manipulate people, vanquish one's enemies and obtain material or political gains. In Thailand, where magical thinking tends to be intertwined with Buddhist teachings, the two most powerful forms of such magic are associated with foreign import – Islamic Malay magic in the South and Khmer magic in the Northeast. Out of the two, Khmer magic is perceived as significantly more threatening, likely because its arcane rituals frequently require materials obtained from corpses. Khmer magic is also revered for its potent love spells, protection spells that make one's skin impervious to blades and bullets, and curses that magically insert unusual objects under one's skin.

Belief in magic and reliance on magical rituals is deeply ingrained in both private and public life of Thai people. Reports of magic rituals are included in early official accounts of visits of foreign emissaries and colonial explorers to Siam. Jeremias van Vliet, the head of the Dutch East India Company in Ayutthaya (1629–34), for instance, claims to have witnessed a particularly brutal ritual that involved burying pregnant women under the pillars of the city walls to turn them into vengeful sentinel ghosts.[1] But while such descriptions can be easily dismissed as examples of Orientalist othering, ample evidence for the persistence of magical thinking and magical practice in contemporary Thai society can be found in both anthropological journals and local journalistic coverage. Magic and its rituals are also deeply embedded in many Thai

---

1   Jeremias van Vliet, cited in Marlane Guelden, *Thailand: Into the Spirit World* (Bangkok: Asia Books, 1995), 56–7.

traditions and customs which continue to be evoked by the ruling powers to sustain the nationalistic myth of 'Thainess' and 'uniquely Thai values' – two imaginary categories that have been consistently employed over the years to rebut inconvenient political criticism and stall the democratization of Thai society.

Religious and supernatural knowledge, including the ability to practise magic was for a long time considered one of the necessary conditions of premodern manly masculinity (*chai chatri*) – the ideal of maleness, which by extension also served as the ideal Thai identity.[2] Thai Traditional Medicine recognizes spirit possession, spiritual attack, material or object intrusion (i.e., magical insertion of alien materials into the body of a person), homeopathic magic (i.e., manipulating objects resembling a person, like dolls) and contagious magic (i.e., manipulating objects connected to a person, such as hair, nail clippings or clothing) as the most common sources of illness.[3] Since the late 1980s, we have also seen the proliferation of popular urban spirit medium cults, blending conventional Theravada Buddhism, nationalistic state discourses, animistic and multi-original religious beliefs and practices, and magic in order to accommodate the spiritual needs of a capitalist society driven by pursuit of material success.[4] Astrologers, fortune-tellers, spirit mediums, sorcerers and Chinese geomancers are commonly employed to ensure the success of business enterprises and assist high-ranking army generals and prominent politicians. Numerous records, for instance, attribute both the rise to power and the downfall of the ousted prime minister Thaksin Shinawatra (2001–6) to magic, employed in equal measures by Thaksin himself and by his opponents.[5] Similarly, the subsequent political protests following one army coup (staged in 2006) and leading to another (staged in 2014) resorted to a variety of magical tactics including damaging statues to block their spiritual power,

2   Khet Sriyaphai, cited in Pattana Kitiarsa, 'The Fall of Thai Rocky', in Kathleen M. Adams and Kathleen A. Gillogly, eds, *Everyday Life in Southeast Asia* (Bloomington: Indiana University Press, 2011), 195–217, 201.

3   Alice B. Child, and Irvin L. Child, *Religion and Magic in the Life of Traditional Peoples* (Englewood Cliffs, NJ: Prentice Hall, 1993), 134–9.

4   Pattana Kitiarsa, 'Beyond Syncretism: Hybridization of Popular Religion in Contemporary Thailand', *Journal of Southeast Asian Studies* 36/3 (2005), 461–87, 468.

5   Pasuk Phongpaichit, and Chris Baker, 'The Spirits, The Stars and Thai Politics', a lecture given at Siam Society on 2 December 2008, <http://pioneer.netserv.chula.ac.th/~ppa suk/spiritsstarspolitics.pdf>, accessed 20 August 2020.

casting protective spells and blood curses, and even more bizarrely, employing used tampons and sanitary napkins as a protective shield, since it is widely believed that menstrual blood disrupts magic and renders talismans and amulets ineffective.[6]

While it may be difficult to pinpoint the exact origin of contemporary magical practices used in Thailand, as they tend to blend concepts and rituals from many sources (from Brahmin and Taoist rituals to Malay and Khmer sorcery), in Thai collective imaginary, and by extension in Thai popular culture, Khmer magic reigns supreme. Khmer magic is consistently portrayed as particularly sinister, due to its use of abject materials in its rituals (from hair clippings and nail pairings to sweat, blood, vaginal secretions, menses, aborted foetuses and corpses). One of the most common magical commodities obtained from corpses used in such magic is *nam man phrai*, literally translated as 'spirit oil' – a magical oil reportedly produced by means of burning a candle under a chin of a newly deceased cadaver, preferably someone who died an unexpected and violent death. The collected substance is then used as the main ingredient in love potions. One drop of such oil is said to be enough to ensnare any unsuspecting victim and turn them into one's sexual slave. Other common materials collected from corpses are the dust from cremated bones and the wax which is applied to the face of the deceased.[7] Khmer sorcerers are also said to be capable of projecting invisible missiles, or magically inserting a variety of objects into the bodies of the living. Some of the common objects include pieces of cloth, animal hide, wooden splinters, or pieces of metal, but you can also come across accounts that mention live animals, such as geckos or baby turtles that have miraculously materialized inside the victim's internal organs.[8]

Needless to say, this kind of magic is perfect material for horror and indeed the abuse of magic is the second most common theme in Thai horror films after ghost stories (although the two often come together). A common characteristic feature of such films is their shift of focus from the actual magical ritual to

---

6   Katarzyna Ancuta, 'That's the Spirit!: Horror Films as an Extension of Thai Supernaturalism', in Peter J. Bräunlein and Andrea Lauser, eds, *Ghost Movies in Southeast Asia and Beyond* (Leiden: Brill, 2016), 131–2.

7   Guelden, *Thailand*, 117–18.

8   Ibid., 114; Ancuta, 'That's the Spirit!', 132.

portraying the (often graphic) consequences of the spell or the curse. In doing so, the films gloss over the role of the male sorcerer performing the ritual, and focus solely on his female customer who is unanimously condemned for using dark magic and branded as an evil magic woman (despite the fact that she is often relatively ignorant of the process). Male customers casting similar spells are not given much space in the movies. A woman using services of a Khmer sorcerer, however, is immediately portrayed as a practitioner of dark arts and if she actually becomes adept at performing magic herself, her evil becomes unbound. This is exactly the premise of *The Art of the Devil* trilogy that offers, arguably, the most complex portrayal of Khmer magic in Thai horror film.

The Art of the Devil trilogy is not much of a trilogy, as the first film is not directly related to the other two. The first film in the series, *Khon Len Khong* (2004), was directed by a veteran director Thanit Jitnukul. It tells a story of a jilted mistress who uses black magic to destroy her lover and his family, and then goes after his former family to complete the task and take over his estate. With its plot mimicking never-ending Thai soap operas, which often blend supernatural elements with family drama, the film failed to excite the audience or the critics at the time of its release. One year later, in 2005, a group of seven filmmakers who chose to call themselves The Ronin Team[9] – Kongkiat Khomsiri, Isara Nadee, Pasith Buranajan, Seree Phongnithi, Yosapong Polsap, Putipong Saisikaew and Art Thamthrakul – released another movie called *Long Khong*, which was marketed under the English name *Art of the Devil 2* even despite its lack of connection to Jitnukul's film. This was followed by a sequel to *Long Khong*, also by The Ronin Team, which was named *Long Khong 2* or *Art of the Devil 3*, adding to the confusion. The middle film in the trilogy, *Long Khong*, which is certainly the most coherent of the three, will be the focus of my discussion.

The Thai title, *Long Khong* is difficult to translate, but the word *khong*, which often simply indicates an 'object', is used when referring to an act of casting spells or curses, as these are frequently tied to various objects, which are either planted near the victim, or manipulated by the originator of the spell. In the case of love spells, these are often two intertwined wax figurines, or dolls;

9   The name was reportedly chosen as most of these filmmakers used to be mentored by Jitnukul but were now expected to stand on their own (like the masterless samurai).

we also have objects that are being projected under the skin of the victim as invisible missiles. The film opens with a reference to such a practice – we are shown a man fishing in a river. Minutes later the same man, who now appears to be in agony, is taken to a local witch doctor. During the ritual, metal fish-hooks resembling the ones he used to catch his fish, begin to miraculously emerge from various parts of his body and the man finally dies from blood loss. Another scene in the film, reveals a cursing ritual where a Khmer shaman puts fish-hooks into the body of a fish which is used for magical transference.

Long Khong tells a story of magic gone wrong. The beginning of the film focuses on a group of high-school students in a rural province. When one of them discovers that his stepmother – a very attractive local teacher, Panor, is having an affair with a school gym instructor, his friends convince him to film them and expose their secret. The plan goes wrong and the kids get caught, which leads to a disturbing scene of sexual abuse used as a form of punishment. Time moves on and most of the group is now studying in Bangkok, with the exception of Panor's stepson, Ta, who stayed behind in the village. The group gets reunited to attend Ta's father's funeral and then, as they visit his (and Panor's) house by the river, strange things start happening. As the young protagonists begin to die mysterious supernatural deaths, we begin to realize it is Panor, who has become a powerful Khmer sorceress herself, taking revenge on Ta's friends for ruining her life.

Even today, *Long Khong* remains one of the most extreme examples of body horror in Thai cinema.[10] Some of its most memorable scenes include depictions of cannibalism (from eating the raw flesh of a corpse to eating a stew with body parts), a boy having his flesh burnt off the bones with an acetylene burner, a girl gouging her own eyes out with her fingernails, live geckos bursting out of a boy's skin, a man having his toenails ripped out with pliers, a grandma eating a live cat and a whole array of fairly regular (in comparison) gruesome deaths. Through a series of plot twists, it is revealed that almost all of the film's protagonists dabbled in magic and visited the same Khmer sorcerer. Kim (the main female student lead) placed a love spell on Ta, the most popular athlete

10   Quite interestingly, in an interview I conducted with one of the film's directors and scriptwriters, Kongkiat Khomsiri, he revealed that one of his sources of inspiration was a rather obscure 1980s German exploitation film *Nekromantik* (1987) by Jörg Buttgereit, which is focused on necrophilia.

at school. More disturbingly, their classmate, Por, placed a similar spell on Ta's stepmother, teacher Panor. The affair between Panor and the gym coach was also the result of a similar love spell. After the kids got sexually abused by the coach they visited the sorcerer as a group to place a curse on him (which resulted in the death-by-fish-hooks scene described before). Por also placed an additional curse on Panor, as he was jealous of her other affair. When Panor – humiliated and plagued by insufferable pain – eventually sought help of a local female witch doctor, she was told there was only one way to remove the curse – she needed to kill and eat the flesh of the sorcerer who had cursed her. She did that, and as a result, she took over his power.

The sequel (or rather prequel) to the film reveals even more mind-bending twists. Panor seduces Ta's father, which makes him poison his first wife, Duen. Duen's family kidnap Panor and ask a Khmer sorcerer to replace her soul with Duen's as a way of resurrecting her. Duen–Panor then tortures and murders her ex-husband (Ta's father) in revenge. Then the ritual backfires and Panor regains control of her body, which of course sends her on a murderous rampage. The final shots of the film reveal that the chain of events was started by Panor herself, who – originally, a rather unattractive teenager – asked the Khmer shaman for a spell to make everyone love her.

Throughout the two films, we are constantly given the message that there is nothing as evil as a woman abusing magic. The two male sorcerers introduced in the films are portrayed as professionals and adventurers. The female witch doctor, who does not practise black magic, is depicted as knowledgeable but ultimately powerless. It is the act of female rage that transforms Panor into the sorceress but the power she gains ultimately drives her insane. In Thai beliefs, women are said to be uniquely predisposed to being invaded by spirits due to their weak or disorganized *khwan* – vital essence.[11] This is why women (especially menstruating and pregnant women) are said to attract the wandering spirits, why they are commonly 'chosen' by spirits to act as spirit mediums, and why they often suffer the results of the misuse of magic. Unsurprisingly, two of the most powerful and feared Thai spirits – *phi pop* and *phi krasue*, are

11   Thomas A. Kirsch, 'Complexity in the Thai Religious System: An Interpretation', *The Journal of Asian Studies* 36/2 (1977), 241–66, 258–9.

typically recognized as witch-like *phi*,[12] gendered as female, and often portrayed as a form of punishment on women who abuse black magic.

In contrast, male practitioners of Khmer magic (and other related practices) are not given much space within Thai horror films. They appear more frequently in action/adventure films, where their magic is used to render them invincible and give them an advantage over their enemies. Films like *Necromancer* (*Chom Khamang Wet*, dir. Piyapan Choopetch, 2005) and *Khun Phan* (2016) and *Khun Phan 2* (2018), directed by Khongkiat Khomsiri, that pit bandits against stalwart policemen, portray the mastery of magic as one of the attributes of hard masculinity. While such portrayals may seem pure fantasy, they are in line with Thai popular beliefs prevalent till today. Though it may be hard to believe, Khun Phan is a historical figure – Phantharak Rajjadej (born in 1903), a renowned crime-fighter in the Southern province of Nakhon Si Thammarat who lived to be 108. In a similar fashion, Chavorat Jaruboon, a former Thai prison executioner, recalls one prisoner whose protective amulets blocked the firing squad's guns and made shooting him impossible until they were removed.[13] The magic used in male-oriented films is only identified as Khmer if used by the villains. Although the heroes may be subjected to the same rituals, the presence of a magical Buddhist monk is usually used to offset the negative image of magic associated with Khmer sorcery.

Drawing on the rich texture of authentic magical beliefs and practices, Thai films produce representations of magic that are then projected back into society. Khmer magic functions in such representation as the ultimate source of evil and a great corrupting force, especially to women. Magical prowess is taunted as an attribute of manliness if used in moderation. With real-life practitioners of magic frequently resorting to film aesthetics to promote their business, it is impossible to tell whether we are dealing with films imitating life or life imitating films. But perhaps it does not matter after all.

12 The Thai word *phi* is used to categorize a variety of spirits and supernatural entities, which, given their unique constitution and properties, may correspond to diverse lexical categories in English – from ghosts and spirits to demons and monsters.

13 Chavoret Jaruboon, with Nicola Pierce, *The Last Executioner: Memoirs of Thailand's Last Prison Executioner* (Bangkok: Maverick House Asia, 2006), 140–1.

Álvaro Martín Sanz

The Beauty and the Beast in *The Shape of Water* (2017)

> In fairy tales, monsters exist to be a manifestation of something that we need to under-
> stand, not only a problem we need to overcome, but also they need to represent, much
> like angels represent the beautiful, pure, eternal side of the human spirit, monsters need
> to represent a more tangible, more mortal side of being human: aging, decay, darkness
> and so forth.[1]

This quote by the Mexican filmmaker Guillermo del Toro represents his
position towards one of the main components of his films, the monster as a
magical and unknown creature. Throughout his entire career, del Toro's films
have included, through different representations, a constant revision of the
figure of the monster. Dismissing approaches based exclusively on the terror
of the unknown, the filmmaker shows the monster as a stranger in a reality
in which it is out of place, despite the lack of any visible break between the
everyday and the magical and supernatural world. In this sense, the monster
nature refers to the human condition. As Jasia Reichhardt argues:

> Only a human being or a humanoid can be a true monster. No monstrous cupboard,
> chair, plant or teapot could engender real fear, horror and fascination all at once. The
> essential condition for a monster is that the human characteristics it possesses must not
> be changed too far.[2]

---

1   Guillermo Del Toro, 'The Power of Myth', YouTube (2019), <https://www.youtube.
     com/watch?v=hmKCbJOu1uA>, accessed 20 July 2020.
2   Jasia Reichhardt, 'Artificial Life and the Myth of Frankenstein', in Stephen Bann, ed.,
     Frankenstein, Creation and Monstrosity (London: Reaktion Books, 1994), 139.

In this way, del Toro makes a new approach to magical realism character-ized by its use of special effects in the film medium and by a narrative that goes beyond the magical elements, postulating critical notions towards social reality. Magical realism, as conceived by Colombian writer Gabriel García Márquez, establishes a relationship between two apparently contra-dictory orders in such a way that reality is invaded by fantastic elements that do not provoke any kind of rupture or disharmony. 'The supernatural is not presented as problematic.'[3] Surprise comes as a result of the combi-nation of real and unreal elements, concrete and abstract, tragic and absurd. Magic is accepted as a hidden part of the real world, being able to present itself through varied connotations such as the wonderful, the fantastic, the baroque, the grotesque, the social or the critical.[4] From this, in this chapter, I will undertake a close reading of Guillermo del Toro's *The Shape of Water* to explain how the filmmaker adopts a framework of magical realism in order to create a credible universe from children's fantasy that serves to build a parallel reality. Magic, represented in the figure of the monster, works as an escape from everyday life (see Figure 14). Cinema is shown as a technology 'capable of performing illusions'[5] that give a new dimension to literary genres.

3   Amaryll Chanady, *Magical Realism and the Fantastic: Resolved Versus Unresolved Antinomy* (New York: Garland, 1985), 23.
4   Octavio Lanni, 'El realismo mágico', *Boletín de estudios Latinoamericanos y del Caribe* 40, 70.
5   Colin Williamson, *Hidden in Plain Sight: An Archaeology of Magic and the Cinema* (London: Rutgers University Press, 2015), 10.

Figure 14. Elisa Esposito (Sally Hawkins) and the Amphibian Man (Doug Jones) in *The Shape of Water*, dir. Guillermo del Toro (Fox Searchlight Pictures et al., 2017).

The Shape of Water is del Toro's twelfth film as a director. The film was premiered at the main competition in the seventy-fourth Venice International Film Festival, where it was awarded the Golden Lion for 'Best Film'. After that, the film received several awards and nominations in film festivals worldwide culminating in thirteen nominations at the ninetieth Academy Awards, where it won in the categories of Best Picture, Best Director, Best Production Design and Best Original Score. Thanks to this extensive journey, *The Shape of Water* is, by its own merits, the most successful work of the Mexican filmmaker to date. In numbers, *The Shape of Water* grossed $63.9 million in the US and $195.2 million internationally.[6] In this way, del Toro is one of the greatest exponents of Mexican transnational cinema, his two comrades, Alejandro González Iñárritu and Alfonso Cuarón, being the other two.[7]

---

6   'The Shape of Water', Box Office Mojo (2018), <https://www.boxofficemojo.com/mov ies/?id=theshapeofwater.htm>, accessed 20 July 2020.

7   Deborah Shaw, *The Three Amigos. The Transnational Filmmaking of Guillermo Del Toro, Alejandro González Iñárritu, and Alfonso Cuarón* (Manchester: Manchester University Press, 2016).

Set in the 1960s, the plot tells the story of Elisa Esposito, a young mute girl that works at a top secret research facility as a cleaning lady who finds a monstrous figure, an Amazonian amphibious humanoid captured for scientific experimentation. Feeling sorry for the creature, Elisa rescues the amphibian man from being vivisected, and eventually falls in love with it. Her friends help in her rescue mission: Zelda, an African American co-worker, Robert, a Soviet spy working as a scientist, and Giles, a gay graphic designer that lives next door. Del Toro claims to have been inspired by Jack Arnold's *The Creature from the Black Lagoon* (1954), in which, with a similar initial idea, an amphibian creature falls for the female protagonist, but they end up separated from each other.[8]

In this sense, the plot establishes a threatening reality, taking place in a military laboratory and a Cold War context that resonates with a utopian future in line with Trump's 'Make America Great Again' message.[9] The protagonist nevertheless emerges unharmed as from a children's fairy tale. Despite the ugly-aesthetic style that surrounds the first moments of the film, with desaturated colours and ruined decorations that build a decadent atmosphere, the filmmaker transmits calm and tranquillity via Alexandre Desplat's melodic soundtrack, while showing the monotonous daily routine of the protagonist with stabilized shots. With this initial contrast, the Mexican filmmaker proposes the integration, through filmic forms, of an inharmonious universe, setting up the dynamics that will be developed during the rest of the film. The viewer sees the ugliness, but at the same time is captured by the optimistic spirit of Elisa, whose daydreams and way of seeing reality bring her closer to Jean-Pierre Jeunet's Amélie Poulain (*Le Fabuleux Destin d'Amélie Poulain*, Claudie Ossard Productions et al., 2001). In line with this, film critic Renuka Vyavahare describes how del Toro manages to create a combined world of fairy tale and reality:

> Reading from the word go; the visionary filmmaker paints a visual and emotional master-piece that strikes an incredible balance between reality and fantasy [...]. More than its visual brilliance, what captivates you the most is del Toro's ability to capture the minutiae of his ordinary characters' everyday life. An unlikely amalgamation of supernatural,

8   T. Gray, 'Love and Danger on the "Water" Front', *Variety* (2018), <https://variety.com/2018/film/awards/shape-of-water-inspiration-from-monstermovie-1202659976/>, <https://doi.org/10.1080/17400309.2011.585854>, accessed 20 July 2020.

9   John Richardson, '*The Shape of Water*: An Allegorical Critique of Trump', *The Conversation* (2018), 1–5.

spiritual and sci-fi elements, The Shape of Water at heart, is a simple tale of hope and empathy. It rebuilds your faith in love, which isn't and shouldn't be defined by a certain shape or form.[10]

In this sense, Adji explains how 'del Toro's realistic narrative tries to portray how these different figures live their lives, support and interact with one another'.[11] For the author, *The Shape of Water*'s main message is about 'embracing otherness'. Thus, when the monster manifests itself, far from causing fear, it fosters empathy and tenderness. It is the uniqueness of its physical characteristics that makes it able to join the wide amalgam of the rest of the characters, also marginalized by their different conditions. 'Monsters are not only physically threatening; they are cognitively threatening',[12] in that same way, we could add, the main characters are also threatening. Andrew Tudor, arguing about monsters, says that 'to fracture a naturalistically represented physical order is, simultaneously, to affirm both the precariousness and the significance of that order'.[13] Therefore, del Toro's protagonist characters in *The Shape of Water* are out of place providing mutual help to each other in front of a rigid, unjust and oppressive system. 'Monsters are in a certain sense challenges to the foundations of a culture's way of thinking.'[14] That is why

there exists the concept of cleansing a society of impure things; the monster comes to function as a sort of scapegoat, taking on all the impurities that society needs to cast out and then being sacrificed, killed in often ritual ways, so that the impurities are destroyed along with the monster.[15]

10   Renuka Vyavahare, '*The Shape of Water* Movie Review', *Times of India* (15 February 2018), <https://timesofindia.indiatimes.com/entertainment/english/movie-reviews/the-shapeof-water/movie-review/62934788.cms>, accessed 20 July 2020.

11   Alberta Natasia Adji, 'Falling for the Amphibian Man: Fantasy, Otherness, and Auteurism in del Toro's *The Shape of Water*', *IAFOR Journal of Media, Communication & Film* 6/1 (2019), 59.

12   Ann Davies, 'Guillermo del Toro's Monsters: Matter Out of Place', in Ann Davies, Deborah Shaw, and Dolores Tierney, eds, *The Transnational Fantasies of Guillermo del Toro* (New York: Palgrave Macmillan, 2014), 29–43, 30.

13   Andrew Tudor, *Monsters and Mad Scientists: A Cultural History of the Horror Movie* (Oxford: Basil Blackwell, 1989), 124.

14   Peter Hutchings, *The Horror Film* (Harlow: Pearson Education, 2004), 35.

15   Davies, 'Guillermo del Toro's Monsters', 30.

Magical Realism

Thus, in order for the appearance of the monster to not generate a break with the aesthetic and narrative approaches of the film, del Toro uses a universe impregnated with some of the methods of magical realism. As stated by Faris 'one of the most immediately striking ways in which magical realism imbricates the extraordinary within the ordinary is the accumulation of realistic details to describe an impossible event'.[16] Thus, in *The Shape of Water*, the impossible moments are surrounded by a whole series of plausible and realistic characteristics that leave the viewer wondering about the possibility, however remote it may be, 'what if'. The hidden presence of the supernatural creature in a realistic-looking secret military laboratory, is the first and foremost of these forays. But there are also other scenes that use this strategy to create images of beauty impregnated with magical realism. Thus, we can mention the scene in which Elisa gives an underwater kiss to the creature in a flooded bathroom (see Figure 15). This scene, reminiscent of a similar one in *Delicatessen* (Constellation et al., 1991) by Jean-Pierre Jeunet, is presented with a whole series of details that frame it in everyday reality: water seeping into the cinema downstairs or pouring out of the door while the theatre owner complains.

Figure 15. Elisa (Sally Hawkins) and the Amphibian Man (Doug Jones) in *The Shape of Water*, dir. Guillermo del Toro (Fox Searchlight Pictures et al., 2017).

16   Wendy B. Faris, *Ordinary Enchantments: Magical Realism and the Remystification of Narrative* (Nashville, TN: Vanderbilt University Press, 2004), 90.

Similarly, the final scene is presented as the natural conclusion to a fantastic fable that emerges from a real environment: Elisa is drowning in the sea until the creature saves her by providing her with gills (see Figure 16). From the harbour, the rest of the characters, worried, contemplate the surface of the water, missing the miracle that takes place below. Following the concept of magical realism announced by Roh: 'el misterio no penetra en el mundo representado, sino que palpita tras él' [the mystery does not penetrate the represented world but beats behind it].[17] In both cases, the importance of Desplat's music should be highlighted, giving continuity to the scenes, enhancing the magic of the moment and making the sequences more cinematically unforgettable. In any case, it is worth noting how the narrative takes advantage of the film medium to create powerful images that also, thanks to advances in computer animation and special effects, perfectly integrate the magical aspects into everyday reality.

Given these scenes, following Spindler[18] we are able to categorize *The Shape of Water*'s magical realism as 'Anthropological magical realism'. This type has two voices, one rational and realist and one that indicates a belief in magic. 'The word "magic" in this case is taken in the anthropological sense of a process used to influence the course of events by bringing into operation secret or occult controlling principles of Nature.'[19] The contradiction between these two voices 'is resolved by the presence in the text of a specific cultural world-view, a *Weltanschauung* where the mythical and the rational coexist'.[20] In del Toro's work, the magical voice is represented both by the creature and by the look of naivety that the character of Elisa poses on a grey and cruel world. The rational voice is set in all the background characters of the story that do not believe in the supernatural. The unifying vision that overcomes the contradiction is composed by the gaze of the scientists who work in the laboratory and for whom magic can be summed up as all those facts for which

---

17   Emil Volek, 'Realismo Mágico entre la modernidad y la postmodernidad: hacia una remodelización cultural y discursiva de la nueva narrativa hispanoamericana', *Inti: Revista de literaturahispánica* 1/31 (1990), 5.

18   William Spindler, 'Magical Realism: A Typology', *Forum for Modern Language Studies* XXIX/1 (1993), 75–85.

19   Ibid., 80.

20   Eva Aldea, *Magical Realism and Deleuze. The Indiscernibility of Difference in Postcolonial Literature* (London, New York: Continuum Literary Studies, 2011), 3.

science still has no explanation. Del Toro's canon is the showcase of 'numerous creatures – even entire worlds – that lie parallel to or beneath our own accepted reality'.[21] Thus, for the filmmaker, the magic is hidden in all the facts of the natural world that have not yet been illuminated by instrumental reason.

Therefore, for del Toro, magic is neither necessarily dangerous nor are all monsters potentially harmful. As Judith Halberstam comments:

> The danger of monsters lies in their tendency to stabilize bias into bodily form and pass monstrosity off as the obverse of the natural and the human. But monsters are always in motion and they resist the interpretive strategies that attempt to put them in place.[22]

In this sense, *The Shape of Water* deconstructs the terrifying monster archetype in order to create a magical and mysterious figure that the protagonist falls in love with. Magic manifests its captivating qualities in all the scenes that reflect this process of falling in love. 'Their love scenes are lyrical and sensual and despite all odds, they live happily ever after.'[23] The Mexican filmmaker reflects mainly the seduction process in a sequence that presents an ellipsis that shows the passage of time, where we see several times how Elisa choses to spend her free time at the laboratory with the creature. These images, accompanied by period music, show how the reality and the fantastic converge in the feelings of empathy between the two characters, who share lunch, listen to music or dance together. In this way, as Lupercio Madero points out, *The Shape of Water* becomes a confluent love story that is at the same time an ode to otherness.[24]

21   Rebecca Janicker, 'Myth and Monstrosity: The Dark Realms of H. P. Lovecraft and Guillermo del Toro', in Davies, Ann, Deborah Shaw, and Dolores Tierney, eds, *The Transnational Fantasies of Guillermo del Toro* (New York, NY: Palgrave Macmillan, 2014), 45–60, 48.

22   Judith Halberstam, *Skin Shows: Gothic Horror and the Technology of Monsters* (Durham, NC: Duke University Press, 1995), 85.

23   Hayley Arizona Roche, 'Celebrating Imperfection through Perfect Images: Guillermo del Toro's Work', *Studies in Arts and Humanities* 5/2 (2019), 89.

24   Salvador Iván Lupercio Madero, '*El laberinto del Fauno* y *La forma del agua*: La representación femenina y el amor en el cine de Guillermo del Toro', *El ojo que piensa. Revista de cine* 20 (2019), 58.

Figure 16. The Amphibian Man (Doug Jones) and Elisa (Sally Hawkins) in *The Shape of Water*, dir. Guillermo del Toro (Fox Searchlight Pictures et al., 2017).

We can conclude this essay by asserting that *The Shape of Water* is, up to the present moment, the natural culmination of the representation of the figure of the monster in Guillermo del Toro's cinema. The Mexican director uses narrative resources typical of magical realism in order to create a realistic atmosphere dotted with fabled qualities. He uses the medium film to construct a magical artifice that makes the viewer travel to another reality. This is in line with the primordial work of film as pointed out by Rachel O. Moore.[25] The objective of the magical realism proposal is to harmonize the protagonist of the story, the figure of the monster, with the surrounding reality. In this sense, the filmmaker goes beyond his previous works. Not only is the monster no longer terrifying, but it is an outcast being defined by its own differences, just like the rest of the human characters. The dissonance caused by the appearance of

---

25   Rachel O. Moore, *Savage Theory: Cinema as Modern Magic* (London: Duke University Press, 2000), 163.

Magical Realism

monsters like the faun in *Pan's Labyrinth* (2006) or *Hellboy* (2004) becomes in *The Shape of Water* a motive for curiosity, discovery and, eventually, love. In this way, the surrounding magic also envelops the process of falling in love, making the impossible possible and offering a moral portrait of empathy and the need to understand the other.

Josephine Diecke and Noemi Daugaard

The Colour Purple as a Signifier of Shamanism in *Black Panther* (2018)[*]

Throughout film and television history, the colour purple is never employed innocently. Specifically, when connected to the representation of witches, sorcerers and evil magical counsellors in fairy-tale, fantasy and science-fiction films, the colour is chosen not only to signal the magical nature of the character, but also to hint at their ambivalence. Purple signifies 'difference from the ordinary': it is connected to the aspect of magic but superimposed with ulterior identity components such as exotic 'otherness', power and deviance from social norms. These layered identities have been fostered by long-standing Western cultural discourses and connotations surrounding the colour purple, its complex function and meaning. In this context, Ryan Coogler's 2018 film *Black Panther* proposes a new, Afrofuturistic perspective on magic and the colour purple.[1]

In the realm of colour symbolism and colour psychology, purple is understood as being close to mysticism, art and philosophy.[2] In the problematic and pseudo-scientific book on colour and personality, *Colour in Your World*, Faber Birren associates distinct personalities with specific colours, thus indicating a series of simplistic interpretations and stereotypes that result in a categorical systematization of colour and human character. For instance, he states that purple is associated to 'artists, mystics, those of

---

[*] This contribution has received funding by the Swiss National Science Foundation (SNSF).

[1] The term Afrofuturism was coined in 1993 by Mark Dery, see Mark Dery, 'Black to the Future. Interviews with Samuel R. Delany, Greg Tate, and Tricia Rose', in Mark Dery, ed., *Flame Wars. The Discourse of Cyberculture* (Durham, NC: Duke University Press, 1994), 735–78.

[2] Faber Birren, *Color in Your World* (New York: Macmillan, 1978), 28.

philosophic bent'.[3] Birren goes on to connect the colour purple with qualities of prophets and with a propensity for exotic cults. Albeit problematic and rigid, categorizations of colour such as this are common. More recent works from film and media studies such as Joshua Yumibe's *Moving Color* (2012), Sarah Street and Joshua Yumibe's *Chromatic Modernity* (2019) and the collection *Color Mania* (2020), edited by Barbara Flueckiger, Eva Hielscher and Nadine Wietlisbach, offer alternative readings of culturally and socio-politically charged colour symbolism in film and media.[4] However, approaches to colour analysis that focus on a supra-temporal and supra-national interpretation of individual colours such as the colour purple are still circulating and, all too often, revert back to simplistic schemes, ignoring the multifaceted function that colour can have. In *If it's Purple, Someone's Gonna Die*, for instance, Patti Bellantoni writes that purple holds 'a powerful sway in the realm of the noncorporal, the mystical, and even the paranormal' as well as the 'ritual, magic, and the spiritual'.[5] However, instead of illuminating the various interconnections and identity-forming markers associated to these realms, Bellantoni reverts to the rather simplified conclusion that, if it's purple, someone's gonna die.

This narrow take on colour can be found in film productions, for example, in *The Thief of Bagdad*,[6] *Die Geschichte vom kleinen Muck*[7] or *The Little Mermaid*.[8] In these movies, warm purple tones are used in specific settings and costumes for characters that combine not only aspects of magic and supernatural powers, but also incorporate exoticist and orientalist discourses as they have been consolidated throughout centuries of Western colonialism and

---

3   Ibid., 27–8.

4   Joshua Yumibe, *Moving Color. Early Film, Mass Culture, Modernism* (New Brunswick: Rutgers University Press, 2012), Street Sarah, and Yumibe, Joshua, *Chromatic Modernity. Color, Cinema, and Media of the 1920s* (New York: Columbia University Press, 2019); Barbara Flueckiger, Eva Hielscher, and Nadine Wietlisbach, *Color Mania. The Material of Color in Photography and Film* (Zurich; Winterthur: Lars Müller; Fotomuseum Winterthur, 2020).

5   Patti Bellantoni, *If It's Purple, Someone's Gonna Die. The Power of Color in Visual Storytelling* (Oxfordshire: Taylor & Francis, 2005), 190.

6   Dir. Raoul Walsh, Douglas Fairbanks Pictures, 1924.

7   Dir. Wolfgang Staudte, Deutsche Film (DEFA), 1953.

8   Dir. Ron Clements, and John Musker, Walt Disney Pictures, 1989.

cultural imperialism. As discussed by Edward Said, centuries of Western imaginations of 'the Orient' have reiterated stereotypical depictions of people and places coded as 'oriental', which still shape the representation and discourses circulating today.[9] For reasons of space, these discourses cannot be elaborated upon in this chapter.

While these discourses on colour and their connection to Orientalist imageries reveal themselves to be rather conventionalized and often based on mechanisms of Othering, it is important to underline that colours and their usage should never be simplified. As a case in point, while Ryan Coogler's *Black Panther* employs purple in agreement with conventionalized Western visual traditions, it exceeds them by modifying the ways in which the colour purple interacts with the topics of magic, royalty and power. Here, the colour purple stands not just as a marker of Othering, but it functions as a vessel for the unification of magic, nature and technology in the Afrofuturistic world of Wakanda.[10]

Connecting ideas from the past with visions of the future in a contemporary present is the most important trait of *Afrofuturism*. Indeed, as theorists such as Mark Dery,[11] Alondra Nelson[12] and Lisa Yaszek[13] point out, the associated media practices and narratives explore the possibilities of 'black futures derived from Afrodiasporic experiences'.[14] Using a mix of formal and aesthetic characteristics from science-fiction, history and fantasy, a series of artworks in the realms of literature, visual arts, photography or the moving images draws alternative empowered worlds: here, African traditions are not limited to unlocalized and exoticized appropriations by Western colonizers, but celebrate the cultural diversity and technological lead of an imagined uncolonized Africa and African diaspora. In 2018, *Black Panther* joined this

9   See Edward W. Said, *Orientalism* (New York: Knopf Doubleday Publishing Group, 1978).

10   A comparable use of colour can be found throughout the Marvel comic books which, however, must be left aside in this chapter.

11   Mark Dery, 'Black to the Future', 179–222.

12   Alondra Nelson, *Afrofuturism. A Special Issue of Social Text* (Durham, NC: Duke University Press, 2002).

13   Lisa Yaszek, 'Afrofuturism, Science Fiction, and the History of the Future', *Socialism and Democracy* 20/3 (November 2006), 41–60.

14   Ibid., 42.

tradition of Afrofuturistic storytelling, introducing alternative identity construction mediated by magic and shamanism as an instrument of collective empowerment and liberation. As Okaka Opio Dokotum recently pointed out, the film takes us on

> an epic journey, from a mystical past rooted in the power of nature through an enslaved and violent diaspora, through a rich diversity of social cultures, through an imagined amalgam of nature resources and native ingenuity to a final victory for the human race, courtesy of African wealth, innovation, compassion and benevolence.[15]

In this context, we argue that the 'imagined amalgam' mentioned by Dokotum also concerns *Black Panther's* attribution of meaning to colour in general and to the colour purple in particular. As we will show in the following, the movie shies away from long-standing visual traditions of utilizing purple as a marker of Othering shaped by a white hegemonic and racist ideology. Instead, *Black Panther* challenges this tradition by positively connoting the colour purple. It is not staged in opposition to other colours or 'non-colours' such as white, grey, beige or black, typically read as good, but as a necessary part of the overall colour spectrum. At the same time, the colour acquires a special standing through its active attribution of technologically or spiritually improved features by People of Colour themselves.

By adhering to core conventions of the genre and to the Marvel universe, the film shows us the past, present and future events of the imagined country of Wakanda and its leading warrior king T'Challa, aka Black Panther (Chadwick Boseman). Right at the beginning of the film, in a 3D-animated prologue, we learn about Wakanda's founding myth from T'Challa's uncle N'Jobu (Sterling K. Brown):

> Millions of years ago, a meteorite made of vibranium, the strongest substance in the universe, struck the continent of Africa affecting the plant life around it. And when the time of man came, five tribes settled on it and called it Wakanda. The tribes lived in constant war with each other until a warrior shaman received a vision from the Panther goddess Bast who led him to the Heart Shaped Herb, a plant that granted him superhuman strength, speed, and instincts. The warrior became King and the first Black Panther, the

---

15 Okaka Opio Dokotum, *Hollywood and Africa. Recycling the 'Dark Continent' Myth from 1908–2020* (Oxford: NISC (Pty) Ltd, 2020), 247.

protector of Wakanda. [...]. The Wakandans used vibranium to develop technology more advanced than any other nation, but as Wakanda thrived the world around it descended further into chaos. To keep vibranium safe, the Wakandans vowed to hide in plain sight, keeping the truth of their power from the outside world.[16]

While the camera dynamically follows the story of the meteorite's impact by panning and zooming in and out of single story lines, the colour scheme is restricted to four dominant hues: grey-brown for most of the earthly elements such as human figures and objects; a warm yellowish-orange for diffused lights; a glowing neon-blue characterizing the vibranium's energetic path; and a similarly striking, dark neon-purple representing the stimulating magical power of the Heart Shaped Herb. And with this colour scheme, the most important narrative and aesthetic patterns of the film are introduced, including the key motivations of all conflicts and agreements to come.

In *Black Panther*, the character bearing the strongest association with the colour purple is shaman Zuri (Forest Whitaker). As guardian of Wakanda's traditions, rituals and spiritualism, Zuri inhabits a position intrinsically connected to the founding myth of Wakanda. While the depiction of Zuri echoes long-standing visual discursive strategies connecting the colour purple with magic, it also presents further aspects, thus surpassing these conventionalized schemes by playing with supposedly standardized functions and colour symbolism.

According to the national myth, the Panther Goddess Bast leads the first Black Panther, a shaman, to the Heart Shaped Herb, the magical plant that transfers supernatural strength, speed and instincts onto him – powers that his successors will inherit. Thus, the central role of shamanism and Wakanda's godly and magical origin are established from the beginning. As a consequence, Zuri represents just one in a long line of shamans in charge of cultivating, preparing and administering the Herb, a protector of natural magic, who plays an intrinsic part in Wakanda's prosperity. Furthermore, the shaman is the gatekeeper to the Ancestral Plane, a dimension the Black Panther is allowed access to after consuming the juice of the Heart Shaped Herb, and where it is possible to consult the elders.

16 N'Jobu in *Black Panther*, dir. Ryan Coogler (Marvel Studios/Walt Disney Pictures, 2018), 00:00:15–00:01:38.

In the film, the Heart Shaped Herb is depicted in a glowing neon-purple and tended to by the shaman and his female helpers. Unsurprisingly, they are all dressed in the same purple hue of the Herb. While other Wakandan tribes, and, specifically, the Merchant Tribe, also wear purple garbs, the connection between the shamanistic magic and the Herb is more intense, an almost natural given. For instance, already in the opening scene, in which we see a younger Zuri in Oakland, acting as a spy for his king, the sweater he is wearing – albeit decidedly Western and conforming to American streetwear – is conspicuously purple.

By decidedly associating the colour purple with magic and with the shaman, *Black Panther* reiterates a well-established visual tradition coding purple as the colour of the magical and supernatural. Nevertheless, the film refuses to comply to these conventions in significant ways. Indeed, while magical characters have long been depicted wearing purple or even having purple skin – think of the sea witch Ursula in *The Little Mermaid* or the magical counsellor in *Die Geschichte vom kleinen Muck* – this association was also recurrently negatively connoted – but not so with shaman Zuri. He is far from being stereotyped, for instance, in form of the trope of the 'Magical Negro'.[17] In popular depictions, witches, sorcerers and consultants with magical powers commonly reveal themselves to be evil, two-faced and working only for their own gain or, in the case of the Magical Negro, for a supposedly superior white protagonist.[18] Conventionally, the colour purple denotes a layering of different mechanisms of Othering: not only do these characters exhibit magical abilities, but they are also construed as an 'exotic Other' as opposed to Western characters.

---

17   See Krin Gabbard, *Black Magic. White Hollywood and African American Culture* (New Brunswick, NJ: Rutgers University Press, 2004); Susan Gonsalez, 'Director Spike Lee Slams "Same Old" Black Stereotypes in Today's Films', *Yale Bulletin&Calendar* (2001), <http://archives.news.yale.edu/v29.n21/story3.html>, accessed 28 July 2020; Matthew W. Hughey, 'Cinethetic Racism. White Redemption and Black Stereotypes in "Magical Negro" Films', *Social Problems* 56/3 (2009), 543–77.

18   See Dustin Whitlock, 'How Marvel Avoids Racist Stereotypes, Embraces CGI in "Black Panther"', *clarionledger* (2019), <https://www.clarionledger.com/story/magno lia/entertainment/2018/02/16/how-black-panther-avoids-racist-stereotypes-embra ces-cgi/345004002/>, accessed 28 July 2020.

Contrarily to this, the portrayal of Zuri is not based on mechanisms of Othering; nor is he reduced to being an aid to white leads. Zuri is a fundamental and intrinsic part of the rituals of Wakanda, a hero who sacrifices his life for the king's. His character is thus much more rounded, a complex and multidimensional being, rather than the traditional, simplistic and negative depiction of a 'magical Other'. The colour purple, while clearly underlining his magical abilities and associating him with the Ancestral Plane, does not codify him as different, ambivalent or dangerous; instead, he is an indispensable member of the Wakandan community (see Figure 17). Consequently, by re-codifying the shaman's identity and intrinsically linking it to the colour purple, the film appropriates enduring discourses on magic and colour and allows the objects of these discourses to become subjects and regain power over their own representation.

Figure 17. Shaman Zuri (Forest Whitaker), initiating the coronation ceremony in *Black Panther*, dir. Ryan Coogler (Marvel Studios/Walt Disney Pictures, 2018).

Even though Patti Bellantoni's earlier mentioned analysis of the colour purple as marker of death might be simplistic, another observation of hers is very fruitful: 'We found purple is a colour that inspires associations with the non-physical. It sends a signal that someone or something is going to be transformed.'[19] Indeed, in *Black Panther*, purple serves as an indicator of transitions. Being detached from physical, corporal and earthly logic in general,

19   Bellantoni, *If It's Purple, Someone's Gonna Die*, 191.

purple opens the gates to supernatural and transcendent worlds that can be specific yet elusive at the same time. Reinforced by its shimmering, glowing or otherwise striking properties, the colour stands out against the green and brown landscapes of Wakanda, the warm red hue of the ceremonial sand in the herbal garden or the clean black and white look of princess Shuri's (Letitia Wright) high-tech design lab.

One of the few places in which purple takes on a dominant role in the set design is the Ancestral Plane. After ingesting the Heart Shaped Herb, both T'Challa and N'Jadaka enter an Astral Dimension to meet with their respective dead fathers. Notably, in the first encounter of King T'Challa with former King T'Chaka (Atandwa Kani), this intermediate world resumes the colour scheme of the animated flashback of the film's prologue: the energetic blue of the vibranium colours half of the sky and is reflected by the environment, while neon-purple stripes hover over the clouds and stars (see Figure 18). The striking colour scheme highlights the particularity of this location and puts it in strong contrast to present day Wakanda. A comparable visual approach can be found in the American mystery web television series *The OA*,[20] as the multi-verse shown therein also reveals a transcendental world marked by shades of purple and blue, which can be entered through near-death experiences.

Figure 18. T'Challa (Chadwick Boseman), visiting the ancestral plane in *Black Panther*, dir. Ryan Coogler (Marvel Studios/Walt Disney Pictures, 2018).

20   Created by Zal Batmanglij, Brit Marling (Plan B Entertainment, Anonymous Content, Netflix, 2016–19).

As king of Wakanda, the eponymous Black Panther is responsible for protecting the hidden country with all of the mystic and innovative tools his people have to offer. While Zuri serves as gatekeeper of the Heart Shaped Herb's strengthening and healing powers, and Shuri takes care of designing and developing Afrofuturistic vibranium technologies, King T'Challa incorporates both traditions in order to save Wakanda's future. Mediated by the usage of colours, this union challenges the traditional dichotomy of science vs. shamanistic magic and, as such, incorporates the essence of Afrofuturism and its intersection of African culture and traditions and technology.[21] In T'Challa's character, the transformational power of Wakandan technology and shamanic magic meet the conventionalized use of the colour purple as marker of supernatural transition. To visualize these transformation processes, the colour pervades and penetrates the human body in various ways. For instance, while ingesting the Herb concoction, T'Challa's body, and later N'Jadaka's, reacts to the invigorating drink by lighting up the affected veins with a purple glow. In a similar way, the Herb's healing energy runs through Agent Ross' (Martin Freeman) bullet wound after inserting a vibranium powered Kimoyo bead into his skin. In many instances, the curing qualities of the Herb merge with the supernatural strength of vibranium through protective gadgets and garments such as sound-nullifying boots or the Panther habit. The process of activating the suit and using its capacity to charge and revert kinetic energy itself is accompanied by partly regular, partly irregular purple patterns, thereby revealing the power of the vibranium that has been inserted into all these gadgets (see Figure 19).

In conclusion, in drawing upon Afrofuturism, *Black Panther* realizes the promise of the movement. To Mark Dery's question 'Can a community whose past has been deliberately rubbed out, and whose energies have subsequently been consumed by the search for legible traces of its history, imagine possible futures?',[22]

---

21   See, for instance, Ytasha L. Womack, *Afrofuturism. The World of Black Sci-Fi and Fantasy Culture* (Chicago: Chicago Review Press, 2013).

22   Dery, 'Black to the Future', 180.

Figure 19. The Black Panther (Chadwick Boseman), wearing the Panther habit in *Black Panther*, dir. Ryan Coogler (Marvel Studios/Walt Disney Pictures, 2018).

the film answers with a clear yes and proposes an empowered vision of community. However, it goes further than that: by re-appropriating Western discourses on the 'exotic Other' and the Western cultural history of colour and attributing new meanings and connotations to both, the film allows for new conceptions of Black African identities independent from, or in spite of, Western cultural and political hegemony, combining technological prowess with indigenous cultural and spiritual practices. A further crucial aspect that cannot be ignored, is the representation of a Black superhero that *Black Panther* provides, thus counteracting the often remarked upon 'exclusion of people of color from sf's future'[23] and providing important representation.

Although *Black Panther*'s Afrofuturistic universe absorbs a number of conventionalized tropes of supernatural powers and myths, the production team shied away from generalized attributions to (Western) magic. Indeed, when asked about the connection between vibranium's power and the Herb ceremonies, Marvel Studios president, Kevin Feige, denied direct

---

23   Bould, Mark, 'The Ships Landed Long Ago. Afrofuturism and Black SF', *Science Fiction Studies* (2007, 34,2. SF-TH Inc., 177–86).

connotations to magic by stating: 'That's partially spiritual. We certainly don't call it magic, but there's vibranium that has been interwoven within that soil and that land for thousands of years, so there are other things going on with it.'[24]

Whether the producers of the franchise call it magic or not, *Black Panther*'s Afrofuturistic narrative and aesthetics are clearly shaped by a mix of conventional and unconventional customs surrounding the colour purple as an indicator for supernatural powers in objects, characters, or mystic places. Within this film, however, the sovereignty over the associated discourse is assigned to people of colour. For once, the construed identities are not linked to negative connotations – despite their association with the colour purple. *Black Panther* withstands the traditional Western audiovisual representation of the colour purple as being a signifier of 'other', magic, danger, or abnormal. Thus, when the white character, Agent Ross, suspiciously states that bullet wounds do not just magically heal overnight, the Wakandan princess and design expert Shuri responds in a slightly amused manner: 'They do here. But not by magic, by technology.'[25]

24   Anthony Breznican, 'Black Panther Trailer Decoded. Ryan Coogler Reveals Secrets of the New Marvel Movie', *Entertainment Weekly* (2017), <https://ew.com/movies/black-panther-trailer-decoded-marvel-ryan-coogler-kevin-feige/>, accessed 28 July 2020.

25   Shuri in *Black Panther*, 01:09:55–01:10:00.

Part III

Stage Magic in Its Golden Age

Beatrice Ashton-Lelliott

The Magician Autobiography

The Victorian period saw a rise in the popularity of professional conjurers. Alongside these performers a new and specific genre of autobiography emerged: that of the magician autobiography. These carefully choreographed, generally episodic narratives gave readers a unique, yet often fictionalized, insight into the origins and daily lives of famous performance magicians. The most well-known examples of this writing include Jean-Eugène Robert-Houdin's *Memoirs of Robert-Houdin* (1859), Signor Antonio Blitz's *Fifty Years in the Magic Circle* (1871), Dr H. S. Lynn's *The Adventures of the Strange Man* (1873) and *A Magician's Tour, Up and Down and Round about the Earth* (1890) by Harry Kellar. These autobiographies are key texts in considering the experience and narratives of performance magic across the nineteenth century, marking the beginning of the period which magic historians have referred to as the 'Golden Age of Magic'.[1]

The magician autobiography as a genre text frequently engages with the reality of illusions within Victorian society and purports to tell the 'truth' of a magician's life and experiences. This is often in direct conflict, however, with the many mythologized elements of the narratives and the profession of performance magic itself. By considering the magician autobiography as an artefact and as a genre, we can begin to see their connecting threads and the parallel themes used to establish their typical narrative construction. These shared themes range from colonial commentary and political engagement to international travel and accusations of being in league with the devil. This chapter explores both the texts individually and the similarities which emerge

1   Historiographical opinions on this term vary, but the 'Golden Age of Magic' is generally accepted to be between 1850 and 1930, as stated in texts such as: Ricky Jay, Mike Caveney, Jim Steinmeyer, and Noël Daniel, eds, *Magic: 1400s–1950s* (Cologne: TASCHEN, 2013).

from a parallel analysis, revealing the topics which preoccupied Victorian performance magicians and their readership.

Jean-Eugène Robert-Houdin (1805–71) is frequently described by past and present magic historians as the 'father of modern magic'.[2] He is also credited by scholars as being the catalyst for the reformation of the magician figure in society and culture.[3] Whereas in previous centuries conjuring had been largely confined to urban streets or rural fairs, as the nineteenth century began magicians were moving from vagrant, impoverished, mobile archetypes to performing in upper-class drawing rooms, parlours, and eventually in theatres and even at royal soirées. Robert-Houdin dedicated his career to transitioning from his own artisan roots to establish himself as a society figure and respected performer, and publishing his autobiography was a crucial step in cementing his reputation.

As he began to perform less often in public, Robert-Houdin published his *Memoirs*[4] in 1859, which acts as a foundational text concerning the development of stage magic in the nineteenth century and how Robert-Houdin used the literary form to exaggerate his own persona. *Memoirs* follows Robert-Houdin from boyhood and mechanical apprenticeship to the beginnings of his magic career, into the peak of his fame and concluding with his ambassadorial

2   Virtually every critical text featuring Robert-Houdin contains this phrase, see, for example: Christian Fechner, *The Magic of Robert-Houdin: An Artist's Life* (Boulogne: Editions F.C.F, 2002), 4; Graham M. Jones, 'The Family Romance of Modern Magic: Contesting Robert-Houdin's Cultural Legacy in Contemporary France', in Francesca Coppa, Lawrence Hass, and James Peck, eds, *Performing Magic on the Western Stage: From the Eighteenth Century to the Present* (New York: Palgrave, 2008), 33–60; Michael Mangan, *Performing Dark Arts: A Cultural History of Conjuring* (Bristol: Intellect, 2007), xxiv.

3   See Mangan, *Performing Dark Arts*; James Cook, *The Arts of Deception: Playing with Fraud in the Age of Barnum* (Cambridge, MA: Harvard University Press, 2001); Sofie Lachapelle, *Conjuring Science: A History of Scientific Entertainment and Stage Magic in Modern France* (New York: Palgrave, 2015).

4   Titled *Confidences d'un prestidigitateur* in the original French. Two English editions of *Memoirs* emerged in the nineteenth century: one translated by Sir Lascelles Wraxall (1828–65), originally in two volumes with a translator's preface published in May 1859 in London, and one 'edited' and prefaced by Dr Robert Shelton Mackenzie (1809–80) published in September 1859 in Philadelphia. The 'American' translation of Robert-Houdin's text is identical – Mackenzie's only change is an added index and preface.

mission during the French colonization of Algeria. The narrative is structured in a way reminiscent of a traditional *bildungsroman*, but Robert-Houdin's family and domestic life, particularly his first and second wife and children, are often conspicuous by their absence. The text is often highly sensationalized, with the author himself often addressing his 'reader' directly and asking: 'Why should I not convert this fiction into a reality?'[5] These early comments speak to the performative nature of Robert-Houdin's life, even offstage, and asks the reader explicitly to suspend their disbelief whilst reading the autobiography in the same manner as observing a magic trick.

Memoirs is most notable in a narrative sense for the magician's use of the character of Torrini, a travelling mountebank and disgraced former aristocrat who trains a young Robert-Houdin in the art of conjuring, acting as a mentor and surrogate father figure. Torrini is now, however, regarded as an entirely fictitious invention by the author with Paul Robert-Houdin, the magician's grandson, describing Torrini as a 'literary device'.[6] The contemporaneous magic historians H. J. Burlingame and Thomas Frost both took the Torrini story at face value and repeated Robert-Houdin's account in their own texts,[7] giving Torrini a life of his own which lasted well into the twentieth century. Katharina Rein has noted that 'while it is widely known [...] by the spectators that magicians lie onstage, their credibility seems to have been mostly unquestioned by readers when it came to their life stories',[8] and the persistence of the Torrini myth even amongst researchers of magic history is a key example of this trust of often fictionalized accounts.

Jean Chavigny first put forward the idea that he was fictional in the 1943 following unsuccessful attempts to research Torrini's life through archival work – although Christian Fechner notes that Chavigny's 'affirmation was

5   Jean-Eugène Robert-Houdin, *Memoirs of Robert-Houdin*, trans. Lascelles Wraxall (London: Chapman and Hall, 1859), xiv.

6   David Price, *Magic: A Pictorial History of Conjurers in the Theater* (New York: Cornwall Books, 1985), 70.

7   See Thomas Frost, *The Lives of the Conjurers* (London: Chatto & Windus, 1881) and H. J. Burlingame, *History of Magic and Magicians* (Chicago: Charles L. Burlingame & Co., 1895).

8   Katharina Rein, 'Fantastical Lives', in Suzanne Sauvage, Christian Vachon, and Marc C. Choko, eds, *Illusions. The Art of Magic* (Milan: 5 Continents Editions, 2017), 52–63, 56.

not unanimously accepted'[9] by magic historians at the time. Robert-Houdin created a suitably dramatic life for this character, who spends much of the narrative grieving the death of his son at his own hands through a failed Bullet Catch trick and personal rivalries with real-life contemporaries. That Torrini is a total fiction can be taken as a key example of how the fabrications put forward in magician autobiographies may conflict with the expected 'integrity or honesty'[10] of the Victorian gentleman and whether these traits were compatible with the deception inherent in the conjuring profession.

Later in the nineteenth century, other magicians realized that writing an autobiography could be one avenue to increase their popularity, income and advertising. *Fifty Years in the Magic Circle* by 'Signor' Antonio Blitz (born Antonio Van Zandt) was published in 1871 with the lengthy subtitle of: 'Being an Account of the Author's Professional Life; His Wonderful Tricks and Feats; with Laughable Incidents, and Adventures as a Magician, Necromancer, and Ventriloquist'.[11] The 'laughable' nature of the text is important in considering the intentions of *Fifty Years* as a text, as many of its vignettes are clearly relayed for comedic value and entertainment. This is in great contrast to Robert-Houdin's *Memoirs* which, although not without its own comedic moments, is altogether more focused upon conveying the seriousness of conjuring as a profession, its artistry and building a lasting legacy of importance for its author.

Fifty Years was distributed with a different sort of readership in mind. It was first published 'by subscription only'[12] and is dedicated to Blitz's 'American friends and patrons'.[13] Thus, whilst Robert-Houdin's text enjoyed international success, receiving a front-page review from Edmund Saul Dixon in Charles Dickens's *Household Words*, Blitz's initial readership was most likely predominantly American, despite Blitz himself being British and enjoying widespread media attention for his British tours. The nineteenth-century magic historian Henry Ridgely Evans writes that Blitz was born in the 'village of Moravia',[14] perpetuating a myth that Blitz himself created and again highlighting the

---

9   Fechner, *The Magic of Robert-Houdin*, 48.
10   Mangan, *Performing Dark Arts*, 104.
11   Antonio Blitz, *Fifty Years in the Magic Circle* (Hartford, CN: Belknap & Bliss, 1871), i.
12   Ibid.
13   Ibid., iii.
14   Henry Ridgely Evans, *The Old and the New Magic* (Chicago: The Open Court Publishing Company, 1906), 178.

ways in which autobiographical texts helped magicians to propagate false information for entertainment purposes. Blitz was actually born in Deal, England, with a posthumous insert announcing Blitz's death in a copy of *Life and Adventures of Signor Blitz*[15] admitting that the magician was born in 'Kent County, England'.[16] *Fifty Years,* although taking a very different approach to *Memoirs,* was clearly inspired by the prior text and sought to capitalize off of its popularity, helping to establish the microgenre of magician autobiographies.

As with Robert-Houdin's pretences to authenticity, Blitz states in his introduction to *Fifty Years* that his 'whole object has been to present facts – to draw from truth, not fiction – to present events as they occurred, rather than appeared',[17] whilst on the other hand noting later that he 'never made a memorandum, therefore have written entirely from memory' and that as a result 'there may be some slight inaccuracies in regard to dates and circumstances; if so, they will in no way invalidate the facts'.[18] This highlights Blitz's unique interpretation of what a fact truly means and his own view of it as a transient definition, whilst also presenting the impression to the reader that his autobiography acts as an outlet to present his 'true' life and private self, yet this again is a deception in itself.

In their autobiographies, both magicians often describe being accused of supernatural acts and the suspicion which they face in rural areas whilst on tour. Whilst Robert-Houdin often seeks to move away from these associations by focusing upon his rise to the upper echelons of society, Signor Blitz embraces them, frequently highlighting episodes in which he is accused of criminal behaviour[19] or having satanic powers. One of the most telling incidents of Blitz's

---

15   Another (identical in content) edition of *Fifty Years in the Magic Circle.* This copy is held in the Charles Sanders bequest at the University of Michigan Library.

16   Antonio Blitz, *Life and Adventures of Signor Blitz* (Hartford, CN: T. Belknap, 1872), iv.

17   Blitz, *Fifty Years in the Magic Circle,* v.

18   Ibid., vii.

19   The magician summarizes these suspicions in a comment from a child: 'Signor Blitz, ma told me you could take money out of other people's pockets!' (Blitz, *Fifty Years in the Magic Circle,* 429). Katharina Rein has noted that Howard Thurston, the later stage partner of Kellar, epitomized these concerns as a teenager, developing 'several con games' with his brother and thus 'combining sleight of hand with criminal activity' (Rein, 'Fantastical Lives', 60–2).

Magic Lives

engagement with diabolic imagery is presented to the reader through a clearly formulaic incident. Blitz describes being introduced to strangers in the street:

> 'That man?' answered the person addressed. 'That is Signor Blitz, the ventriloquist and magician.'
>
> 'The devil!'
>
> 'No, not quite, but rather a near relation. You can go on, driver.'[20]

These one-liners are primarily presented in dialogic format, recreating the moment in the present tense for the reader in an act of counterfeit honesty. Blitz's reliance upon dialogue positions the reader as the main focus of his autobiography, clearly determined to, as Robert-Houdin also admits, entertain his reader. By contrast, however, Robert-Houdin relies upon first person narration, presenting his text as granting the reader access to his private, personal thoughts, as opposed to Blitz's expositional dialogue.

Memoirs, arguably, is more successful in its counterfeited authenticity due to Robert-Houdin and his translator's narrative and technical choices, relying on the *mise en abyme* of Torrini's history and others to situate the autobiography as a kind of frame story. *Fifty Years* acts more as a series of loosely connected vignettes, each designed to solidify the themes Blitz establishes such as his assumed links with the devil, in opposition to the sequential *bildungsroman* style of *Memoirs*. In terms of how magicians constructed their public identities through their writing, Blitz's autobiography in particular suggests a much more fragmented identity with a reliance upon popular genres and humorous episodes, whereas Robert-Houdin's work acts as an origin story and documentation of his attempts to elevate conjuring.

Other notable texts in the magician autobiography genre include Dr H. S. Lynn's *The Adventures of the Strange Man* (1873) and Harry Kellar's *A Magician's Tour, Up and Down and Round about the Earth* (1890), which provide a foil to the more well-known works of Robert-Houdin and Blitz. Lynn and Kellar's texts follow similar formats to their predecessors, with their main difference being that whilst Lynn's is written in the traditional first person, Kellar's features the fictional narrator of a demon following his master

20   Blitz, *Fifty Years in the Magic Circle*, 257.

(Kellar). Lynn (born Hugh Washington Simmons) enjoyed relative popularity in his day and inspired several imitators (which he himself laments in *Strange Man*) but is largely unremembered today. His autobiographical text documents his international travels, acting often as a travelogue for readers and demonstrating colonial attitudes, particularly in his thoughts regarding Chinese audiences and colleagues. Harry Kellar (born Heinrich Keller) is, by contrast, still a relatively popular figure due to his persistence into the twentieth century and his working relationship with Harry Houdini in later life. Although both texts touch upon the author's childhoods, they both chiefly narrate world tours and global encounters, hoping perhaps to emphasize the international appeal of Anglophonic magic. Kellar in particular, through his use of the tongue-in-cheek demon narrator as a framing device, follows the Blitz school of autobiography, seeking to appeal to reader's interest in the pretended supernaturalism of his performances.

Through their autobiographies then, magicians sought to distinguish themselves as individuals, and yet in doing so they created a genre which only further embodied the homogenous 'conjuring fraternity'.[21] The thematic and episodic symmetry of these texts is clear in their parallels, with their commonality demonstrating a varied yet unified genre. Magician autobiographies act as a notable artefact through which we can gain an insight into how conjurers wished to be perceived by readers and audiences during the nineteenth century in what was typically a highly ephemeral profession. Whilst some magicians sought to use the autobiographical form to build a lasting professional legacy, advertise their skills and highlight their dedication to the craft, they ultimately all shared one purpose in common with the magic shows of their authors: to entertain.

---

21   George Sexton, *Spirit-Mediums and Conjurers: An Oration* (London: J. Burns, 1873), 3.

Christopher Pittard

The Bullet Catch

The bullet catch is one of the paradigmatic magic tricks and one with a long history, first described in Jean de Chassanion's *Histoires Memorables des Grands et Merveilleux Jugemens et Punitions de Dieu* (1586), influentially developed in Henri Decremps' *La Magie Blanche Devoilee* (1871; translated by Thomas Denton as *The Conjuror Unmasked*), and popularized as 'the gun delusion' by John Henry Anderson in the 1840s. A member of the audience is invited to inspect a gun and to load it with a bullet marked to be identifiable, and then fire it at the magician. If the trick works correctly, the magician catches the bullet and presents it for inspection. But the trick can also fail, most famously in the example of the pseudo-Chinese conjuror Chung Ling Soo (William Robinson), killed while performing it at the Wood Green Empire in 1918, and in injuries reported by performers in the 1840s including Anderson and Antonio Blitz.[1] These reports (often fictionalized) of physical danger give the routine its significance; Katharina Rein suggests that the bullet catch represents a rupture in the surface of illusion, in that the audience's readiness to be tricked by a sleight of hand is threatened by the bullet catch's potential to be fatal, implying that the feat and its attendant risks are genuine.[2] But there is another component to the bullet catch's status as paradigmatic magic trick: it self-reflexively embodies the agonistic structure of performance magic itself. Jehangir Bhownagary

1   Jim Steinmeyer, *The Glorious Deception: The Double Life of William Robinson, aka Chung Ling Soo, the Marvellous Chinese Conjurer* (New York: Carrol and Graf, 2005); Antonio Blitz, *Fifty Years in the Magic Circle* (Hartford, CT: Belknap and Bliss, 1871), 138–9.

2   Katharina Rein, 'Rupturing Illusionism: The Bullet Catch', *Early Popular Visual Culture* 16/2 (2018), 157–71.

suggests that conjuring comprises a tripartite conflict, in which the performer starts from a mimetic position of portraying an existing world of physical laws, engages with the audience in a perceptual struggle, and eventually (if the magician is competent) creates a state of vertiginous pleasure.[3] But if the bullet catch dramatizes the individual conflict between audience and magician, in the nineteenth century this becomes mapped onto wider political contexts, with the imagery of the Victorian bullet catch often caught up in national and international conflicts, situating the routine within discourses of war rather than its less honourable antecedents in the duel.

My focus is on two nineteenth-century examples of the bullet catch. The first is by the 1820s and 1830s conjuror Khia Khan Khruse, a Portuguese performer who masqueraded as an Indian juggler starting his career with Ramo Samee's troupe. Khruse has a particular place in cultural history as the model for Charles Dickens' conjuring alter ego Rhia Rhama Rhoos in the 1840s, but had gained earlier notoriety for having been falsely reported to have died performing the bullet catch at Dublin's Pall Mall music hall in 1818.[4] In fact, Khruse continued to extensively tour the UK well into the late 1820s with an act combining sleight of hand with acts of physical endurance and contortionism (billed as his 'Protean Transformations'); the bullet catch therefore became a useful marketing tool, turning its performer into a cultural legend.

A vivid account of Khruse's performance of the bullet catch appears in the soldier Benson Earle Hill's military memoirs *Home Service* (1839), when Hill and his friend Colonel Ford act as volunteers:

> [A] pistol was handed round for inspection, the Indian requesting, in as good English as he could muster, that some gentleman would load it with powder *and bullet*, also paraded, and fire at Khan at fourteen paces, Khia pledging himself to catch the ball in his tawny

---

3   Jehangir Bhownagary, 'Creativity of the Magician', *Leonardo* 5/1 (1972), 31–5.

4   On Dickens' parody of Khruse, see Christopher Pittard, 'The Travelling Doll Wonder: Dickens, Secular Magic, and *Bleak House*', *Studies in the Novel* 48/3 (2016), 279–300. On the rumour of Khruse's death, see Edwin A. Dawes, *The Great Illusionists* (Secaucus: Chartwell, 1979), 170–1.

fist. [...] We carefully examined the weapon; there was no false chamber into which the ball could fall, the powder was genuine Pigott and Andrews, and the

'Bullets were made of lead, lead, lead!'

Instead of contenting himself with the ordinary nick or cross upon the ball, the Colonel carefully cut 'a broad R', or arrow, the mark which distinguishes his Majesty's naval and military stores. I loaded, and, as sailors say, 'rammed home wad, shot, and cartridge', then offered the charged tube to my companion, who declined with a smile-

'No, my dear boy, *you* shall have the honour of shooting the fellow; take good aim at him, and mind the chandelier.'

[...]

'Him Saib ready?' demanded the Asiatic.

Signifying assent, I asked him where he meant to stand, that I might step out the number of paces agreed on.

'I tan here, you no fright, if kill me I forgive, but me catch de ball, and no debil in it!'

The pit of the theatre was floored over, and I counted out the fourteen steps between me and my willing victim.

'All ready, say!' cried whitey-brown.

I took a deliberate aim at his body, and, I almost blush to confess, with a certainty of seeing him fall dead from the shot, as no deception had been practiced in the loading. The ladies held their hands to their ears, the trigger was pulled, and 'ping!' went the bullet, if ever I heard a bullet fly through the air. Khia Khan gave a leap, which I thought was the effect of his death-wound, and then advanced, showing his fine set of teeth to the greatest possible advantage, with his right hand clenched, saying:-

'Him got him! what him mark?'

'The broad R.'

'Ah, me no know what Saib mean, him dis, I tink;' and, opening his palm, there lay the identical piece of lead so carefully marked by the colonel.

Thunders of applause followed this extraordinary display; the danger past, even the ladies joined in expressing their unqualified delight at having witnessed so wonderful a trick.

I turned to my companion; he appeared somewhat disconcerted, and said to me- 'If that fellow were to offer to be rammed into Queen Elizabeth's pocket-pistol at the castle, for the purpose of obtaining an expeditious passage to Calais, I wouldn't allow the powder to be served out for the purpose, for, from what I have just witnessed, I think that in a minute after you had put the port-fire to the vent, he'd be walking in the *Place*, without one gunpowder spot on his muslin.'[5]

While Khruse's performance takes place in the civilian space of the theatre, the imagery of war encroaches. Hill's account takes on additional colonial dimensions through its commercialized references to armoury: the 'genuine Pigott and Andrews' powder, the bullet bearing the symbol of 'his Majesty's naval and military stores', indicative of a pervasive commercial British power (the pseudo-Indian Khruse will, effectively, be killed by an advertisement). The colonial context of Orientalist conjuror facing a Western soldier is obvious; more striking is the way in which Khruse is hypothetically co-opted into the service of England in historical narratives of war, turned into an Indian bullet fired from an English pistol.

The theorist Paul Virilio might refer to Khruse's imaginary transformation into a speeding bullet as a process of becoming dromological, a machine of speed. For Virilio, war and visual entertainments are imbricated; in *War and Cinema* Virilio explores 'the osmosis between industrialised warfare and film', the manner in which cinematic ways of seeing arise out of militaristic modes of perception, and vice versa as cinematic technologies become increasingly central to modern weapons.[6] As Virilio puts it, '[o]nce the cinema was able to effect surprise […] it effectively came under the category of weapons'.[7] Though *War and Cinema* only passingly mentions performance magic, conjuring's status as a precursor to modern cinema suggests its potential for cultural connections to earlier forms of warfare, and it is the bullet catch which provides the clearest connection.[8] Hill's account of taking aim at Khruse combines machinic precision with the threat of bodily response in the retelling: 'I took a deliberate aim at his body, and, I almost blush to confess, with a certainty of seeing him fall dead.' Hill anticipates the

---

5   Benson Earl Hill, *Home Service: Or Scenes and Characters from Life at Out and Head Quarters* (London: Henry Colburn, 1839), 168–70.

6   Paul Virilio, *War and Cinema: The Logistics of Perception* (London: Verso, 1989), 73.

7   Ibid., 10.

8   Virilio briefly discusses intersections between militarism and magic in *The Art of the Motor* (Minneapolis: University of Minnesota Press, 1995), 65–8, noting that one of the first performers of an invisibility effect was the martially named Colonel Stodare.

ambiguity Virilio identifies in the act of taking aim 'as a geometrification of looking, a way of technically aligning ocular perception along an imaginary axis that used to be known in French as the "faith line" (*ligne de foi*)'.[9] This model highlights the subjectivity of the one firing, the element of belief that this is the correct line of fire. But Virilio notes that, historically, the contexts of 'faith' and 'belief' disappear from the act of taking of aim; 'the ideal line appears thoroughly objective', eliding interpretative subjectivity.[10] Written accounts of the Victorian bullet catch, with their emphasis on the act of aiming, imply the tension between an automated aim and the 'faith line', between objective geometry and subjective interpretation.

The martial imagery that surrounded accounts of the bullet catch in the nineteenth century also helped to dissociate the act from the less reputable agonistic context it more closely resembled: the duel. The bullet catch lopsidedly parodies the duel, with one shooter instead of two, but in accounts like Hill's the magic trick is just as bound by strict physical procedures. That the bullet catch should become associated with the racially indistinct Khruse is of a piece with the early nineteenth-century critique of duelling as a form of barbarism. John Leigh notes that, for eighteenth-century commentators, the duel had no precedent or equivalent in classical culture, and therefore could not be 'necessary to a definition of honour or integral to an idea of civilization'.[11] 'Barbarous' became the most frequently used adjective to describe duelling in the eighteenth and nineteenth centuries. Despite the fact that it is Hill who fires the pistol, it is Khruse who embodies the barbarity of the duel.

Over the Victorian period, performances of the bullet catch move away from the barbarism of the duel (individuals pitted against each other for no discernible reason) and reconceptualize it as an honourable military encounter of miniaturized war. No longer the conjuror against a sole combatant, or even the audience, this was the conjuror against an army, often resituating the routine in specific geopolitical conflicts (most notoriously Chung Ling Soo's recasting of the routine as a drama of the Boxer Rebellion).

---

9   Virilio, *War and Cinema*, 3.
10   Ibid.
11   John Leigh, *Touché: The Duel in Literature* (Cambridge, MA: Harvard University Press, 2015), 8.

This movement of the bullet catch from barbaric duel to honourable war led to such absurd spectacles as the soldier-turned-conjuror Ernesto Patrizio catching a cannonball, a routine inspired by his battlefield experiences in the Austrian-Italian war of 1866.[12]

If Patrizio's performance was the aesthetic culmination of bullet catch as war, then the political culmination of this process occurs in my second example, Jean-Eugene Robert-Houdin's *Memoirs* (1859). In its most famous episode, Robert-Houdin is asked by Napoleon III to quell an uprising being fomented by the Marabout tribe leaders in Algeria, who are using conjuring techniques to influence the populace against the French military. Robert-Houdin's task is to replicate these feats in order to demonstrate that they derive not from any mystical powers, but are simply sleights of hand. One of the tricks Robert-Houdin uses to accomplish his mission is a variant of the bullet catch, in which he catches the bullet in an apple. The scene is an exact inversion of Hill's account; it is written from the perspective of the magician rather than the audience; the conjuror is western, the audience racially other; Hill's care in taking aim contrasts with Robert-Houdin's 'opponent' taking aim 'immediately, without the slightest hesitation.'[13] If in the early nineteenth century the duel was criticized as a barbarous practice that was simply an aristocratic indulgence resolving disputes of no real consequence, then the reappearance of this imagery in Robert-Houdin's bullet catch serves a real military-political purpose.

The appearance of the bullet catch at the climax of the *Memoirs* also calls attention to the book's problematic status as biography. Much of the early section of the book is taken up by the embedded biography of the magician Torrini, a magician forced into a change of identity (from the Comte de Grisy) and an itinerant lifestyle following the death of his son when the bullet catch goes fatally wrong. In 'The Son of William Tell', the volunteer is invited to fire at Torrini's son, who catches the bullet in an apple, but the working of the trick lies in the use of false bullets:

12   Milbourne Christopher, *Magic: A Picture History* (New York: Dover, 1991), 140–1.

13   Jean-Eugene Robert-Houdin, *Memoirs of Robert-Houdin: Ambassador, Author and Conjuror* (Philadelphia, PA: George Evans, 1859), 387.

Till now I had never dreamed of any danger in the performance of this trick, and, indeed, I had taken all possible precautions. The false bullets were contained in a small box, of which alone I had the key, and I only opened it at the moment of action. That evening I had been peculiarly careful; then how can I explain the frightful error? I can only accuse fatality. So much is certain – a leaden bullet had been mixed with the others in the box, and was inserted in the pistol.

Conceive all the horror of such an action! Imagine a father, with a smile on his lips, giving the signal which will deprive his son of life – it is frightful, is it not?

The pistol was fired, and the spectator, with cruel adroitness, had aimed so truly that the bullet crashed through my son's forehead.[14]

The Algeria scene uses the bullet catch to resolve the tensions prompted by this earlier episode, with Robert-Houdin likewise 'catching' the false bullet in an apple. Over the course of the *Memoirs*, then, the bullet catch is rehabilitated from pointless family tragedy to useful tool of international politics. But there is a further tension in this reappearance of imagery from the earlier part of the book. While Robert-Houdin's Algerian bullet catch was a historically verifiable event, the Torrini narrative is now regarded as almost certainly entirely fictional.[15] When Torrini thus asks us to *conceive* all the horror of killing his son, this is precisely what Robert-Houdin himself is doing in creating his fictionalized surrogate father figure, deploying a fictional bullet catch early in his *Memoirs* in order to lend weight to a historically recorded performance near the end.

Yet, for all the verified events of the Algeria chapters, the bullet catch was an inherently unreliable narrative. Khia Khan Khruse's rumoured death in 1818 seems to contrast with Hill's eyewitness account of the bullet catch, yet on closer inspection Hill's apparent attention to procedural details nevertheless misses the crucial sleight of hand that makes the trick work, and the retelling is marked by embarrassment – 'I blush to recall'. In Robert-Houdin, the bullet catch marks the hinge between historical event and fiction masquerading as

14   Ibid., 129.
15   Graham M. Jones, 'The Family Romance of Modern Magic: Contesting Robert-Houdin's Cultural Legacy in Contemporary France', in Francesca Coppa, Lawrence Hass, and James Peck, eds, *Performing Magic on the Western Stage: From the Eighteenth Century to the Present* (New York: Palgrave, 2011), 33–60.

biography. To return to the agonistic structure mentioned above, and as I have argued elsewhere, Bhownagary's tripartite structure of magic needs a fourth stage – (mis)narration, the magic residing not so much in the event on stage, but in the way it is told to us by others.[16] The nineteenth-century bullet catch becomes a powerful engine of fictional narrative.

16　　Pittard, 'Travelling Doll Wonder', 292.

Katharina Rein

Women in Stage Magic around 1900

Performance magic has a long and problematic history of gender imbalance. In 2019, the Magischer Ring Austria (The Magic Circle Austria) dedicated an issue of the club's periodical *aladin* to women in magic. In the first article, Hanno Rhomberg, editor-in-chief and president of the organization, suggests that the battle of the sexes (which he places in quotation marks) has, in fact, been one of 'the masses against the powerful'. He backs up this questionable claim by the illogical statement that 'in history, since the remote past, we have been seeing an *oppression* of men and women by the powerful, who usually show a male face'.[1] Who exactly those suppressors might be and how they 'show a male face' without being male suppressors (as Rhomberg implies) remains a mystery. The chaotic article ends with a passing side-sweep against gender-sensitive language and a postulation that 'the usual statements of women politics on the "gender pay-gap" [sic!] [are] are dubious and wrong'.[2] These, according to Rhomberg, serve to justify the discrimination against men in the 'battle of the sexes' that is merely alleged by feminists. Judging by this article, performance magic (at least in Austria) not only has a long history of (systemic) sexism but also a severe problem with it today.

---

1   Hanno Rhomberg, 'Frauen und Männer – Kampf der Geschlechter?', *aladin. Fachzeitschrift des Magischen Ring Austria* 2 & 3 (2019), 6–8, 6: 'Wir sehen in der Geschichte von alters her eine *Unterdrückung* von Männern und Frauen durch Mächtige, welche meist ein männliches Gesicht zeigen', emphasis in original.

2   Ibid. '[...] die üblichen Aussagen der Frauenpolitik zum „Gender-Pay-Gap" [sic!] [sind] unseriös und falsch'.

The decades around 1900, considered 'an era of unprecedented cultural visibility and voice for women',[3] saw a rising number of women entering the entertainment business. This chapter focuses on the discourse around women in stage magic in their roles as magiciennes and assistants at the time usually considered the 'Golden Age of Conjuring'.[4] Given the limited length of this chapter, this can only be a cursory glance. A broad discourse – or rather, two that are intertwined with one another – that cannot be touched upon here, concerns witchcraft, occultism and modern spiritualism. The main adversary openly fought by magicians during magic's Golden Age, were spiritualist mediums. This war was founded on the magicians' assertion of moral superiority: while mediums claimed supernatural abilities for themselves and fooled their patrons, magicians, thus ran the narrative, performed similar feats with similar methods but openly admitted to presenting illusions for the sake of entertainment. The conflict – mostly male magicians, constructing themselves as rational and 'enlightened', debunking predominantly female mediums, constructed as deceitful and greedy 'magical women' – stands in the shadow of the witch-hunt. While I have written more extensively on the interplay of magicians and spiritualists elsewhere,[5] this chapter sheds some light on women in modern performance magic, where they were (and still are) un(der)credited, objectified and praised for their looks rather than their skills.

3   Susan A. Glenn, *Female Spectacle: The Theatrical Roots of Modern Feminism* (Cambridge, MA: Harvard University Press, 2002), 216.

4   While opinions on the exact year dates vary, this is usually a period of c. 50–90 years around 1900. I am following Jim Steinmeyer's periodization that focuses on the time from 1845–1936 (see *Hiding the Elephant: How Magicians Invented the Impossible* [London: Arrow, 2005]) rather than shorter time frames as proposed, for instance, by Mike Caveney (in 'The Masters of the Golden Age', in Noel C. Daniel, ed., *Magic, 1400s–1950s* [Cologne: Taschen, 2009], 338–97) that take on a more US-centred perspective, considering only the decades after the 1880s, when the popularity of magic had made its way across the Atlantic.

5   See Katharina Rein, *Techniken der Täuschung. Eine Kultur- und Mediengeschichte der Bühnenzauberkunst im späten neunzehnten Jahrhundert* (Marburg: Büchner Verlag, 2020), 278–88. This book is currently under contract for publication in English under the title *Techniques of Illusion. A Cultural and Media History of Stage Magic in the Late Nineteenth Century* (London: Routledge).

Looks and sexuality take centre stage in reviews and promotional material concerning female magicians. For instance, Melinda Saxe, a Las Vegas magic star of the 1990s, usually posed with exotic animals, on motorcycles or huge canons, in skimpy underwear (occasionally combined with a cape). What is often missing in these promotional materials are the magic props that, along with smart, formal attire, are a staple in male magicians' iconography (who also usually appear fully dressed). While dress codes were different in the Victorian period, women in the entertainment industry did not enjoy the highest moral standing. Women's restrictive societal role encompassed them staying at home and pleasing their husbands when they returned from work. 'Sex, submission, and complacency were the characteristics expected of women', Angela Marie Sanchez writes, 'not unlike those expected of magicians' assistants.'[6]

As with many other lines of work, women were, for a long time, deemed unfit for the magical profession altogether. Writing for the periodical of The Magic Circle, 'the most prestigious magic club in the world',[7] in 1980, the organization's historian Edwin Dawes states that Mademoiselle Patrice' (active around 1890, more about her below) success as a conjuress 'is phenomenal, as good conjuring requires qualities very seldom indeed found in a woman, and she may perhaps be taken as the exception which proves the rule that ladies do not make good *prestidigitateuses*'.[8] The author thus responds to the existence of a highly skilled female magician by repeating his prejudice that there can be no such thing. And if the factual situation seems to prove him wrong, then he must be looking at the exception to the rule, which, in turn, can be declared to support his gender bias.

Part of what supposedly made women unfit for the magical profession, was their alleged inability to keep secrets. This was based on the cliché of the loquacious and impulsive woman that mindlessly gives away all kinds of things if she is allowed sufficient speaking time. Francesca Coppa identifies a constructed contrast between the male magicians' self-asserting culture of secrecy and the presentation of women on stage. '[F]emale assistants', she writes,

---

6   Angela Marie Sanchez, *Conjuring the Modern Woman: Women and Their Representation in the Golden Age of Magic* (Senior Thesis, University of California, 2012–13), 39.

7   The Magic Circle, <https://themagiccircle.co.uk>, accessed 20 January 2021.

8   Edwin A. Dawes, 'A Rich Cabinet of Magical Curiosities: 67. Mademoiselle Patrice – Lang Neil's Vanishing Lady', *The Magic Circular* 74/803 (January 1980), 107–9, 107.

Female Conjuring

are clearly framed as hired help and not as part of the rarefied social circle of magicians, where knowledge is shared and transmitted; [...] they are depicted within the magic act as hypnotized, asleep, unconscious, or mentally vacant – that is, literally not in possession of the requisite mental equipment for the magician's job of keeping secrets.[9]

As this culture of secrecy began to be institutionalized in organizations, their membership was restricted to men. The Magic Circle introduced regular membership for women only in 1991. Nineteen years later, it counted around eighty women among its 1,500 members.[10] In the eighty-six years of the organization's existence prior to 1991, the only way for women to gain access to it was by means of an honorary membership. Female magicians, here, needed to achieve something outstanding enough to merit this honour, while male magicians could join by demonstrating magic skills – basically by being magicians.

Yet, according to Amy Dawes, at the time of The Magic Circle's foundation, 'a significant nucleus of professional magiciennes existed, and conjuring as a popular hobby for ladies was being advocated'.[11] The best-known and most commercially successful US-American conjuress around 1900 was Adelaide Herrmann (née Adelaide Scarcez, 1853–1932) who enjoyed an exceptionally successful solo career after her husband's death. Adelaide skilfully capitalized on his fame, strategically presenting herself as the widow of Alexander Herrmann (1844–96), America's premier magician. In Alexander's lifetime, she was a co-star in his show, 'presenting several of the illusions by herself'.[12] She also made creative decisions and took on management and business duties.[13] Julia Henderson has shown that Adelaide Herrmann's public image was carefully

9   Francesca Coppa, 'The Body Immaterial: Magicians' Assistants and the Performance of Labor', in Francesca Coppa, Lawrence Hass, and James Peck, eds, *Performing Magic on the Western Stage. From the Eighteenth Century to the Present* (New York: Palgrave Macmillan, 2008), 85–106, 86–7.

10   'Inside the Magic Circle of London', *The Londonist* (5 May 2010), <http://londonist. com/2010/05/inside_the_magic_circle_of_london>, accessed 20 January 2021.

11   Amy Dawes, 'The Female of the Species: Magiciennes of the Victorian and Edwardean Eras', *Early Popular Visual Culture* 5/2 (July 2007), 127–50, 130.

12   Jim Steinmeyer, *The Glorious Deception: The Double Life of William Robinson, aka Chung Ling Soo the 'Marvelous Chinese Conjurer'* (New York: Carroll & Graf Publishers, 2005), 116.

13   Ibid.

constructed to bridge conformity and change: she 'contributed to an emerging turn-of-the-century female identity by alternately reinforcing and resisting contemporary ideas about female gender roles'.[14]

Part of this were her appearances on stage in male clothing (see Figure 20). By performing in men's evening wear, she appropriated the attire that was part of the nineteenth-century-magicians' carefully constructed identity as respectable entertainers[15] and made use of its pragmatic benefits: sleight-of-hand feats developed by men use props and tools adapted in size to male bodies – an arbitrary circumstance that, in turn, served as an excuse to argue that women were unfit to become magicians, having too small hands to manipulate the usual props.[16] Moreover, sleight-of-hand tricks were designed to be performed in male clothing, relying on relatively spacious (dinner) jackets with concealed (as well as visible) pockets and sleeve pulleys. These are impossible to accommodate in women's evening gowns, particularly in the ones that were in fashion around 1900. Adelaide's cross-dressing not only circumvent this gendered exclusion, it also challenged social constructions of gender identity. Further, it was a particularly daring act, considering that we are speaking of a society in which it was legally prohibited to wear clothes of the opposite gender in public.[17]

14   Julia Henderson, 'The Female Illusionist Revealed: Adelaide Herrmann's Expression of Womanhood through Fin de Siècle Material Culture, 1869–1928', *Journal of American Drama and Theatre* 25/2 (Spring 2013), 37–58, 37.
15   Ibid., 48.
16   See Sanchez, *Conjuring the Modern Woman*, 34.
17   See Henderson, 'The Female Illusionist Revealed', 48.

Figure 20. Adelaide Herrmann in men's formal wear. The Magic Circle Archive.
Reproduced with permission from The Magic Circle.

After her husband's sudden death in 1896, Adelaide first continued the
show of 'Herrmann the Great' by 'casting' his nephew Leon as the leading
magician. However, they soon parted ways and in Summer 1899, at the age of
46, Adelaide launched her solo career. This, as Julia Henderson points out,
was a remarkable thing to do 'in a culture that valued youth and in which
the majority of female performers did not perform past marriageable age'.[18]
While, shortly after, a newspaper announced that she was engaged to a Russian
baron,[19] Adelaide in fact did not remarry. Instead, she became the first woman
to headline in vaudeville and performed with outstanding success for almost

18   Ibid., 57.
19   'May Become a Baroness', *Perrysburg Journal* (Ohio, 30 March 1900), reproduced in
      Adelaide Herrmann. Queen of Magic, ed. Margaret Steele (North Bergen, NJ: Bramble
      Books, 2012), 321.

three decades. She was planning another tour at the age of 73, when she fell ill and passed away on 19 February 1932.

While it was common for male magicians at the time to publish auto-biographies, Adelaide Herrmann was, as far as we know, the only magicienne to embark on such a project. But she in no way lagged behind her male col-leagues when it came to glossing over events from her life.[20] Her memoirs omit occurrences such as her arrest for slapping a policeman in the face, or her trouble with the US customs authorities when she attempted to smuggle rare silk from Mexico, concealed underneath a voluminous skirt.[21]

Adelaide also published a number of articles, for instance, encouraging girls and women to practise sleight-of-hand and giving instructions for illu-sions.[22] Another magicienne who advocated conjuring as a 'capital accomplish-ment for ladies'[23] as an author, was Mademoiselle Patrice (Augusta Patrizia de Rella). While Herrmann's career was exceptional around 1900, Patrice's path seems to be more representative. She was a highly skilled conjuress who was constantly undercredited as a professional and objectified by male colleagues. In line with the reduction of women to the role of men's appendices, she was mostly acknowledged as the student and assistant of the magician Charles Bertram, with whom she famously performed the 'Vanishing Lady' illusion in London in 1886, or as the wife of author C. Lang Neil. Neil wrote several books on magic, among them *The Modern Conjurer* (1902), the first one to use photographs to illustrate the illusions described. However, Neil was never a performing magician, which means that his interest in and expertise on magic may have come from his wife. Although Patrice's own professional career was often acknowledged, she remains in the shadow of her male colleagues. For

---

20 On the illusionism of magicians' autobiographies see Beatrice Ashton-Lelliott's chapter in this volume. See also Katharina Rein, 'Fantastical Lives', in Suzanne Sauvage, Christian Vachon, and Marc H. Choko, eds, *Illusions. The Art of Magic* (Milan: 5 Continents Editions, 2017), 52–63.

21 See 'Mrs. Herrmann Tried for Assault', *New York Times* (12 May 1895) and 'Under Her Skirts', *Los Angeles Times* (6 December 1897), both reproduced in *Adelaide Herrmann*, 314–16.

22 Adelaide Herrmann, 'Magic as a Home Amusement', *The Woman's Home Companion* (June 1900), reproduced in *Adelaide Herrmann*, 257–63.

23 Mademoiselle Patrice, 'Conjuring – A Capital Accomplishment for Ladies', *Lady's Magazine* 2/9 (September 1902), 312–28.

instance, while, like her stage partner Charles Bertram, she regularly performed for members of the Royal family at Sandringham House, unlike him, she was not billed as 'The Royal Conjurer' or anything similar.

Testifying to how their male colleagues viewed female magicians is Bertram's comment on Patrice's body in his autobiography *Isn't It Wonderful?* (1896). When describing their 'Vanishing Lady' illusion, he remarks that the tall woman 'weighed a little over nine stone [c. 60 kg, KR] – so that she was not by any means *petite*.'[24] Bertram justified this remark by saying that Mademoiselle Patrice' physical presence 'greatly enhanced the effect of her disappearance',[25] thus giving the comment a contextual significance in the rendering of the performance. Edwin Dawes, however, writing eighty-four years later, in 1980, quotes Bertram's passage and adds:

> It is perhaps ungallant to remark that some sixteen years later, when photographs for *The Modern Conjurer* was [sic] taken, Mdlle Patrice had indisputably put on weight and it seems doubtful that she could still have retained her role as a Vanishing Lady.[26]

In 2002, Amy Dawes joined in the chorus of posthumous body shaming and threw in a comment on Patrice' ageing. Referring to the photographs in the same publication (see Figure 21), she remarked that '[i]n these [pictures], Mlle Patrice appears as an exceedingly formidable and matronly figure, making it difficult to recall the appeal of her earlier prettiness.'[27] Apparently, being pretty and petite (and, by implication, young) was crucial for women on magic stages not only in 1886 but still in 2002. An example of a male magician's abdominal girth or receding hairline being the recurrent topic of derogatory commentary for more than a century remains to be found.

24   Charles Bertram, *Isn't It Wonderful? A History of Magic and Mystery* (London: Swan Sonnenschein & Co., 1896), 125.
25   Ibid.
26   Dawes, 'A Rich Cabinet of Magical Curiosities: 67', 107. Dawes is referring to *The Modern Conjurer and Drawing-Room Entertainer* by Mademoiselle Patrice' husband Charles Lang Neil that features her as a performer.
27   Dawes, 'The Female of the Species', 133.

Figure 21. Mademoiselle Patrice demonstrating her 'method for ladies' of 'The Handkerchiefs and Soup Plate' illusion, in Charles Lang Neil: *The Modern Conjurer and Drawing-Room Entertainer* (Philadelphia, PA: J.B. Lippincott, 1902), 218, Fig. 2. Available online: The Library of Congress, <https://www.loc.gov/item/ltf91000543>, accessed 20 January 2021. Public domain.

For the largest part of the nineteenth century, performance magic was dominated by men to such an extent, that women barely figured in it at all: magicians' assistants were usually male, and the women who did appear onstage were the magicians' fiancées, wives or mistresses. In view of this, Angela Marie Sanchez suggests that the reason Adelaide Herrmann performed in male clothing in her husband's show throughout the 1870s and 1880s also 'speaks to the popularity of male assistants during the early vaudeville years'.[28] It was only in the following decades that women gained greater presence on magic stages, and only in the course of the twentieth century that the scantily dressed female assistant strutting across the stage as a sexy personification of misdirection has become standard.

28   Sanchez, *Conjuring the Modern Woman*, 17.

Female Conjuring

Around 1900, some of the most iconic stage illusions were carried out by men only: Houdini started his career performing with his brother Theodore 'Dash' (who later got a sort of spin-off show of his own as Hardeen), Chung Ling Soo's primary assistant (and stage manager) was Fukado Kametaro, Howard Thurston performed with Guy Jarrett. The person floating in mid-air in John Nevil Maskelyne's legendary levitation illusion was not, as we might imagine, a slender woman, dressed in white, semi-transparent gowns, but his business and stage partner George Alfred Cooke.[29] Even the notoriously misogynistic 'Sawing a Woman in Half' illusion initially featured a male 'victim': Horace Goldin, one of the two illusionists who claimed to have invented it, first 'sawed' in halves a male assistant,[30] before rectifying what Jim Steinmeyer called a 'mistake in casting'[31] by replacing him with a young woman. Magician Val Andrews remarked that '[t]he idea of cutting thru such a fragile and delightful being made the situation so much more dramatic and alarming'.[32] This quote indicates that this illusion was made particularly sensational by the apparent destruction of a *woman*, who was perceived as helpless and fragile. What is more, this is done by a man who thereby breaks with his role as her strong protector. Interestingly, Adelaide Herrmann, too, seems to have performed the Sawing with a female assistant,[33] thus sticking to the by then established standard gendering of this illusion.

As I have argued elsewhere, this staging of brute force directed towards the female body, which became extremely popular during the 1920s – as women around the world began to gain suffrage – may be regarded not only

29   The cast of *The Enchanted Fakir*, the magical playlet in which this illusion was performed, is listed in a programme sheet of the Egyptian Hall in the V&A Collections, Department of Theatre and Performance.

30   See Clinton Burgess, 'Seventeenth Annual Banquet of the Society of American Magicians', *The Sphinx. An Independent Magazine for Magicians* 20/4 (June 1921), 129–31, 131.

31   See Jim Steinmeyer, 'Above and Beneath the Saw', in *Art & Artifice and Other Essays on Illusion* (New York: Carroll & Graf Publishers, 2006), 77–106, 88.

32   Val Andrews, 'The Unsuspected. The Magician's Assistant as a Secret Aide', in Frances Ireland Marshall, ed., *Those Beautiful Dames* (Chicago: Magic Inc., 1984), 16–18, 16.

33   'Mme. Hermann [sic!] to Saw Woman in Half', *The Billboard* (8 October 1921), 8.

as a re-oppression but also as a transfer of power: as the magician slips into a decorative role, he entrusts the success of the illusion entirely to his female co-performer.[34] However, because this distribution of responsibilities is not conveyed on stage, Coppa has argued that while 'female skill and labour' is the secret to this feat, the 'true illusion of the Sawing is, of course, female passivity'[35]: on stage as well as in publicity material, the female assistant's body is presented as inactive except for obeying the magician's command.[36] If magiciennes were undercredited and objectified, female assistants were uncredited and literally treated like objects when they were put into boxes, cut in pieces and put back together.

Coppa states that 'the essence of magic is the effacement – or perhaps more accurately, the displacement – of labor'.[37] It is worth noting that this is true for all labour, not only the assistants'. The modern style of magic, Wally Smith has pointed out, creates the impression of supernatural forces at work by displacing agency – away from any person involved in the production of a magic show: the magicians' behaviour is meticulously scripted, their movements carefully choreographed, and their patter as laboriously rehearsed as their sleight-of-hand. Yet, in the show, all of these elements have to appear incidental, casual and natural, thereby denying the magicians' agency in the illusion. The labour of the backstage workers, engineers and mechanics, too, is entirely neglected in the performance.[38] In case of the assistants who appear on the stage, however, this 'displacement' of labour is most apparent to the spectators. Therefore, the ability to hide their efforts

34   See Katharina Rein, 'Sawing People in Half: Sensationalist Magic Tricks and the Role of Women on Stage in the Early Twentieth Century', in Alberto Gabriele, ed., *Sensationalism and the Genealogy of Modernity. A Global Nineteenth Century Approach* (New York: Palgrave Macmillan, 2016), 163–91.

35   Coppa, 'The Body Immaterial', 93.

36   For instance, in the 'Broomstick Suspension' analysed in Frédéric Tabet's and Pierre Taillefer's chapter in this volume, during which it is bent into various positions in mid-air.

37   Coppa, 'The Body Immaterial', 86, 91.

38   Wally Smith, 'Technologies of Stage Magic: Simulation and Dissimulation', *Social Studies of Science* 45/3 (2015), 319–43, 331–2, 338.

is a highly valued quality in magicians' assistants,[39] and the best ones were praised for their capacity and willingness to endure great physical strain and sometimes pain.

The most well-known one to receive recognition for these abilities was Olive Robinson (Augusta Pfaff, 1863–1934, see Figure 22), who was 'more than once described [...] as the best magician's assistant in the world' by Harry Kellar.[40] Steinmeyer portrays her as 'tiny, well under five feet tall, with a slender figure'[41] – qualities that were credited in her nickname 'Dot'. 'Dot was the ideal size for a magician's assistant', he writes, 'fitting easily into cabinets, suitably light and slender.'[42] Together with her husband William E. Robinson (1861–1918), she alternately worked for the USA's premier rival magicians, Alexander Herrmann and Harry Kellar. When her husband launched his career as the 'Chinese' magician Chung Ling Soo, Olive performed in his show and took on some management and backstage duties. Attesting to her toughness as an assistant, Steinmeyer mentions that in one of the illusions 'Dot was regularly burned by the blasts of steam, leaving her with ugly scars on her hands and arms.'[43]

39   See, for instance, Val Andrews, 'The Unsuspected. The Magician's Assistant as a Secret Aide', in Frances Ireland Marshall, ed., *Those Beautiful Dames* (Chicago: Magic Inc., 1984), 16–18.

40   Will Dexter, *The Riddle of Chung Ling Soo* (London, New York: Arco Publishers Ltd, 1955), 48.

41   Steinmeyer, *The Glorious Deception*, 65.

42   Ibid., 67.

43   Ibid., 299.

Figure 22. Olive 'Dot' Robinson and Harry Kellar presenting the 'Astarte' illusion, 1889. Photographed by Rothengatter & Dillon. New York Public Library, The Miriam and Ira D. Wallach Division of Art, Prints and Photographs: Picture Collection, <https://digitalcollections.nypl.org/items/682b3eae-455d-09c7-e040-e00a18065 8fb>, accessed 20 January 2021. Public domain.

After her husband was fatally shot during a bullet-catching performance in London in 1918, Olive produced a music hall show featuring some of his illusions, but it was unsuccessful.[44] Similarly, several other magicians' wives and former assistants, like 'Colonel' Stodare's widow or Lafayette's former assistant Mlle. Selbini, tried to continue the shows after the leading, male magicians' deaths. Like Olive Robinson, they were unable to establish independent careers. This underlines that Adelaide Herrmann's long and distinguished career

44   See ibid., 412–15.

Female Conjuring

was, after all, a major exception for that time. Perhaps the reason why assistants had a much harder time launching their own careers (than Herrmann who appeared as a co-performer in her husband's show from the start) is precisely the publicly staged erasure of their agency, skill and labour.

Acknowledgement
I would like to thank Frank Cifarelli for carefully proofreading this chapter.

Frédéric Tabet and Pierre Taillefer

'The Suspension Ethéréenne' under the Photographer's Lens

> I certify that Professor De Vere and Miss Lily Edith have given me great satisfaction by their talented performances. They have achieved a great success. I tender them my hearty thanks.[1]

By the time Jacques Offenbach takes over as the manager of the Théâtre de la Gaîté in Paris in mid-1873, Clairville and d'Ennery's fantasy spectacular *La Poule aux oeufs d'or*, *The Hen That Laid the Golden Eggs*, a blockbuster of the genre has been running since early January. In April, the show benefits from the addition of a new visual attraction: the 'graceful poses'[2] of Miss Lily Edith, suspended mid-air. At around the same time, performers from the production make their way in front of Gaston et Mathieu's camera lens, the photographers taking a series of publicity shots in the form of *carte de visite* portraits.[3] Sporting a variety of costumes, Miss Lily Edith is thus photographed performing the illusion that, since the time of Robert-Houdin (1805–71), has been known as the 'Ethereal Suspension'.

One of the foundations of theatrical magic shows is that the techniques employed cannot be detected. To present apparently impossible effects – appearances, vanishes, levitations and the like – illusionists are continually forced to innovate, either by introducing novel methods or reinterpreting the

---

1   Jacques Offenbach, 'Professor De Vere's Modern Marvels', in *The David Baldwin Magic Collection 2* (Chicago: Potter & Potter, 2018), 292.

2   'Nouvelles des arts et des théâtres,' *Le Constitutionnel* 92 (2 April 1873), 3.

3   Gaston et Mathieu registered the photographs on 26 June 1873. Bibliothèque nationale de France, 'Miss Edith', 1387–8, [*Registre des estampes et des photographies déposées en 1872 et 1873*] (Paris: Bibliothèque nationale de France, 1872–3), [351].

standard repertoire in unconventional ways. The photographic act – the imaginary realm in which it operates, its processes, its apparatus – is increasingly embraced as a justification for (re)presentation, but the principles behind it are also exploited and manipulated. Studying illusionists' use of photography, and the images of Miss Lily Edith's ethereal suspension in particular, exposes the relationship between the professional practitioners of both disciplines, especially as regards the concept of trickery.

Photography on the Stage

Having been the capital of the sciences in the eighteenth century, Paris became the entertainment and leisure capital for its nineteenth-century inhabitants.[4] Against this backdrop of a culture favourable to theatrical novelties, research into optical magic – already begun towards the end of the Enlightenment in the form of Rabiqueau's studies and Robertson's phantasmagoria projections – keep pace with technological advances in how to control light. After making their debut at the Royal Polytechnic Institution in London, the spirits of Professor Pepper (1821–1900) appear, in turn, on the Parisian stage in 1863, most prominently in the auditorium of the illusionist Robin (1811–74). Simultaneously, as an increasing number of theatres became electrified, Dr Lynn (1831–99) and, later, Buatier de Kolta (1847–1903) lay the foundations for 'black art' techniques that enable a performer to remain invisible in darker areas of the stage. In both cases, a lighting-based magical scripture emerges: managed and controlled, beams of light remodel spaces and render appearances deceptive.

The second half of the nineteenth century sees this refined magic coincide with significant photographic advances. Technical innovations (flexible film, fast emulsion), aesthetic innovations (small formats, *cartes de visite*, colouring)

---

4   Alain Corbin, *L'Avènement des loisirs. 1850–1960* (Paris: Flammarion, 1995); Julia Csergo, 'Extension et mutations du loisir citadin', *L'Avènement des loisirs 1850–1960* (Paris: Flammarion, 1995), 121.

and social innovations (the emergence of professional photographers, lower costs) radically transform the way in which the new process is viewed. While magicians may not play an inventive role in the field of photography, they are at least privileged observers of it. Those who make a living from the two disciplines continually rub shoulders and experiment in closely neighbouring spaces. In the Bois de Boulogne's Parc du Pré-Catelan, which opens in 1856, a dozen lodges host the most popular entertainments of the Second Empire, Bénita Anguinet's Théâtre de Magie and the Bisson brothers' photographic pavilion among them. The Bissons also take a number of photographs of both the exterior and interior of the nearby illusionist's theatre. After applauding Anguinet's magic routines, Parisian high society is just as astonished when posing, on horseback or in a coach, in front of the camera lens.[5] Encounters here often involve friendly relationships – Alfred de Caston and the photographer Étienne Carjat; Robert-Houdin and the similarly Blois-based Mieusement – and sometimes familial ties, as is the case with the virtuoso manipulator Tufferau (1829–1903), who just so happens to be the younger brother of the photographer Edmond Tufferau (1826–1903). André Voisin (1807–75), the Second Empire's most famous manufacturer of illusion apparatus, even tries his hand at professional photography, building a photographic studio in the site adjoining his shop.[6] A few years later, he and his confrère Robin register a patent for the use of portrait-bearing passes to regulate theatre subscriptions.[7]

Lastly and most significantly, photographers and illusionists share a half-century-long common fate at 8 Boulevard des Italiens, starting when Hamilton, Robert-Houdin's successor as the director of the Soirées Fantastiques, sublets the floors above his theatre to the famed photographer Disdéri.[8] In 1854, the vestibule of the Théâtre Robert-Houdin thus plays host to an exhibition of Disdéri's work,[9] and one of the first exhibitions in the theatre's foyer in 1857

5   'Nouvelles diverses', *Le Ménestrel* 24/25 (24 May 1857), 4.
6   'Liste générale des adresses de Paris' *Annuaire-almanach du commerce* (Paris: Firmin Didot Frères, 1862), 545.
7   'Brevet d'invention, mode de contrôle, photographie', *Recueil général des lois et des arrêts* (Paris: Larose et Tenin, 1870), 203–4.
8   *Minutier central des notaires* (Paris: Archives nationales), XXX/920.
9   'Galerie photographique de M. Disdéri', *La Lumière* 4/45 (11 November 1854), 179.

includes a sizeable area dedicated to photography.[10] After Hamilton comes a series of illusionists, the last of whom is Georges Méliès, while Disdéri's studio passes through Désiré Lebel,[11] Émile Tourtin[12] and Clément Maurice in turn, the latter a photographer and, later, operator of the Lumière cinematograph. Press coverage of local incidents – destruction caused by a leak in 1881,[13] major fires in 1892[14] and 1901[15] – also regularly evoke the proximity and intertwined destiny of the two establishments.

Illusionists soon adopt and exploit the voguish new medium. Photography becomes merchandise: it serves as advertising and is disseminated across the public sphere. Just as people collect portraits of crowned heads of state, so they assemble photographs of showmen like Jean-Eugène Robert-Houdin and Alfred de Caston in scrapbooks.[16] From the 1860s, the likes of Bénita Anguinet and Josef Velle offer photographs or photo albums of themselves as raffle prizes during their shows.[17] Photographic prints, moreover, make their way onto illusionists' stages, becoming props in their shows. Alfred de Caston creates 'thought photographs'[18] and uses *cartes de visite* bearing his portrait to note his predictions, dating and signing them before letting spectators keep them as souvenirs.[19] Audiences also enjoy 'La photographie Brunnet' and 'La photographie Verbeck',[20] routines in which

10   'Chronique', *La Lumière* 7/17 (25 April 1857), 67.

11   Disdéri's business partner from 1857 to 1865.

12   'Les tramways en France: Les tramways du Havre', *Le Monde illustré* 18/879 (14 February 1874), 110.

13   'Faits divers', *Le XIXe siècle* 11/3448 (7 June 1881), 3.

14   'Faits divers: Le feu au théâtre Robert-Houdin', *L'Intransigeant* 4519 (27 November 1892), 3.

15   Henri Petitjean, 'L'Incendie du boulevard des Italiens', *Le Figaro* (1 February 1901), 3–4.

16   Charles Gaudin, *Catalogue général des illustrations contemporaines photographiées format carte de visite* (Paris), 1862.

17   'Théâtre de Valence', *Le Courrier de la Drôme et de l'Ardèche* 35/70 (24 March 1866), 3.

18   'Salle du Vaux-hall, au Parc', *Le Moniteur belge* 29/340 (December 1859), 4869.

19   Frédéric Tabet, and Pierre Taillefer, *The Lion and the Rose Searching for the Father of Modern Mentalism* (Turin: Masters of Magic, 2015), 67–103.

20   Verbeck, *Programme* I154(9) (Nantes: Archives municipales, 1880), 42.

portraits appear on blank cards.[21] 'La photographie des dames' is a feature in the illusionist Pickman's programme of 1884; at the end of this effect, 'every lady may take her portrait with her, and can have it framed if she wishes'.[22] Even learned animals profit from photographic fever, as is the case with Minos, a dog that can recognize photographic portraits laid before him.[23]

In the nineteenth century, illusionists' photographic iconography often involves the same themes. The magician poses, occasionally with a prop representing his or her show (a slate for Alfred de Caston, a ball or a magic wand for Josef Velle, a couple of cards impaled on a sword for Mme Delemarre), in a full-length portrait. Photographs of the magician's stage and set, meanwhile, as with the Théâtre de Magie in the Pré-Catelan and the Théâtre Robert-Houdin, are devoid of human presence, each show's full range of props instead being exhibited specially for the photographer.[24] Shots depicting a magic effect are rarer. Eugène Thiébault does, however, produce a series that serves as a visual evocation of the spectres that appear at the Salle Robin[25]: the photographer replaces the theatre's optical apparatus with trick photography (double exposures). This change in technique is needed because the artificial lighting of the time prevents the effects of not just stage lighting, but also optical magic, from being captured in a photograph. Yet by changing the technique, the status of these images becomes ambivalent: are these shots popular because of Robin's fame or that of his ghosts? Do people like them because of the ambiguity of their relationship to spirit photographs, which are emerging in the United States at this point, or because of how clever the trick photography they feature is? The kind of trick employed changes the very nature of the depiction. Other problems connected to the photographic medium reveal themselves in a series of shots of Miss Lily Edith's ethereal suspension (see Figure 23).

21 'Société royal du Sport nautique de la Meuse', *La Meuse* (Liège) 10/278 (25 November 1865), 2.

22 Pickmann, Programme from the théâtre de Limoges, 22 February 1884 (Pierre Taillefer collection).

23 Jules Prevel, 'Courrier des théâtres', *Le Figaro* 23/99 (April 1877), 2.

24 Bisson frères, *Vues du Pré-Catelan, Bois de Boulogne* (Paris: Bisson frères, 1856), 23; *R. H.* (Paris: Cinémathèque française, ca. 1890), CF. P.371-042.

25 Laurence Senelick, 'Pepper's Ghost Faces the Camera', *History of Photography* 1/7 (1983), 62–72.

Figure 23. *Professeur de Vere: Le Fakir et sa fille enchantée Miss Lily Edith*
(Paris: Choumara; London: C. de Vere, [1873]). (François Voignier collection). Photo by
François Voignier.

Photographic Suspension

In September 1847,[26] Robert-Houdin had presented the first version of his
'suspension éthéréenne', which was – according to his own account – one of
the tricks that earned the most applause in his show.[27] Presented as exempli-
fying the magic of science,[28] the illusion had such an impact on the collective

26   Jean-Eugène Robert-Houdin, *Confidences et révélations* (Paris: Delahays, 1868), 427.
27   Ibid., 299.
28   Ibid.

imagination that it served as a source of inspiration to Jules Verne.[29] The staging – apparent from engraved and photographic depictions[30] – used by Miss Lily Edith and her husband Charles de Vere[31] when presenting the effect a quarter of a century later is entirely different. Her elbow resting on a staff, Miss Lily Edith remains suspended in the air, lying on nothing at all (see Figures 24a and 24b). Under chromatic limelight,[32] she is held aloft, her costume then changing to represent a series of characters: a dancer, Little Red Riding Hood (see Figures 25a and 25b), a Scot, France, Mercury (see Figures 26a, 26b and 26c), Renown, a priestess of Bacchus.[33] The illusion as exhibited on the stage of the Théâtre de la Gaîté seems to go still further than both Robert-Houdin's invention and the illusion conveyed by photographic media: combining the mechanical principles of the suspension and the optical principles of black-art productions, the 'fakir', Charles de Vere, ultimately removes the supporting staff from beneath his wife's elbow,[34] leaving Miss Lily Edith levitating with no apparent means of support.[35]

This routine, as presented by Miss Lily Edith and her husband in Paris, is a success.[36] Billed as 'The Fakir and His Enchanted Daughter, Miss Lily Edith', the illusion will go on to be exhibited in Belgium, England and Lyon, as well as at the largest fairs in France. Booklets illustrating the eight poses in

29 Jules Verne, 'Autour de la lune', *Journal des débats politiques et littéraires* (13 November 1869), 2.

30 Paris: Bibliothèque nationale de France, NA-250 (box 15) and N-2 (EDITH-EDOUARD); Paris: Musée Carnavalet, PH50080.

31 Lily Edith, who later finds fame as Okita, just so happens to be the young wife of the English illusionist Charles de Vere. Her identity is confirmed in 'Tribunal de commerce', *Feuille Officielle des îles Saint-Pierre et Miquelon* 19/1 (5 January 1884).

32 'Professor De Vere's Modern Marvels', *The David Baldwin Magic Collection*, 292; see also Charles Dupanty, 'Échos des théâtres', *Le Soleil* 1/35 (3 April 1873), 3.

33 'Chronique', *Journal de Lyon* 3/178 (1 July 1873), 2.

34 'La Soirée théâtrale', *Le Figaro* 20/99 (9 April 1873), 3.

35 This improved version is, incidentally, the one that Charles de Vere will, much later, go on to sell. Charles De Vere, *Grands Trucs et illusions* (Paris: De Vere, ca. 1900), 3.

36 Honoré Daumier offers a caricature of this illusion on 26 June 1873: *Le Charivari* 36/37 (7 February 1867), 3.

Figure 24a. 'Le magnétisme – The magnetism', *Professeur de Vere: Le Fakir et sa fille enchantée Miss Lily Edith* (Paris: Choumara; London: C. de Vere, [1873]). François Voignier collection. Photo by François Voignier.

Figure 24b. Gaston et Mathieu (Paris), Miss Lily Edith suspended, portrait-*carte de visite*, 1873. Paris, Musée Carnavalet, PH50080. Photo by Musée Carnavalet.

Figure 25a. 'Chaperon rouge – The Little Red Riding Hood', *Professeur de Vere: Le Fakir et sa fille enchantée Miss Lily Edith* (Paris: Choumara; London: C. de Vere, [1873]). François Voignier collection. Photo by François Voignier.

Figure 25b. Gaston et Mathieu (Paris), Miss Lily Edith as Little Red Riding Hood, portrait-*carte de visite*, 1873. Paris, BnF, NA-250 (box 15). Photo by Frédéric Tabet.

Figure 26a. 'Mercure – Mercury', *Professeur de Vere: Le Fakir et sa fille enchantée Miss Lily Edith* (Paris: Choumara; London: C. de Vere, [1873]). François Voignier collection. Photo by François Voignier.

Figure 26b. Gaston et Mathieu (Paris), Miss Lily Edith as Mercury, portrait-*carte de visite*, 1873. Paris, BnF, NA-250 (box 15). Photo by Frédéric Tabet.

Figure 26c. [Gaston et Mathieu (Paris)], Miss Lily Edith as Mercury, stereoscopic image, 1875. Paris, BnF, N-2 (EDITH-EDOUARD). Photo by Pierre Taillefer.

engraved form are sold at fifty *centimes* each, as the photographs taken for the Théâtre de la Gaîté, must have been, too (see Figure 23). As their repertoire changes, Charles de Vere and Miss Lily Edith continue to exploit their photographic effigies as advertising tools.[37] These photographs have a value that, if not considerable, is at least symbolic, as in 1884, following a dispute with the management of Henry 'Duperrey' Daunay's travelling theatre, with which the couple have been appearing, a legal judgement forces the establishment's manager to return four photographic portraits to Miss Lily Edith.

The photographic depictions of Miss Lily Edith's suspension raise two questions about how a magic effect can be captured in an image. The first is one of structural incompatibility, which is related to the difficulty to freeze a magical moment, whereby a large number of magic effects do not lend themselves to a magic 'moment' being captured. In his study of the psychology of magic, Alfred Binet thus notes that no illusion is apparent from the series of photographs of illusionists that he has had taken.[38] The Russian film director Sergei Eisenstein will create a cinematographic model from this observation, since, as is the case in the world of illusion, the ability to perceive an effect (something disappearing or simply an image moving) has its origins in different still images being mentally pitted against one another.[39] Suspension falls under the category of 'effects of transition', that depend 'upon the gradual and visible development of some mysterious change'.[40] With these illusions, it is possible to freeze-frame the point at which the change takes place. By introducing a *pause* into the presentation of the effect, a particular moment can be presented to the photographer's lens, with the pause held for as long as it takes for the negative to react. The same illusion of the ethereal suspension, which lends itself to the photographic medium especially well, is thus exhibited for

---

37　'Les Merveilles modernes par De Vere' reproduced in Edwin A. Dawes, 'Ionia and the Family De Vere', *The Magic Circular* 72 (1978), 198.

38　Alfred Binet, 'La Psychologie de la prestidigitation', *Revue des deux mondes* 64/125 (15 October 1894), 922.

39　S. M. Eisenstein, *Notes pour une Histoire générale du cinéma* (Paris: AFRHC, 2013), 116.

40　Nevil Maskelyne, and David Devant, *Our Magic: The Art in Magic* (New York: E.P. Dutton, 1911), 78.

the photographic lens by the American illusionist Madame Young[41] as well as the French illusionist Jehanne d'Alcy.[42]

The second problem is one of spatial incompatibility. For the image to be sufficiently well lit, all the subjects have to change location and be set up in photographic studios. These light-based constraints mean that it is impossible to capture optical-magic effects. In addition, with the illusions removed from their performance context, some of the methods used are revealed, thereby exposing how sophisticated the mechanical workings are. It is certainly possible to move the mechanical rig used in the suspension, but in a studio, it is impossible to use the floor to camouflage it – as was done at the Théâtre Robert-Houdin, for example.[43] Depicting the horizontal suspension in the vertical format of portrait-*cartes de visite* presents a further challenge: two images that have come our way actually show Miss Lily Edith resting on her staff, but in a vertical position, while a third depicts her at a less-than-forty-five-degree angle with respect to the staff, the points of her shoes and the fingers of one of her hands reaching the edge of the image and compromising the effect's clarity. The stereoscopic image, which comes from the same session,[44] offers a means of resolving the spatial limitation, as it involves a square format that better lends itself to a full view – in both two and three dimensions – of the illusion.

***

The major advances that the art of illusion makes in the nineteenth century go hand in hand with the phenomenon of shows finding more permanent homes in theatres, where the audience's point of view, as well as light and sound, can be controlled. The majority of magic routines developed in such settings are inseparable from the framework surrounding them. Illusionists' transition to the photographic medium provides, on the one hand, proof of how

41   'Lot 53, Aerial Suspension', *Dai Vernon/Bruce Cervon Magic Collections* (Chicago: Potter and Potter, 2010), 16.

42   Christian Fechner, *La Magie de Robert-Houdin*, vol. 3 (Boulogne: Éditions FCF, 2005), 325.

43   Ibid.

44   The stereoscopic view seems to be a reprint made for a new set of shows, as Vigié registered it on 3 April 1875. Bibliothèque nationale de France, 'Lily Edith', 606, [*Registre des estampes et des photographies déposées en 1874 et 1875*] (Paris: Bibliothèque nationale de France, 1874–5), [318].

quick magicians are to assimilate the new technology into their programmes and practices. On the other hand, it reveals how effects need to be changed in order to render them compatible with the new capture-based framework. By understanding the constraints imposed by and limitations of these media, magicians subvert capture-based norms and thereby create trick images and sounds: the awkward base of Miss Lily Edith's illusion is thus – voluntarily? – removed from the frame.

More generally, this study reveals the art of illusion's social function. From the first denunciations of spiritualism through to the early days of the cinematograph, illusionists' new photographic iconography prompted, in the first instance, spectators to engage in a critical reading of photographic objectivity. In the second instance, at a point we locate in the early twentieth century, the omnipresence of photographic trickery created conditions that allowed a playful form of appropriation to emerge, first though photographic recreations and, increasingly, via amateur cinema.

Acknowledgement
The authors would like to offer their most sincere thanks to Maxwell Pritchard for his careful translation of this article, and to François Voignier for sharing documents from his collection.

Part IV

Magic Crossing Media Boundaries

Frank Kessler

The Féerie

'A very old and broken magician, having rendered an important service to his protégés, asked only one favour in return: they should cut his own body into pieces and throw these into a white-hot furnace so that he could be reborn young and healthy.' And so it happened – on a stage in Paris. This scene as well as the machinery that was employed to make this magical rebirth happen was described in detail in 1873 in J. Moynet's seminal book on stage technology in France (Figure 27).[1] It is a scene from *Le Roi Carotte*, a play with music by Jacques Offenbach, which premiered on 15 January 1872 at Théâtre de la Gaîté. The play is generally categorized as 'Opéra-bouffe-féerie' and it belonged thus to the very popular nineteenth-century French stage genre called féerie [fairy play]. The féerie was a form of spectacular theatre combining fantastic action, often based on fairy tales, with music, songs, ballets, extravagant costumes and sumptuous sets. As the action often involved fairy godmothers,[2] wizards, witches or demons performing acts of magic, each féerie included numerous trick effects such as the one from *Le Roi Carotte*.[3] According to Moynet, some of those tricks had first been used in English Christmas pantomimes before

---

1   J. Moynet, *L'Envers du théâtre. Machines et décorations* (Paris: Hachette, 1873), 95–6. Unless noted otherwise, all translations from French or German are mine.

2   In the French tradition, 'fée' refers generally to the character of the fairy godmother and not to fairies as 'the little people', as in the British tradition. See Katharine Briggs, *The Fairies in Tradition and Literature* (London, New York: Routledge, 2002). She states '[...] with Perrault the Fairy Godmother entered England. The Fairy Godmother was a new character among the Personae of Fairyland [...]', 222.

3   On féerie see also Frank Kessler, 'La Féerie: un spectacle paradoxal,' *Lendemains* 152 (2013), 71–80 and Kessler, 'The *Féerie* Between Stage and Screen', in André Gaudreault,

being shown in France, and indeed some features are common to féeries and pantomimes.[4]

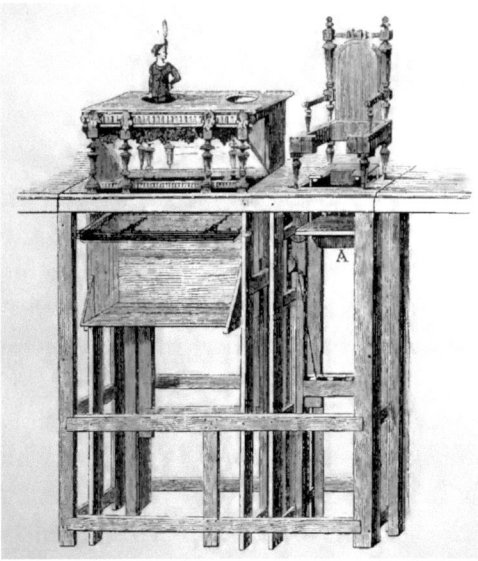

Figure 27. Set-up for the trick in *Le Roi Carotte*, in J. Moynet, *L'Envers du théâtre. Machines et décorations* (Paris: Hachette, 1873), 95, Fig. 19.

Magic on the Stage and Stage Magic

Magic in many forms was a central ingredient in féeries, in particular sudden appearances of supernatural beings such as fairies, sorcerers or diabolic creatures, as well as disappearances or transformations of objects or characters. Being part of the enchanted universe of the féerie, such performances of magic, contrary to those of professional conjurors and stage magicians in

---

Nicolas Dulac, and Santiago Hidalgo, eds, *A Companion to Early Cinema* (Malden, MA, Oxford: Wiley-Blackwell, 2012), 64–79.

4   Moynet, *L'Envers du théâtre*, 91.

their shows, did not imply that the actors and actresses had acquired specific skills to be able to accomplish them, apart from being able to move swiftly according to the instructions that they received. The magic was first and foremost the product of the theatrical machinery and the work of the stage-hands that were hidden from the audience's eyes, while the spectators were doubtlessly well aware of the fact that something was happening behind the scenes which created the marvellous events that they could see materialize on the stage.

While during the very same period stage magicians, too, resorted to advanced technologies to accomplish their amazing feats, they took pains to make sure that the set-up of the stage did not betray the intervention of forces other than the incredible dexterity or stupefying capacities of the performer. Audiences obviously knew that there was something that 'did the trick', but contrary to the spectators in a theatre they could not easily account for the miraculous exploits they witnessed by attributing them to a machinery that they knew existed behind the scenes. As Katharina Rein argues, in such magic shows 'the virtuosity of the performers competes with the capacity of the audience to find out their method'.[5] Stage magicians were always eager to be at least one step ahead of their audience's knowledge about their routines.[6]

In a féerie, a genre that in the late nineteenth century was said to be appreciated above all for its 'naiveté', the relation between the onstage magical events and the spectators was different. A successful féerie had to 'charm' its audience, the 'small and big children' as the French writer Émile Zola put it.[7] The function of the tricks was described in 1885 by the author of an encyclopaedia of theatrical terms as 'rendre réel aux yeux du public' [make appear real to the eyes of the audience] the marvellous and magical elements of the play, that is, to contribute efficiently to the spectators' immersion into the enchanted

---

5   Katharina Rein, *Techniken der Täuschung. Eine Kultur- und Mediengeschichte der Bühnenzauberkunst im späten neunzehnten Jahrhundert* (Marburg: Büchner Verlag, 2020), 170.

6   Rein, *Techniken der Täuschung*, 165–75. See also Katharina Rein, 'Vanishing Technology: Transparency of Media in Stage Magic', in Nele Wynants, ed., *Media Archaeology and Intermedial Performance. Deep Time of the Theatre* (Cham, CH: Palgrave Macmillan, 2019), 99–114.

7   Émile Zola, *Le Naturalisme au théâtre* (Paris: G.Charpentier, 1881), 357.

universe that the féerie presented.[8] At the same time, however, the audience also had to be astonished by the tricks. Their novelty, their complexity or the smoothness of their execution was critically assessed by spectators and journalists alike. But the issue was not in the first instance to understand 'how it was done', but rather to appreciate the spectacular effect that a trick produced.[9]

Féeries presented thus a different kind of magic than magic shows. Rather than making the spectators wonder how a specific feat had been accomplished, they aimed at overwhelming them with a firework of attractional moments, from the sets and costumes to the ballets and songs, with trick effects as a central element. These in particular attracted the journalists' attention and thus were part of the spectacle's marketing strategy. As a féerie was a rather expensive production, publicity was crucial for it to be profitable financially. But while tricks were highlighted in the press mainly as individual attractions, their success with the audience depended on their integration into the action.

The abovementioned scene from *Le Roi Carotte* was not a central one in the plot, but rather a detour for the heroes' quest: the magician Quiribi promises them a magic lamp if they help him to be reborn a young man. So the complex procedure, in the course of which Quiribi's head was taken from his body and placed in the centre of a table where it continued talking while his limbs and torso were thrown one by one into the furnace, was purely conceived as one of the spectacular moments of *Le Roi Carotte* that characterized the féerie as a genre. According to Moynet's detailed description, the entire dismemberment of the magician was performed in full view of the audience and made possible by a clever use of fake limbs, trap doors and mirrors. So in this case, the technicians of the Théâtre de la Gaité worked with a combination of traditional stage techniques and a clever arrangement of mirrors that they may in fact have borrowed from stage magicians who at the time used them in similar ways. However, the specific integration of this set-up into the narrative action as well as the props that they resorted to were original and apparently impressive enough for Moynet to select this trick as an example for his book.

8   Arthur Pougin, *Dictionnaire historique et pittoresque du théâtre et des arts qui s'y rattachent* (Paris: Firmin-Didot, 1885), 748.

9   See Frank Kessler, and Sabine Lenk, '"*Rendre réel aux yeux du public*": Stage Craft, Film Tricks and the *Féerie*', in Nele Wynants, ed., *Media Archaeology and Intermedial Performance* (Cham, CH: Palgrave Macmillan, 2019), 83–98.

Both stage magicians and theatre technicians moved within a competitive professional field where they had to surpass others by surprising the audience with novel tricks and effects. While the former needed to create conditions that seemingly excluded the use of technical tools so that they themselves could take centre stage as performers, the latter worked behind the scenes to 'make appear real to the eyes of the audience' the magical powers that intervened in the universe presented in the play. Just like stage magicians, the producers of féeries were always on the lookout for the latest technical developments that might allow new spectacular effects. But they used them differently, because in a féerie the tricks had to contribute to the creation of an enchanted world that the audience could enjoy in its 'naiveté' and at the same time admire the exploits of its makers.

Stage Magic and Screen Magic

Even before the turn of the century, the new medium of moving pictures adopted the genre into its product range. In 1899, the French filmmaker Georges Méliès produced his first féerie, *Cendrillon* [Cinderella], as did his competitors Pathé frères with *La Belle et la bête* [Beauty and the Beast]. A few years later, probably from 1902 onwards, the genre category 'Féeries et contes' became standard in Pathé's sales catalogues for about a decade. There were some important differences, though, between theatrical and cinematic féeries. The films were comparatively long for their time, consisting generally of several tableaux, yet their duration rarely exceeded ten to fifteen minutes. Also, films inevitably lacked certain ingredients of stage féeries such as witty dialogues and songs as well as the music that was specifically composed for the play. While féerie films were often hand- or stencil coloured, they were also offered as black and white prints, so not all of the spectators saw them in the colourful splendour that theatre audiences experienced. Given their length and, in many cases, the additional cost for coloured prints, féeries were more expensive than other films, and thus exhibitors used them as highlights of their programmes. Therefore, their production values had to be flaunted. Consequently, elaborate sets, costumes and ballets were an important element in cinematic féeries, yet tricks quite clearly were the central attractions and largely determined the structure of the films.

Once the subject as such was determined, in stage féeries the action was constructed by first of all deciding upon the major effects it should contain and in which scenes they should appear. Once this decision was taken, the other scenes could be written to establish a narrative connection between them.[10] In an article published in 1932 in which Méliès looked back on his days as a filmmaker, he described his working method in very similar terms. He, too, started out by determining the effects and tricks, whereas the scenario was little more than the thread which linked them together.[11]

To achieve his trick effects Méliès, who had constructed his own studio, but also his competitors at Pathé frères, did use some stage techniques, in particular trap doors. However, what distinguished filmed féeries from stage performances was the possibility to employ the specific means of the cinematic medium, most prominently the substitution splice, but also multiple exposure, apparent size depending on the distance of an object or person in relation to the camera, or dissolves. The substitution splice, that is, the splicing together of two different, slightly modified takes in an identical framing in order to create an apparent temporal continuity, was used first and foremost for sudden apparitions, disappearances and transformations, sometimes combined with pyrotechnical effects. Dissolves, on the other hand, allowed to show gradual apparitions, disappearances or transformations. By means of double or multiple exposure spectres could be shown moving across the scene, characters could be doubled, tripled, quadrupled, etc. In combination with different distances to the camera, characters could appear as dwarfs or giants. Another technique, which Méliès did not employ, contrary to Segundo de Chomón who worked for Pathé, was frame-by-frame animation which made objects magically move 'on their own'.

In practice, different devices could be combined within one scene. In his 1906 film *Les quatre cents farces du diable*, which included footage that he had contributed to the stage production of *Les 400 coups du diable* one year

10   See Kessler, 'The *Féerie* between Stage and Screen', 67.
11   Georges Méliès, 'L'importance du scenario', *Cinéa et Ciné pour tous réunis* 24 (1932), 23–5.

earlier, Georges Méliès incorporated a scene with two characters trying to have a meal in an inn that was run by Satan himself. Whenever they try to sit down, the table and the chairs disappear and reappear elsewhere in the room. This was achieved by both stage traps and substitution splices, with cardboard tables being raised and lowered, as well as real tables disappearing by means of a splice. While such a combination may seem counterproductive as it underscored the artificiality of the cardboard tables and the relative simplicity of the device that was used to make them appear and disappear, it also flaunts the effect obtained by the cinematic device. Even though by 1906 substitution splices were certainly no longer a novelty, their specific quality as cinematic tricks was emphasized by the contrast.

Méliès himself saw the different trick techniques as more or less equal, though, as all of them could contribute to the creation of stunning effects. He affirmed: 'I introduced to the kinematograph mechanical, optical, magic, and other tricks. When all these techniques are competently used together, I do not hesitate to say that it is possible today to achieve the most impossible and improbable things in kinematography.'[12]

Conclusion

Magic was a central ingredient to the féerie both as a stage and as a screen genre. Within the universe of the féerie, magic was performed by sorcerers and sorceresses, by fairies and demons, by djinns and diabolic creatures. The task of the makers of féeries, both theatrical and cinematic, was to make appear such acts of magic as a reality, albeit a fictional one, to the eyes of the audience. In order to achieve this, they had to resort to sophisticated technologies. As a genre, the féerie aimed at enchanting the spectators through the richness of the fantastic and magical world that was displayed, but also

12   Georges Méliès, 'Kinematographic Views' [1907], Appendix B in André Gaudreault, *Film and Attraction. From Kinematography to Cinema* (Urbana, Chicago, Springfield: University of Illinois Press, 2011), 148.

to make them marvel at the incredible wonders that could be shown onstage and onscreen. The audiences came to enjoy the 'naiveté' of the spectacle, but at the same time had high expectations which the producers tried to meet. Contrary to stage magic, onstage and onscreen féerie magic did not challenge spectators to try and unveil its secrets. It simply aimed at making them wonder.

Matthew Solomon

Georges Méliès' *Escamotage d'une dame chez Robert-Houdin* (1896)

Georges Méliès is perhaps the best-known of all magician-filmmakers, whose trick films adapted tropes of stage illusion to the specific technological and material possibilities of the new medium of cinema. The earliest of Méliès' trick films known to survive is *Escamotage d'une dame chez Robert-Houdin* ('Star' Film, 1896), hereafter referred to as *Escamotage d'une*, which was titled *The Vanishing Lady* in Méliès' American sales catalogues *dame*, where it is listed at a length of 'about 65 feet', corresponding to a screening time of about one minute if Méliès' lost film *Conjurer Making Ten Hats in Sixty Seconds*, which is likewise listed at a length of 'about 65 feet', is to be believed, although projection speeds varied greatly.[1] In *Escamotage d'une dame*, Méliès performed a variation of The Vanishing Lady, an illusion which Buatier de Kolta had introduced ten years earlier, although it had become something of a cliché by 1896 (Figure 28). Magician Charles Bertram, whom de Kolta licensed to perform the illusion in London, wrote in 1896, '[o]f course, hundreds of imitators sprung up. No place of entertainment was complete without its vanishing lady.'[2] Along with numerous theatrical imitations, British film producer Robert W. Paul made a film of the illusion featuring Bertram, as did several American

1   *Complete Catalogue of Genuine and Original 'Star' Films (Moving Pictures)* (New York: Geo. Méliès, 1903), 10. See also Paolo Cherchi Usai, *Silent Cinema: A Guide to Study, Research, and Curatorship* (London: British Film Institute Publishing, 2019), 179–85, 376.

2   Charles Bertram, *Isn't It Wonderful? A History of Magic and Mystery* (London: Swan Sonnenschein and Co., 1896), 127.

film producers with their own performers, including a Biograph version in 1897 and an Edison version in 1898, the latter featuring another early magician-filmmaker, Albert E. Smith.[3] The woman who appears in Méliès' version is Jehanne d'Alcy, who was a performer in Méliès' magic theatre, the Théâtre Robert-Houdin and much later became Méliès' second wife in 1925.[4] Although Méliès later claimed it was an 'exact reproduction of the famous trick of Buatier de Kolta', the film in fact expanded considerably on the original illusion.[5] Indeed, Méliès' *Escamotage d'une dame* combined The Vanishing Lady with two other illusions, the appearance of a skeleton in the empty chair and the transformation of the skeleton into a living person.[6]

3   Ian Christie, *Robert Paul and the Origins of British Cinema* (Chicago: University of Chicago Press, 2019), 274; Charles Musser, *Edison Motion Pictures: An Annotated Filmography, 1890–1900* (Pordenone, Italy: Le Giornate del Cinema Muto; Washington, DC: Smithsonian Institution Press, 1997), 467. See also Musser, *The Emergence of Cinema: The American Screen to 1907* (New York: Charles Scribner's Sons, 1990), 231, 271–2.

4   'Escamotage d'une dame chez Robert-Houdin', *Les Amis de Georges Méliès* 1 (1982), 10–11; '"Escamotage d'une dame chez Robert-Houdin": Le premier rôle de Jehanne d'Alcy', *Cinémathèque Méliès* 22 (1993), 45–9.

5   Georges Méliès, 'En marge de l'histoire du cinématographe (Suite)', *Ciné-Journal* 888 (3 September 1926), 11 (my translation).

6   Matthew Solomon, *Disappearing Tricks: Silent Film, Houdini, and the New Magic of the Twentieth Century* (Urbana: University of Illinois Press, 2010), 33–5.

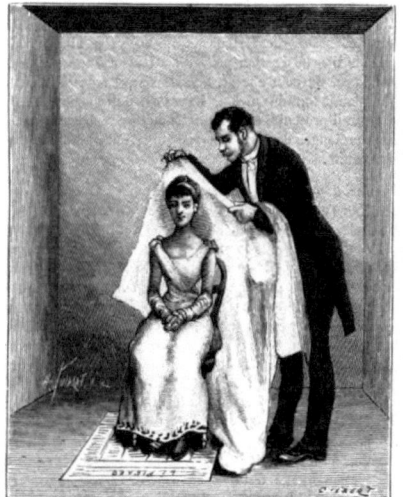

Figure 28. Illustrations that accompanied a published explanation of 'La Femme Escamotée' in La Nature, no. 946 (18 July 1891), 176.

Despite nominally performing the vanish in the genteel style of Robert-Houdin, Méliès' film is comical inasmuch as the magician conjures a skeleton instead of the woman seemingly by mistake. He recoils in surprise when he sees it in the chair, and succeeds in making the vanished woman reappear only when he drapes the cloth over the chair and tries another time. While the fabric covers both the disappearance and the reappearance of the woman, the appearance of the skeleton occurs in full view of the audience, yet another departure from the typical way of presenting The Vanishing Lady. Typically, the vanished woman reappeared from the wings or in the theatre, as she does in the British film *Sing As We Go!* (1934), in which the trick was accomplished onscreen with de Kolta's theatrical method (and reportedly one of the specially prepared chairs he used to perform the illusion).[7]

In many versions of The Vanishing Lady as it was performed onstage, the covering placed over the woman disappeared at just the moment when it was removed: the person and the cloth thus *appeared* to vanish at the same

7   Jasper Maskelyne, *White Magic: Story of Maskelynes* (London: Stanley Paul & Co., Ltd, 1936), 73.

moment, leaving only the chair and the newspaper beneath it.[8] Bertram insisted, 'The trick was never complete without the veil being made to vanish [...] simultaneously with the lady's disappearance, [...] which caused an especial interest to the audience, and made our performance stand out in contrast to all imitations.'[9] In Méliès' version, the fabric does not disappear: he casts it aside, and then picks it up again to cover the skeleton as it is transformed into d'Alcy, casting it aside again as d'Alcy rises from the chair. Whereas many of the props in a magic show and in countless trick films are brought onstage, used in a trick, and then removed (or else made to disappear), the fabric remains and is central for the mise-en-scène of two distinct and non-consecutive illusions. Like Méliès, many magicians omitted the cloth vanish since it was reportedly more difficult than vanishing the person, and more likely to fail.

Professor Hoffmann's 1890 book *More Magic* concludes with a detailed explanation of The Vanishing Lady illusion that parses the advantages and disadvantages of vanishing the veil, 'an additional effect [...] performed by Buatier and the more ambitious of his imitators':

> If all goes well, the effect is extremely magical, the visible disappearance of the veil enhancing the marvel of the invisible disappearance of the lady. [...] In my own opinion, the additional effect of success is not sufficient to counterbalance the risk of failure, and this element of the feat is best omitted.[10]

As Bertram, who performed the illusion with the vanishing of the veil, pointed out in 1899, 'Many performers tried the trick afterwards: and most of them could "vanish" the lady, but they could not cause the disappearance

---

8   In some stage versions of The Vanishing Lady, the woman came onstage carrying a handkerchief and only the handkerchief remained on the chair after she vanished. In Méliès' version, d'Alcy enters carrying a fan, which remains in her hands throughout the time she is onscreen.

9   Bertram, *Isn't It Wonderful?*, 127–8.

10 Professor Hoffmann [pseud., Angelo John Lewis], *More Magic* (London: George Routledge and Sons, 1890), 455. See also William George Provan Houstoun, 'The Grand Cycle of Conjuring Treatises: *Modern Magic, More Magic, Later Magic* and *Latest Magic*', *Early Popular Visual Culture* 16/2 (2018), 123–45.

of the large silk covering.'[11] The sheer size of the fabric, unlike the much smaller handkerchiefs and silks typically used in conjuring, made it difficult to manipulate and especially challenging to vanish.

If the explanation found in *More Magic* is accurate, the fabric had to be 'very thin soft silk, so as to be capable of being folded or crumpled into very small dimensions' and then rapidly pulled up the sleeve by means of an elastic cord.[12] The draping of the silk was also a crucial part of The Vanishing Lady stage illusion inasmuch as it was used to suggest that she was still in the chair while she was in fact in the process of exiting the stage, only to then reappear in the wings or in the theatre audience. A framework of metal wire held the silk in the shape of the woman's seated silhouette as she descended through a trap door in the stage; it dropped out of sight when the silk was removed. A newspaper placed beneath the chair ostensibly prevented the use of a trap door, but the newspaper was either specially cut and lined up with the opening of the trap door or made of rubber with a concealed slit large enough for a person to slip through.[13]

No trap door was involved in Méliès' film version. Instead, discontinuous shots filmed from the same camera position were cut together, and the draping of the fabric betrays the placement of several of the cuts. Indeed, the fabric appears to be rather thicker than silk and it seems to have been somewhat difficult to manage at several points in the film. As Méliès raises the fabric up after draping it over d'Alcy as she is seated in the chair, part of her is still visible at the point where the cut was later placed. Similarly, as he drapes the fabric over the skeleton, he leaves a corner of the chair uncovered, which is likewise still visible at the point where the cut was later placed. Watched closely, these seemingly inadvertent mishandlings of the fabric betray the fact that the film is not a spatial illusion, but instead is a trick that relies on manipulating temporality.

For French film historians like Georges Sadoul, the placement of the first cut in *Escamotage d'une dame* was a straightforward replacement of the use

---

11   'Royalty's Magician: A Chat with Mr. Charles Bertram' (1899), reproduced in *The Wizard Exposed: Magic Tricks, Interviews, and Experiences* (Glenwood, IL: David Meyer Magic Books, 1987), 98.

12   Hoffmann, *More Magic*, 453. See also 209–10.

13   Albert A. Hopkins, ed., *Magic: Stage Illusions and Scientific Diversions, Including Trick Photography* (New York: Munn and Co., 1897), 42–3.

of a trap door in the theatre. Sadoul pointed out that the film was shot not inside the Théâtre Robert-Houdin, where the lighting would have been insufficient, but instead outdoors in full sunlight on the Méliès family's property in Montreuil (before Méliès' glass-enclosed filmmaking studio was constructed there a year later). Filmed outside on a platform in front of comparatively simple scenery, according to Sadoul, Méliès stopped the camera and held his pose while d'Alcy left the field of view, then resumed filming to create the disappearance effect.[14] However, accounts like this omit a crucial component of the illusion, namely the physical alteration of the strip of negative film, as Jacques Malthête pointed out:

> This effect [stop camera] is always associated with a splice. [...] Every appearance, disappearance or substitution was of course done in the camera but was always re-cut in the laboratory on the negative and for a very simple reason: this trick effect [...] will not work if the rhythm is broken. But the inertia of the camera was such that it was impossible to stop on the last frame of the 'shot' before the 'trick', change the background or the characters, and start up again on the first frame of the 'shot' after the 'trick' without having a noticeable variation in speed.[15]

The instantaneous onscreen disappearances Méliès created were not 'in camera' effects, but instead relied on joining together separate strips of film, a material practice that is the basis of many of Méliès' cinematic illusions and became the virtual *sine qua non* of his filmmaking.

14   Georges Sadoul, *L'invention du cinéma, 1832–1897* (Paris: Éditions Denoël, 1977 [1946]), 391. For similar accounts, see Jean Mitry, *Histoire du cinéma: Art et industrie*, vol. 1 (Paris: Éditions Universitaires, 1967), 117; Jacques Deslandes, and Jacques Richard, *Du cinématographe au cinéma, 1896–1906* (Tournai: Casterman, 1968), 422.

15   Jacques Malthête, letter from 1 May 1981, quoted in André Gaudreault, 'Theatricality, Narrativity, and Trickality: Reevaluating the Cinema of Georges Méliès', trans. Paul Attalah, with Tom Gunning and Vivian Sobchack, in Matthew Solomon, ed., *Fantastic Voyages of the Cinematic Imagination: Georges Méliès's Trip to the Moon* (Albany, NY: SUNY Press, 2011), 42.

Figure 29. Visible traces of a splice in a film print of *Escamotage d'une dame chez Robert-Houdin*, Georges Méliès ('Star' Film, 1896).

Direct evidence of the physical process – and indirect evidence of the chemical process – of re-joining separate strips of film can be seen in surviving positive prints of Méliès' films (Figure 29). The visible splices in these prints reveal how Méliès' most important trick was done, even though his method was far from secret. *The Handbook of Kinematography* is one of the many places where it can be found under the heading 'joining films (Figure 30)'. To make a splice, one first had to cut the strip of film slightly past the last desired frame and scrape the emulsion off. After the frame lines and sprocket holes were properly aligned and film cement was applied, another strip of film could be laid over and affixed to it.[16] This overlap resulted in a thicker join that left a mark visible in subsequent generations of positive prints.

16   Colin N. Bennett, *The Handbook of Kinematography: The History, Theory, and Practice of Motion Photography and Projection*, 2nd edn (London: Kinematograph Weekly, 1913 [1911]), 220–2.

The Materiality of Film Magic

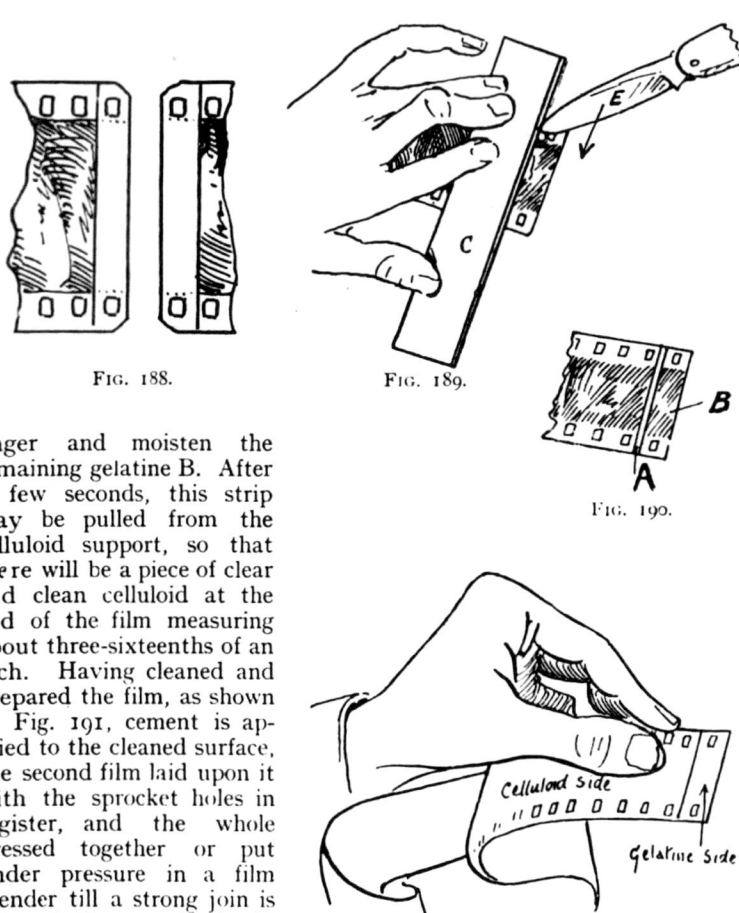

FIG. 188.   FIG. 189.

FIG. 190.

finger and moisten the remaining gelatine B. After a few seconds, this strip may be pulled from the celluloid support, so that there will be a piece of clear and clean celluloid at the end of the film measuring about three-sixteenths of an inch. Having cleaned and prepared the film, as shown in Fig. 191, cement is applied to the cleaned surface, the second film laid upon it with the sprocket holes in register, and the whole pressed together or put under pressure in a film mender till a strong join is effected, Fig. 192. It should be noticed that the film

FIG. 191.

Figure 30. Illustrations depicting the material process of manually cutting and splicing a strip of film in Colin N. Bennett, *The Handbook of Kinematography: The History, Theory, and Practice of Motion Photography and Projection*, 2nd edn (London: Kinematograph Weekly, 1913 [1911]), 221.

In a 1907 article, Méliès provided a revealing account of the origins of the 'very simple trick' which Malthête and others have termed the 'substitution splice'.

One day, when I was photographing as usual in the Place de l'Opéra, the camera I used in the early days (a primitive thing in which the film tore or frequently caught and refused to advance) jammed and produced an unexpected result. It took a minute to disengage the film and to start the camera up again. In the meantime, the passersby, horse trolleys, and other vehicles had, of course, changed positions. When I projected the strip of film, which I had stuck back together at the point of the break, I suddenly saw a Madeleine-Bastille trolley changed into a hearse and men become woman. The substitution or stop-camera trick had been discovered. Two days later, I carried out the first metamorphoses of men into women and the first sudden disappearances that, in the beginning, had such great successes.[17]

This anecdotal account has many of the hallmarks of fiction, but Méliès does specify that he 'had stuck back together' 'the strip of film', indicating that 'substitution' was a more accurate description than the more common appellation 'stop-camera trick'. In French, Méliès qualified it as the 'so-called *stop-camera trick*' ('dit *truc à arrêt*', emphasis in original).[18]

Here, Méliès offers readers a foundational anecdote that echoes another oft-repeated (and even more specious) story of cinema's earliest days which Martin Loiperdinger rightly describes as cinema's 'founding myth': the story of spectators fleeing the eponymous approach of the railroad train in the Lumières' *L'Arrivée d'un train en gare* (1896).[19] Leaving aside the repeated mention of gender in Méliès' Place de l'Opéra story, which deserves feminist analysis along lines pointed out by Lucy Fischer and Karen Beckman, the transformation from trolley into hearse suggests an allegorical reading that is congruent with the transformation from living person to skeleton in *Escamotage d'une dame*.[20]

17   Georges Méliès, 'Kinematographic Views', ed. Jacques Malthête, trans. Stuart Liebman, and Timothy Barnard, in André Gaudreault, *Film and Attraction: From Kinematography to Cinema* (Urbana: University of Illinois Press, 2011), 148.

18   Geo. Méliès, 'Les Vues cinématographiques', in Roger Aubry, ed., *Annuaire général et international de la photographie* 16 (Paris: Plon, 1907), 385, my translation, emphasis in original. See also Malthête in Gaudreault, *Film and Attraction*, 173–4n17, 174n18.

19   Martin Loiperdinger, 'Lumière's *Arrival of the Train*: Cinema's Founding Myth', trans. Bernd Elzer, *Moving Image* 4/1 (2004), 98–118.

20   See especially Lucy Fischer, 'The Lady Vanishes: Women, Magic and the Movies', *Film Quarterly* 33/1 (1979), 30–40; Karen Beckman, *Vanishing Women: Magic, Film, and Feminism* (Durham, NC: Duke University Press, 2003); and Katharina Rein, ' "The Vanishing Lady", the Railway, and Illusions of Movement', in Katharina Rein, ed.,

The Materiality of Film Magic

Analogue film projection involves a continual alternation between a projected still image and a fraction of a second of darkness on the screen when the shutter covers the lens. In *Escamotage d'une dame*, however, this alternation is thematized between life and death: d'Alcy is replaced by a skeleton, but then replaces the skeleton a moment later; the transformations are covered by a veil that makes d'Alcy and the skeleton, respectively, momentarily invisible – not unlike the shutter that flickered behind the lens of the projector showing the film.

This tension between life and death was part of the chemical composition of the celluloid on which the film was originally recorded, printed and duplicated. As a 1913 book about the nitrocellulose industry explained: 'Broadly speaking, the framework of the individual cell – the predominating constituent of plant tissues – the structural basis of all vegetable organisms – is cellulose. It is the plant itself minus its protoplasmic contents.'[21] Celluloid was the stuff of life itself. It may not have been alive, but it had not vanished. Instead, it had been transmuted into film, coated with photographic emulsion and given new onscreen life by camera and projector.

Illusion in Cultural Practice: Productive Deceptions (London, New York: Routledge, 2021), 87–103. See also Pierre Jenn, *Georges Méliès, cinéaste* (Paris: Éditions Albatros, 1984) and Réjane Hamus-Vallée, 'La sauce et le poisson: Pour une esthétique de l'effet méliésien', in André Gaudreault, and Laurent Le Forestier, with Stéphane Tralongo, eds, *Méliès, carrefour des attractions* (Rennes: Presses Universitaires de Rennes, 2013), 97–106.

21   Edward Chauncey Worden, *Nitrocellulose Industry: A Compendium of the History, Chemistry, Manufacture, Commercial Application and Analysis of Nitrates, Acetates and Xanthates of Cellulose as Applied to the Peaceful Arts*, vol. 1 (New York: D. Van Nostrand Co., 1911), 1.

Jamy Ian Swiss

Conjuring on the Small Screen

Is there, then, magic in video-land? Moving images surely capture the fluidity of motion that produces the astonished surprise resulting from a good trick. [...] Some video recordings of magic performances, however, have serious problems of credibility, [...]. How are we to assess an illusion seen on video? Did the assistant vanish from the box because the camera was turned off or because of a real trick? Magic is at its best alive, seen by our own eyes, rather than through the eyes of an illustrator or the lens of a camera.[1]

Conjuring, a part of the variety arts, was created to be experienced live and in person. No conjuring performance will ever be as effective in recorded media as when experienced in the immediacy of live performance. The illusions of conjuring can be seen as, among other things, a kind of special effects achieved within live conditions, and it is that very live-ness, rather than the size or scale of the effect, that lends conjuring its universal appeal and power. The effects of magic are essentially trivial, but the fact that the effect is performed live delivers its profound impact, including a buzzing dissonance in the viewer – 'a burr under the saddle of the mind'[2] – that is at once distinct from the experience of watching cinema.

For magicians, the camera creates other challenges beyond this fundamental dilution of the intended and desired experience. The camera cannot be misdirected, as it stares flatly with its monocular eye. Unlike the viewer's eyes in meat-space, the camera never blinks, and more important, does not shift and follow and focus where the magician subtly directs – or at least, does

---

1   Edward Tufte, and Jamy Ian Swiss, 'Explaining Magic', in Edward Tufte, ed., *Visual Explanations. Images and Quantities, Evidence and Narrative*, 7th edn (Cheshire, CT: Graphics Press, 2005 [1997]), 55–71, 63.

2   Whit Haydn, *Chicago Surprise*, 2nd edn (self-published, 2001 [2000]), 5.

not follow and focus anywhere nearly as powerfully as in live performance, where the magician relies substantially on the skills of misdirection. While non-magicians often mistakenly consider misdirection as a synonym for distraction, misdirection is actually a phenomenon of controlling the viewer's active sense of focus – a complex and varied set of tools of cognitive manipulation and control that comprises a critically important part of the conjuror's special skill set. Magician Tommy Wonder suggested that 'misdirection' should more aptly be termed 'direction' for this reason.[3] Magician William McQueen says to his audiences, 'The hand isn't quicker than the eye; it's just the eye sees a lot of things the mind never notices.' For all the work that contemporary neuroscience is undertaking in its attempts to scientifically investigate and understand conjuring, no better summary of its finding will likely be produced than McQueen's entertaining and illuminating comment.

Yet despite the challenges that recorded and broadcast media present to the success and impact of conjuring, conjuring, like most variety arts, has always attempted to adapt to new channels of opportunity, and it often has been among the first among its variety arts counterparts to do so. At the very birth of cinema, magicians like Georges Méliès[4] served as pioneers of that new medium, both by recording actual magic performances and by creating cinematic versions that relied on editing and other innovative techniques of trick photography rather than the methods of conjuring. Around 1920, Harry Houdini famously starred in a series of films that focused on his escape feats.[5]

While the history of magic is inescapably intertwined with the birth of cinema, and hence addressed in the segment which follows, this chapter will thenceforth focus on the differences in experiencing magic when presented live in a space shared by audience and performer alike, rather than in broadcast media – be it television or video-communications technology (i.e. Zoom) – in

---

3   'It would be far better for us if misdirection had not become an accepted term in magic, and direction had been adopted instead.' Tommy Wonder, and Stephen Minch, 'Getting the Mis out of Misdirection', in *The Books of Wonder*, vol. 1 (Seattle, WA: Hermetic Press, 1996), 9–34, 13.

4   On Méliès see Matthew Solomon's chapter in this volume.

5   See Matthew Solomon, *Disappearing Tricks: Silent Film, Houdini, and the New Magic of the Twentieth Century* (Urbana: University of Illinois Press, 2010).

which the performance is viewed live in real time, but performer and audience are separated by cameras, screens and distance.

The History of Magic on Television

Notwithstanding other films of magicians performing magic, from the time of Méliès forward; or film appearances by professional magicians playing themselves[6]; the birth of broadcast television would have a profound impact on magic. The 1950s and 'The Golden Age of Television' would see the creation of numerous variety shows, some particularly focused on comedy, others on music. In these early days of broadcast television, magicians would routinely appear performing their acts on general variety shows such as *The Ed Sullivan Show* and *Hollywood Palace* in the 1960s.[7]

Two magicians who pioneered magic on television in the 1950s and 1960s were Mark Wilson and Don Alan. While Alan would define a style of professional close-up magic for an entire generation or more to come, Wilson would create a style of performing 'grand illusion' – human scale illusions and apparatus that contained human bodies – still in use today: in which the illusions were typically performed to music in short form, sparing the necessity of creating lengthy scripts for spoken word 'presentations',[8] the traditional

6   For example, Dante the Magician [Harry Jansen] in the 1942 Laurel & Hardy feature film, *A-Haunting We Will Go*, dir. Alfred Werker (Twentieth Century Fox, 1942).

7   Magicians have been appearing on television since its early days: Nicola performed a manipulative routine with billiard balls on television in September of 1931 during a run at the Brooklyn Paramount theatre, eight years before RCA introduced television at the New York World's Fair; see 'Around New York with Max Holden', *The Sphinx* 30/2 (20 April 1931), 37. Additionally, Geri Larsen, of the famed Larsen family, was apparently the first woman to appear on television, starring in her own children's television show in San Francisco circa 1939; see 'Geri Larsen, *MagicPedia*, <http://geniimagazine.com/wiki/index.php?title=Geri_Larsen>, accessed 14 September 2021.

8   'Presentation' is the jargon term magicians use to describe the manner of accompaniment – such as spoken word scripting – above and beyond the basic trick or illusion, in order to clarify, enhance, and connect the effect with the audience.

manner in which the great illusionists of the Edwardian era's Golden Age of Magic had performed them. Wilson would create the first television magic series, *The Magic Land of Allakazam*, which ran from 1960 to 1965.

With the decline of variety shows, magicians needed a new pathway to television exposure. Between 1975 and 1982, Canadian magician Doug Henning, created seven prime-time hour-long television specials. Every special featured a celebrity host who would solemnly assure the audience at the start of the show – as television actor Michael Landon did at the start of the second *World of Magic* special that aired in 1976 – that 'I guarantee there are no camera tricks, no manipulation of videotape, or any other electronic devices'. This approach would serve to define for the era magic's answer to the challenges of television credibility. The fact that the first four of these specials were broadcast live served significantly to validate the legitimacy of the magic, however this aspect was eventually abandoned due to the many challenges it presented.[9]

David Copperfield would adopt, refine and build upon the Henning format, beginning with his first national television special, *The Magic of ABC*, a vehicle for introducing the network's new season, which aired in 1977. Copperfield's subsequent specials would be accompanied by an array of celebrity guests, and shows would conclude with a signature Copperfield 'megatrick' illusion, which over the years would include such ballyhooed features as vanishing a seven-ton Lear Jet, and, in 1983, vanishing the Statue of Liberty.

The issue of camera trickery persisted as an insistent subtext before and after the Statue of Liberty illusion. In the opening moments of that special, Copperfield addressed the subject head on. 'One thing's for sure: It won't be done with camera tricks. All the magic you'll see on your television screen tonight is exactly what you could see if you were right here – part of our live audience.' Yet again, later in the programme, celebrity guest actress Michele Lee repeated the assertion that 'David's magic is performed with absolutely no camera tricks. The illusion you are watching at home is exactly the way he is doing it.'

---

9   In the course of the airing of *Doug Henning's World of Magic IV*, a tiger escaped backstage and managed to consume a number of ducks and baby chicks intended for a heartening show climax. Changes were made on the fly in order to bring the live broadcast to successful completion, but this would be the last special to be broadcast live.

By 1997, Copperfield had mostly run his course as a television performer, while continuing to tour as the most successful stage magician of his time.[10] The gap he left on TV would be filled by David Blaine.

Magic on TV in the Twenty-First Century

In his first television special in 1997, *Street Magic*, Blaine would upend the Henning/Copperfield television magic format and replace it with his own. Gone was the celebrity host intoning promises of fealty to visual purity; gone was the seated studio or theatre audience; gone was the Las Vegas stage model. In the place of these conventions came the signature elements of reality television: the magician was filmed performing on the street, apparently for spontaneously gathered passers-by, and the handheld cameras were often pointed at the audience – typically a crowd of screaming young women – whose reactions provided the all-important sense of credibility of the illusions, while the illusions consisted primarily of close-up magic, rather than boxes inhabited by women for subsequent disassembly and restoration.

Blaine's new format was immediately adopted internationally. In England, Derren Brown, a close-up magician working at restaurants, was cast as a mentalist version of Blaine, and became hugely successful as a result. In Japan, the Japanese-American performer, Cyril Takayama, similarly adapted the Blaine reality-television style. Both Derren Brown and Cyril Takayama would become internationally famous via YouTube clips, presaging the contemporary scene in which magician stars of YouTube, Instagram and TikTok gather followings in the millions, while remaining virtually unknown to anyone other than their young audiences of social media followers.

Other performers embracing the Blaine format would include Marco Tempest, a Swiss magician based in the United States and specializing in magic that was often flavoured with new technology. Criss Angel would create

---

10   He remains a top Las Vegas headliner today, performing at the David Copperfield Theater at the MGM Grand Hotel and Casino.

Mindfreak, the first American magic television series since *Magic Land of Allakazam*. *Mindfreak* was broadcast on small cable networks and audiences that were fractional compared with those of Copperfield and Blaine, but the series ran from 2005 until 2010, and would lead to his being the first magician and headliner to be featured in a Cirque du Soleil show in Las Vegas, namely *Criss Angel: Believe*, which debuted in 2008.

While David Blaine continues to produce television specials periodically at intervals several years apart, the most popular magic television series currently broadcasting is *Penn & Teller: Fool Us!* Their third television series,[11] headed toward its ninth season[12], *Fool Us* is essentially a television variety show, where all the variety acts do magic of one sort or another. The variety occurs within the field, from sleight-of-hand close-up magic to grand illusions, comedy magic to mentalism. This is reframed however from the tradition of variety shows under the contemporary banner of reality TV, hung on the hook of trying to fool Penn & Teller, for which successful entrants receive a trophy, and a single performance on the stage of the Penn & Teller Theater in the Rio Hotel & Casino in Las Vegas.[13]

In his book, *Disappearing Tricks* (2010), Matthew Solomon concluded by observing:

> The recent prominence of magicians on television reminds us of the capacity of moving images to re-present and deceive while raising some of the same issues that troubled audiences who saw Houdini's confounding combinations of non-fiction and fiction film footage during the 1920s. Angel and Blaine both employ the tropes of reality television (location shooting, handheld cameras, partially visible video crews) to present their illusions and sleight-of-hand tricks on television and DVD. These familiar tropes, along with the stunned responses from 'real people' that follow, seem to vouchsafe the authenticity of their tricks.

11   Their first was a variety series, *Sin City Spectacular*, made for one season of twenty-four hour-long episodes on the FX Network in 1998/99 [for which this writer served as magic consultant, writer and associate producer]; the second, entitled *Bullshit!* was produced by Showtime for three seasons, 2003–5, a reality and documentary series debunking pseudo-scientific claims.

12   The eighth season premiered on 1 October 2021.

13   After both shows were temporarily suspended due to the Covid-19 pandemic, they both returned to their respective Las Vegas stages: Copperfield, after a brief opening and closing in November of 2020, reopened his show 21 March 2021; Penn & Teller reopened 22 April 2021 after more than year's absence.

> Fans of each of these rival magicians argue that the other is a 'fake' on Internet message boards, but these accusations suggest that media-savvy audiences for both Angel and Blaine detect deception not just in the performance of these magic tricks, but in their television representation. What has been elided? How much has actually been shot on location? Who are 'real people', and who are confederates? In this way [...], more than a century after Méliès made Jehanne d'Alcy disappears in *The Vanishing Lady*, screen magic continues to provide an arena in which people can probe the methods of media manipulation. Even more importantly, the 'realist' screen magic of contemporary television magicians – like Houdini's films before them – gives us occasion to question the place of illusion not solely in fiction, but in what is ostensibly nonfiction.[14]

Such arguments about the nature of magic as 'real' or 'fake' have failed to abate despite the increasing ubiquity of magic on the small screen. In 2018, Netflix debuted the reality series, *Magic for Humans*, featuring magician Justin Willman. Partly thanks to the presence of sometimes-unconvincing audience assistants, the series sparked a quantity of articles questioning the legitimacy of the magic depicted in the show. One such article, entitled 'When Seeing Isn't Believing', theorized about the importance of credibility in broadcast magic.

> Why is this insistence on magical authenticity such a big deal? You might think that editing and camera placement are merely additional tools to create a final effect – not better or worse than smoke, mirrors, and wires, just different. The reality is a bit more complicated: While editing magic is in some respects its own art form, the often-unspoken code around what magicians are and are not allowed to do on camera – and who gets to make the rules in the first place – can be quite strict.[15]

There would be nothing unusual about the foregoing paragraph had it appeared in a journal for magicians, written by a magician. That it was written by a professional journalist in a public outlet speaks volumes about the underlying issue of credibility in magic, and how widely it is understood, and assumed significant, by the audience.

---

14   Solomon, *Disappearing Tricks*, 128.

15   Eric Thurm, 'When Seeing Isn't Believing', *Vice.com* (11 March 2019), <https://www.vice.com/en/article/mbz54n/when-seeing-isnt-believing-v26n1>,   accessed 11 March 2021.

A New Era: Magic Performances Online, and the Nature of 'Real Magic'

Despite the challenges that recorded and broadcast media present to the success and impact of conjuring, conjuring has always attempted to adapt to new channels of opportunity. At this writing, the world finds itself in the throws of the Covid-19 pandemic, a virus that has shut down live performance around the world and has had, and continues to have, a devastating impact on performers and all those connected with the production of live performing events. In the face of these challenges, many magicians have 'pivoted' and created virtual magic shows performed over video platforms like Zoom, whether presented as corporate and private events, or publicly ticketed shows. At the same time, veteran magicians often find themselves frustrated by the severe limitations of the experience – both for their audiences and themselves alike – and many have declined the pursuit of online shows altogether for these reasons, awaiting the return of in-person performance.

In presenting virtual magic, some performers have pointed the camera at themselves performing their traditional shows – a poor and limited use of the new technology and marketplace – while others have tried to create and utilize material that is 'interactive', in which the home viewer takes an active part, perhaps even using props at a remote distance from the performer; one popular example would be the use of a deck of cards provided by the spectators themselves, utilized in the performance of a card trick at the direction of the performer.

With the advent of virtual magic shows, the issue of video magic credibility is now of concern not merely to a handful of magicians producing broadcast television, but to every magician presenting his or her own virtual show. The debate of where and how to draw the line between what constitutes valid magic that plays by the rules and magic that does not continues apace, because the rules are ultimately self-determined.

Magician Eric Mead operates from a set of fundamental principles that he has clearly articulated in online debate with other magicians.

Magic in TV, or in virtual space today, is tough. The audience is aware of the idea of camera tricks and part of the job if they are to feel amazed is to assure them that's not the case. Where do you draw the line? Real time masking is ok, but editing a pre-recorded clip is not? Why? Forced perspective or doing things out of the frame is ok, but using green screen technology and helpers with green sleeves and gloves is not? Why? For me, we leave the realm of conjuring magician when we employ any camera tricks, as it breaks the unwritten contract (in the case of my virtual show made explicit at the top) that what we are seeing is NOT the result of camera tricks. It's a complex issue. I solve it by assuring my audience there will be no camera tricks, no edits, no special software to help make the magic happen – and then I live by that promise.[16]

The experience of magic is a first-hand experience of the truly impossible. Given the commercial pressures of show business, magicians strive to communicate this experience; given the ease of turning on the television as compared to going to the theatre, audiences tune in to try to have the experience; and both sides share an agreement, of some sort, that has to do with promises made, kept, mutually agreed upon. But no such experience can compare to a genuine object in three-dimensional space suddenly disappearing inches from a participant's eyes, or transforming while tightly held in a spectator's hand. Magic is a form of timeless appeal. One may speculate that it is also a form of literally cosmic appeal, in that its business is the portrayal of the ability to violate universal physical laws of the cosmos. Thus, if an alien civilization was to arrive on earth, while it would likely be incapable of communicating directly with humans, it might be as amazed and entertained as the rest of us witnessing the illusion of sawing a person in half, or of a person floating in air. And so this timeless, and perhaps spaceless, form continues to adapt to every available medium, even one to which it is so poorly suited as television.

16   Facebook page of Eric Mead, posted on 20 February 2021, <https://www.facebook.com/meaderic/posts/10222595441666105>, accessed 11 March 2021.

Roswitha Schuller

'My Friend the Witch Doctor' (1958)

> I told the witch doctor I was in love with you
> I told the witch doctor I was in love with you
> And then the witch doctor he told me what to do

On 4 May 1958, the Californian recording artist Rostom Sipan Bagdasarian, known under his stage name David Seville, presented his single 'My Friend the Witch Doctor' live on the *The Ed Sullivan Show*, broadcast by CBS.[1]

'Witch Doctor' can be considered a magical media artefact in many ways, in terms of its narratology, its technical design, its semiotics of sound. The title of the pop song by songwriter and actor Bagdasarian was inspired by a prototypical North American romance from the 1950s of a man desiring a woman who clearly does not return his feelings. The former seeks the help of his friend the 'witch doctor', who answers in a pop-voodoo-like manner.

> He said that
> Ooo eee ooo ah ah ting tang walla walla bing bang
> Ooo eee ooo ah ah ting tang walla walla bing bang
> Ooo eee ooo ah ah ting tang walla walla bing bang
> Ooo eee ooo ah ah ting tang walla walla bing bang

The song is composed as a duet with two voices alternating, but the two voices share a joint source. Bagdasarian's real voice takes on the part of the rejected lover, while an accelerated version of his voice delivers the comic and childlike pronouncements of his shaman friend. To do this, Bagdasarian's

---

1   This is based on the Fan Wiki songfacts.com, where information about Billboard chart placements can also be found, <https://www.songfacts.com/facts/david-seville/witch-doctor>, accessed 1 September 2020.

voice was first recorded at half speed, and then played back at standard speed leading to the distortion.[2]

This technique of accelerating a track to double its original recording speed was used once again by David 'Dave' Seville in 1958 for his concept of the Chipmunks in Alvin and the Chipmunks, which would become his second number one *Billboard* hit within just a year. The virtual cartoon band Alvin and the Chipmunks in which Seville appeared with the anthropomorphic chipmunks was broadcast by CBS as *The Alvin Show* during the 1961–2 season and continued to develop in many further productions all the way into the 2000s.

Focusing on the points of the song with relevance to magic, the translation of the auditive trick of the pitched voice, which at the time of the original broadcast was not so common to the audience as the sound effect is today, in the scenic events must have seemed especially extraordinary: in agreement with the acceleration on the sound level, the TV image as a split screen begins to move and seems to alter its aspect ratio and its orientation. This happens by way of a certain hand gesture of the figure of the would-be lover, who translates on a semiotic level the magic formulas of the shaman friend not seen in the image and thus is able to control the woman he loves.

The technical device perfected here seems in retrospect like a conceptual anticipation of the effect of page orientation as came to be used as of the 2010s in various digital gadgets, known above all through the introduction of the iPhone (first generation, 2008) and the iPad (first generation, 2010). In using these devices, the gesture of tipping leads to an equivalent tipping of the visual format from the vertical to the horizontal. If page orientation on digital end devices is based technically on a table function that re-layers the digital information to the respective screen orientation (that is, a programming technique), the media magic of the witch doctor is still defined by the physical manipulation of the recorded magnetic tape. Before discussing the relevant technique below, in the following I will present the cultural-sociological framework and contextualize the mise-en-scène of 'My Friend the Witch Doctor'.

2   'How David Seville and the Witch Doctor Rescued Liberty Records', *Black Gold Brooklyn* (11 October 2017), <https://blackgoldbrooklyn.com/how-david-seville-and-the-witch-doctor-rescued-liberty-records>, accessed 1 September 2020.

You've been keeping love from me just like you were a miser
And I'll admit I wasn't very smart
So I went out and found myself a guy that's so much wiser
And he taught me the way to win your heart

My friend the witch doctor he taught me what to say
My friend the witch doctor he taught me what to do
I know that you'll be mine when I say this to you

The mise-en-scène for 'My Friend the Witch Doctor' forms a triad of figures represented in the midst of tropical décor in a split screen. The witch doctor mentioned in the title is not visible: on the left side, we see the female character who is the object of adoration, usually presented in a passive-shocked state.[3] The male character who takes on both the role of the narrative and the director of this scene is positioned on the right side of the image. The use of the split screen was certainly familiar to the audience from the medium of film; as early as 1913, the American thriller short *Suspense*[4] had already introduced a similar split-screen surface. But unlike the medium of film, which in its presentation in the cinema space or as a projection is a reproduction, the TV show is a live visual transmission, albeit one delayed a few seconds. The use of certain hand gestures of the acting characters can thus, just as in a theatrical performance, in a certain sense be interpreted as an interaction with the audience, violating the convention of the fourth wall.

The gesture is used by the performer at the same time as an element of narrative within the scene. By way of the gesture, the 'symbolic movement', as Vilém Flusser[5] calls it, he plays as it were with the narrative and explains it, at least in part, to the audience: he presents himself as shaping the plot, in this concrete case parallels to the marionette operator pulling all the strings apply. But the strings here are the apparatuses of the television studio and the audience is spatially separated from them. In the mix of colonial-romantic motifs that adorn the studio image, it is not quite clear what idealized location the

---

3 Both roles, that of the shaman and the worshipped one, are here staged as figures of alterity.

4 *Suspense*, dir. Lois Weber, and Philipps Smalley (Rex Motion Picture Company, 1913).

5 Vilém Flusser, *Gestures*, trans. Nancy Ann Roth (Minneapolis: University of Minnesota Press, 2014), 3.

Magic as a Pop-Cultural Trope

concrete space of action is intended to represent. Instead, the scene appears as post-colonial eclecticism: the female character wears a kind of safari outfit that reflects the tourist fashion of the day, including a tropical helmet with loosely draped mosquito netting. She is sitting on a directors' chair among stylized tropical plants. The figure of the gentleman, simultaneously an actor, singer and studio guest of the live show, is wearing a conventional suit with a hat. The witch doctor, as already discussed, remains hidden from the audience and exists only in the sung narrative, the lyrics of the pop song. In fact, Bagdarsarian uses the device to play both male characters in the same way that he sings both duet partners in different (technically altered) registers. With his gloved hands, he carries out gestures in place of the non-visible magically gifted shaman, triggering the events of media magic, the distortion and tipping of the left half of the split screen (see Figure 31).

Figure 31. *My Friend the Witch Doctor* chirogrammes, media collage. Markus Hanakam & Roswitha Schuller, 2020.

With lyrics and gestures, Bagdarsarian takes recourse to conventions of ethnic magic in the entertainment industry of the post-war period. The fan-wiki page tvtropes.org includes the 'ethnic magician' in its index of familiar TV and games tropes.[6] The character of the ethnically stylized magician can take on several forms, or represent a mixed form combining several, for example, the mystical and magically gifted native American or also the magician with African, Caribbean, or Haitian roots (the Fan Wiki describes this trope with the term 'Hollywood voodoo').[7] Bagdasarian also refers to voodoo by way of the lyrics, expressed in the repetitive refrain with the voice of the witch doctor.

> Ooo eee ooo ah ah ting tang walla walla bing bang
> Ooo eee ooo ah ah ting tang walla walla bing bang
> Ooo eee ooo ah ah ting tang walla walla bing bang
> Ooo eee ooo ah ah ting tang walla walla bing bang

This link also inspires the image for the cover of the single released by the label Liberty Records (1955–95), which shows the mask-wearing shaman friend as a puppeteer who in both hands holds a wooden cross with strings to control various puppets. The puppets, obviously members of Dave Seville's band, are represented in folkloristic stereotypes that are typical for the post-war pop music culture of the United States: the Mexican with the cymbals, the Chinese figure at the trumpet, another safari tourist playing trombone, and a big band musician wearing a classical dinner jacket on drums.

Also typical of the period is the beginning Disneyfication[8] of the entertainment media which affects both the visual-creative level of popular graphic design as well as the linguistic idiom. 'My Friend the Witch Doctor' can be seen as referring both affirmatively and ironically to the Disneyland episode

---

6   'Ethnic Magician', *TV Tropes*, <https://tvtropes.org/pmwiki/pmwiki.php/Main/EthnicMagician>, accessed 1 September 2020.

7   Kameelah L. Martin pursues a decolonial, feminist revision of the voodoo trope in the American cinema, specifically looking at the appropriation of the subject by Disney Studios. See *Envisioning Black Feminist Voodoo Aesthetics: African Spirituality in American Cinema* (Lanham, MD: Lexington Books, 2016).

8   See Janet Wasko, *Understanding Disney: The Manufacture of Fantasy* (Cambridge: Polity Press, 2001).

'My Friend the Atom'[9] from the year 1957 (the temporal proximity of their respective broadcast dates is suggestive here). This was part of an advertising campaign to promote the peaceful use of atomic energy and the attempt in the form of edutainment to communicate the nature of invisible atomic energy, like the magic of the witch doctor, in a synthesis of real and animated film.

The visual surface that the CBS production team and Bagdarsarian create for the viewers also relies on a visual notion of synthesis. Since *The Ed Sullivan Show* was broadcast live, for the viewer at the TV set at home every action had to appear live, the same is true of the studio appearance of David Seville, which is first introduced by Sullivan. At the beginning of his show act, with the first lines of lyrics, Bagdasarian can still be seen in full screen. The scene then opens to a split screen with the start of the witch doctor's strophe ('Ooo eee ooo ah ah ...') now showing Bagdasarian on the right side and on the left the female actor. Here, Bagdasarian begins undertaking magic gestures, with which he seems to manipulate the left video track. For the spectators, this generates an illusion of a magical gesture that has an influence on live things happening in the image.

A precise examination of the series of images, that is, the individual frames, shows that this scene actually took a different course.[10] The transition from Sullivan's introduction to Bagdarsarian's performance is not carried out by a pan the studio camera, but a five second fade in/out leads from the image of the moderator to the following scene. This shows that the live appearance is actually a video and that the entire video material of the performance, including the scenes in the split screen, was prepared ahead of time. As media scholar Yvonne Spielmann has established for the status of the visual in the video, this effect has impacts in terms of perception typology and cultural semiotics,[11]

---

9   *Disneyland* episode 14, Season 3, original air date 23 January 1957, dir. Hamilton Luske (Walt Disney Pictures, 1954–8).

10   A frame-by-frame analysis of the video is based on a copy of the material that can be seen on YouTube: <https://www.youtube.com/watch?v=9iA_TZ15ruA>, accessed 1 September 2020. The following technical information is based on an interview with Michael Huber, head designer at Österreichischer Rundfunk ORF, a semiotician who teaches at Vienna's Universität für Angewandte Kunst. The interview was held on 9 July 2020.

11   See Yvonne Spielmann, 'Zum Status des Bildlichen im Video', in Andreas Kirchner, Karl Prümm, and Martin Richling, eds, *Abschied vom Zelluloid? Beiträge zur Geschichte und Poetik des Videobildes* (Marburg: Schüren, 2008), 26.

that is, a becoming unstable of the visual experience of the television audience, in this case desired as an illusion that looks like magic.

What manipulations are now undertaken with the video recordings and in what hermeneutic context do the gestures of the right side of the image relate to the material manipulation on the left side? To return to Flusser's phenomenology of the gesture, the causal link between gesture and affect can be called into doubt:

> One way of defining 'gesture' is as a movement of the body or of a tool attached with the body, for which there is no satisfactory causal explanation. To understand a gesture defined in this way, its 'meaning' must be discovered.[12]

Bagdasarian carries out expansive gestures with his two hands, thus showing empty space between his two palms facing one another which he then turns 180 degrees, the left side of the image rotates analogously 180 degrees, the image of the female actor is turned on its head and she is given a scare. Bagdasarian also uses gestures of distortion, when he brings the two palms facing one another closer together, the image of the left is condensed. With his right hand, he undertakes a gesture that looks as if he were drawing an object towards himself; the image on the left is enlarged, making a close-up of the face of the woman visible. The foundation for the distorted views on the left split screen are all video images of the female actor, who increasingly displays a bothered and annoyed expression in the face of her treatment (or enchantment) by the witch doctor.

The gestures of the male character in the performance derive their shape from the imitation of the human interaction with the technical processing devices, like the controller and the mixing console, and seem strangely familiar when viewed today. It is familiar, because the gestures of the users of contemporary devices and gadgets like smartphones or tablets are very similar. But the achievement of synthesis when the hand movement influences the visual and the sound layers equally remains idiosyncratic for the use of gestures in 'My Friend the Witch Doctor'. The meaning of the gesture as a means of scenic and narrative composition is inherent to the history of the performative arts. The gestural only undergoes a change in relation to technological devices, as

12   Flusser, *Gestures*, 3.

is made clear by Bagdasarian's performance. The gestural obtains a new layer of meaning as a device of interface control, gesture recognition is today an area of computer sciences and deals with the bridging capacity of sequences of gestures, capturing that capacity in an algorithm, all the way to image or visual controls. This results in the causality of gestural action that Flusser still called unsatisfactory in his theory of gestures (1991). At around the same time, a research group at Massachusetts Institute of Technology began work on researching tangible image control in 1990[13] and in the process studied pop-cultural artefacts and their visual creations.[14] This new realm of research can look back at a historical tradition. There had certainly been attempts at representing the bridging capacity of certain (scenic) gestures, as for example, so-called *chirogrammes*, graphic studies of hand gestures, that could be gained from the hand and finger poses of commedia dell'arte figures.[15] In the late 1990s, the translation of human gestures to digital forms of application increasingly became a decisive economic factor for technology companies, as Apple made multi-touch gestures its market specific asset. But the wish to maintain the magic for the viewer, as in the case of Bagdasarian, or for the user, as in the case of contemporary consumer devices, remains.

> Come on, oo eee ooo ah ah ting tang walla walla bing bang
> Ooo eee ooo ah ah ting tang walla walla bing bang

Acknowledgement
I would like to thank Michael Huber for generously sharing his expertise with me, and Brian Currid for the translation work.

13   MIT Media Lab: Tangible Media Group, led by Professor Hiroshi Ishii, <https://tangible.media.mit.edu>, accessed 1 September 2020.

14   For example, in an analysis of the film *Minority Report* (2002) by Jennifer 8. Lee: 'You, Too, Can Soon Be Like Tom Cruise in *Minority Report*', *The New York Times* (15 February 2010), <https://bits.blogs.nytimes.com/2010/02/15/you-too-can-soon-be-like-tom-cruise-in-minority-report>, accessed 1 September 2020.

15   See, for example, the chirogrammes by the English natural philosopher John Buwler (1606–56) or the Italian ethnographer Andrea de Jorio (1769–1851).

Michael Wedel

Harry Potter and the Deathly Hallows, Pt. I (2010)

A high percentage of conglomerated Hollywood's most successful films of the past decades, which have shaped our sense of the modern movie block-buster, fall into the umbrella category of 'fantasy' – whether in its 'lower' echelons of science-fiction and horror or as proper examples of 'high fantasy'. Hollywood's recent affinity to fantasy is so close, the presence of the latter's generic elements so pervasive, that attempts at defining its cultural traditions sometimes consider the blockbuster itself as belonging to a pedigree that reaches back to myth and fairy tale.[1]

Apart from thematic and iconographic references, another level of structural affinity between high-concept blockbuster movies and the fantasy genre can be traced along certain shifts in cinematic style and narration. In the age of 'convergence culture', contemporary multi-media enterprises such as the *Harry Potter* franchise are built around big-budget films or film series to exploit their 'brand content' (often derived from bestselling novels) across different media platforms.[2] In this context, filmmaking has increasingly become 'the art of world building, as artists create compelling environments that cannot be fully explored or exhausted within a single

1   Thomas Elsaesser, 'The Blockbuster: Everything Connects, but Not Everything Goes', in John Lewis, ed., *The End of Cinema as We Know It: American Films in the Nineties* (New York: New York University Press), 16.

2   See Maria Dicieanu, 'Harry Potter, Henry Jenkins, and the Visionary J.K. Rowling', in John Alberti and P. Andrew Miller, eds, *Transforming Harry: The Adaptation of Harry Potter in the Transmedia Age* (Detroit, MI: Wayne State University Press, 2018), 93–112.

work or even a single medium'.[3] As Henry Jenkins observes, art direction has assumed a more central role in the conception of franchises, and it is primarily the detailed richness and organizational logic upon which a fictional or alternative world is designed that lends consistency and coherence to a blockbuster franchise and assures both public interest and durable consumer or even fan loyalty.[4]

One way of further investigating his notion of the 'art of world-making' leads me to relate his concept to the theory of fantasy as a literary and cinematic genre. Another points towards a curious omission in Jenkins's model, namely the role of sound design in the era of digital surround and its impact on significant shifts in the audiovisual style of contemporary blockbuster films. Both lines of argumentation will eventually converge in the concept of 'resonance' as the synesthetic correlative to a sense of media magic and spectatorial wonder generated by the fantasy blockbuster film. With the help of this concept, I want to frame a phenomenon that transforms (and transcends) the 'technical wizardry'[5] or 'manual-mechanical trickery'[6] and the 'practical/industrial magic'[7] of special, visual and sound effects into the realm of perceptual sensation. The example with which I would like to suggest the analytical potential of the proposed theoretical shift is *Harry Potter and the Deathly Hallows, Part I* (dir. David Yates, Warner Bros., 2010). Compared to the other films of the franchise, it deploys the most complex and densely textured audiovisual design.

3   Henry Jenkins, *Convergence Culture: When Old and New Media Collide* (New York, London: New York University Press, 2006), 114.

4   Jenkins, *Convergence Culture*, 115.

5   Michele Pierson, *Special Effects: Still in Search of Wonder* (New York: Columbia University Press, 2002), 12.

6   Colin Williamson, *Hidden in Plain Sight: An Archaeology of Magic and the Cinema* (New Brunswick, NJ, London: Rutgers University Press, 2015), 176.

7   Jacqueline Furby, and Claire Hines, *Fantasy* (London, New York: Routledge, 2012), 81; Erik Barnouw, *The Magician and the Cinema* (New York, Oxford: Oxford University Press, 1981), 112. On the relation between cinema technology and magic, see Rachel O. Moore, *Savage Theory: Cinema as Modern Magic* (Durham, London: Duke University Press, 2000), 43–53.

Fantasy and the Poetics of the 'Ontological Rupture'

Jenkins's 'art of world-making' closely corresponds to what has been a staple in thinking about fantasy in literature and film ever since J. R. R. Tolkien's seminal distinction between the 'first' and 'secondary world'. To begin with, there are a number of motifs serving as readily identifiable markers of difference between the 'real' and the 'fantasy' world, including wizards, crystal balls, flying brooms, fairies, magic talismans and talking animals. Among these, Katherine Fowkes has identified three which represent the genre's 'metaphorical center': the phenomenon of magic; acts of metamorphosis and physical transformation; and the ability to fly.[8] Following up on Tolkien's distinction, Fowkes bases her understanding of the fantasy film genre on a 'fundamental break with our sense of reality,'[9] to which all the aforementioned fantastic elements contribute and which constitutes the genre's defining formal characteristic. While this 'ontological rupture' must be 'inherent in the premise of the movie or otherwise integral to the story,'[10] fantasy and mimetic realism are not mutually exclusive categories: 'The use of magic may subvert the normal circuits of cause and effect, but this in no way implies a lack of logic or coherence [...]. Instead, as a trope of fantasy, magic *stands in* for causality.'[11]

Fantasy can hence be described as a genre that produces a type of pleasure at odds with social norms and creates multiple frictions within the regime of realist representation. It is as much 'imaginative and playful in contrast to a world of rationality, work, and conformity'[12] as it is in deviating from aesthetic standards and traditional conventions of cinematic style and image-sound relations. Writing about fantasy literature, Rosemary Jackson has argued that 'the basic trope of fantasy is the *oxymoron*',[13] a semantic and figural self-contradiction which Fowkes, too, sees at the heart of the ontological rupture. As

8   Katherine Fowkes, *The Fantasy Film* (Malden, MA: Wiley-Blackwell, 2010), 5, 50.

9   Ibid., 2.

10   Ibid., 5–6.

11   Ibid., 4.

12   Ibid., 7.

13   Rosemary Jackson, *Fantasy: The Literature of Subversion* (London, New York: Routledge, 2003), 21.

Jackson puts it with reference to Wittgenstein's rabbit/duck paradox, 'fantasy excels at encouraging multiple and even contradictory readings', its 'insistence on "imaginative re-visioning" may be one of the things that binds the genre together, on both a thematic and a viewing level'.[14] Two key aspects can thus be identified: the genre hinges upon a sense of 'ontological rupture' which the consumer is made aware of on one level or another; and it strongly plays on moments of perceptual illusion and ambivalence, on paradoxical constructions and oxymoronic tropes of self-contradiction.

Diegetic Immersion: Film Style and Cinema Aesthetics in the Digital Sound Age

In his discussion of the areas of film production which he sees primarily responsible for the 'art of world-making', Jenkins refers to art direction and production design, the design of costumes and props, the use of special effects technology and computer generated imagery (CGI). The role of sound, or, more precisely, music, is only mentioned in passing. The vital part a blockbuster's soundscapes take in adding shape and dimension, lending presence and credibility to the fictional or fantastic world of a franchise seems dramatically undervalued. This is all the more conspicuous considering the effects of digital surround sound aesthetics, whose truly audiovisual design should be part of any attempt to conceptualize the levels on which this 'art of world-making' operates and how new sound technologies reconfigure the position of the cinema audience vis-à-vis this world.

Digital surround sound systems first appeared in the early 1990s and, compared to Dolby stereo, offered filmmakers a better dynamic range, more channels and a greater flexibility for the placement and transitory panning of sounds within and across a multi-channel environment.[15] Digital surround

---

14   Fowkes, *The Fantasy Film*, 9–10.
15   Mark Kerins, *Beyond Dolby (Stereo): Cinema in the Digital Sound Age* (Bloomington, Indianapolis: Indiana University Press, 2011), 53, 65, 74–5.

sound has radically redefined stereo sound's acoustic 'superfield'[16] in several respects and converted it into what has been called the 'ultrafield'. According to Mark Kerins, the main differences between the 'superfield' and the 'ultrafield' are centred on the ways both 'fields' define the respective relationships between image and sound and between the diegetic world and the audience in the theatre. As regards the sound/image relationship, in the ultrafield the sound retains its function as a frame of reference, anchoring the story and gluing together the narrative. But in place of a constant sonic space it now establishes 'a shifting soundscape that varies with what is seen onscreen'[17] and thereby serves to relate the spatial coordinates for each scene more intricately to the spectator. With respect to the relationship between the diegetic world and its audience, the ultrafield implies a radical change in that instead of placing the audience at a distance from the onscreen world, it seeks to situate the spectator in the middle of the action whenever surround sound is used to its full potential to provide the necessary perceptual 'access points'.

The various traits of digital surround aesthetics, both acoustic (low frequency effects, a larger dynamic range, five discrete full-range channels) and visual (limited use of wide or establishing shots, the fragmentation of space, heavy use of close shots, shooting from within the space of the action, quick cutting, a disregard for classical continuity editing), find their unifying principle in that 'they all work *to immerse the audience in the diegetic world of the film*'.[18] Whereas emotional or narrative involvement into the action of a movie has always been a central concern of cinematic style, the crucial point is that the sense of immersion evoked by the ultrafield becomes a spatial and perceptual given, with the audience now being 'literally placed *in the middle* of the diegetic environment and action'.[19] The space thus created by the carefully manipulated reverberation and resonance of the digital surround ultrafield is an *artificial* space, conceived 'to replace the acoustics of the venue with those

16 Michel Chion, *Audio-Vision: Sound on Screen* (New York: Columbia University Press, 1994), 150–2.
17 Kerins, *Beyond Dolby (Stereo)*, 92–3.
18 Ibid., 130.
19 Ibid., 130–1.

of its own design'.[20] A three-dimensional extension of the diegetic space itself, it is part of the process that Jenkins calls 'the art of world-making'.

If, as Kerins claims, digital surround sound represents a mode of audiovisual aesthetics that supersedes any fixed hierarchy between sound and image, constantly re-negotiating the shape both take for each scene on the basis of technical synchronization and simultaneous audiovisual perception, then it seems particularly suited to the creation of synesthetic effects of resonance: to the creation of moments when sounds take the form of visual impressions, and images collapse into the sheer force and movement of sound. As I would argue, it is precisely when 'the acoustic and the optical mutually affect each other',[21] when we think we hear with our eyes and see with our ears, as visual sounds and sonorous images enter into a reciprocal process of metamorphosis and transformation, exchanging their distinct ontological regimes and sensuous registers, that the fantasy world into which we are drawn reveals itself as being 'different' from within. This sense of 'ontological rupture', marked as it is by a perceptual paradox of synesthetic illusion, takes the shape of an 'audiovisual oxymoron' and may count as a form of 'media magic'. As such it perpetuates a long tradition of magical thinking that set out to enchant the world by plunging into it, seeking its meaning not behind the phenomena of the external world but on the surface of its immediate presence.[22] In a similar vein, the belief in the possibility of pure poetic expression corresponding with magical forms of awareness and apprehension has been based on a radical transgression (or extreme subversion) of an aesthetic order which rigidly aligned the multitude of artistic means with the respective organs of human sense perception. Under the twin-banner of 'rhythm' (synchronization) and 'resonance' (synesthesia) Romanticism rebelled against this order and mapped out a heterogeneous field on which a *sensorium commune* could transverse the static categories of carefully divided faculties of expression and experience.[23]

---

20   Ibid., 125.

21   Jean-Luc Nancy, *Listening* (New York: Fordham University Press, 2007), 82.

22   Karl-Heinz Göttert, *Magie* (Munich: Fink, 2001), 10–12.

23   Veit Erlmann, *Reason and Resonance: A History of Modern Aurality* (New York: Zone Books, 2010), 14–23, 165–83, 185–202, 271–306.

Magic Resonances: 'Disapparition' and the Audiovisual Oxymoron

As Veit Erlmann has argued, the 'acoustic and physiological phenomenon of resonance' has 'played a constitutive role in modern discourses of aurality and rationality'.[24] It is 'inextricably woven into the warp and woof' of a technology-driven modernity but remains beset by the historical imagination of 'a prescientific magic'.[25] With concrete reference to the use of digital surround in the films of the *Harry Potter* franchise, Earlman's conflictual constellation finds its not so distant echo in sound designer Glenn Morgan's description of the nexus between cutting-edge filmmaking technologies and a neo-Gothic retro-aesthetics of sensorial immersion:

> Surrounds are really beneficial for when they support you in the environment in terms of filling it out, turning it into three dimensions. [...] *Harry Potter* is a good example. When you are in the dungeons or the caves, the castles, you really want to feel like *you are submersed* inside the basement or as far down as you can go. And so all of a sudden, now, the surrounds become part of the environment because you hear creaks, and wood, and things that really engulf you and give you claustrophobia.[26]

In many of its individual motifs as well as in its overall design of a world full of covert correspondences and bewildering impressions, the discourse of magic in the *Harry Potter* films draws heavily on elements of the Romantic imagination. But just as no film makes use of the full potential of digital surround aesthetics throughout, not all kinds of magic are presented in the form of an 'audiovisual oxymoron'. The audiovisual design of several scenes in *Harry Potter and the Deathly Hallows, Part 1*, evokes a sense of fluidity in that the images we see – and, by implication, the diegetic world itself – seem malleable. Most strongly perhaps in the top shots with the Dementors hovering over the courtroom in the Ministry of Magic, or when the camera slowly moves around the protective 'wall' Hermione has erected around

24   Ibid., 11.
25   Ibid., 15.
26   Quoted in Kerins, *Beyond Dolby (Stereo)*, 141.

their secret camp in the woods, both shots accompanied by bubbling and gurgling sounds that prepare us for the underwater scene when Ron finally manages to secure the sword of Gryffindor. At other moments in the film, 'visual sound' may take the shape of floating particles and waves or mimic patterns of the sound figures on one of Chladni's glass plates, when 'Wanted'-posters swirl around in the hall of the Ministry of Magic (Figure 32) or when snow is silently falling during Hermione's and Harry's visit to the cemetery of Godric's Hollow.

Figure 32. Corban Yaxley (Peter Mullan) in a whirlwind of 'Wanted'-posters in *Harry Potter and the Deathy Hallows, Pt. 1*, dir. David Yates (Warner Bros., 2010).

Variations in the sound design also depend on the different kinds of magic and supernatural abilities depicted: flying, for example, is repeatedly paired with soft sound effects that harmoniously blend into the symphonic musical score, whereas fantastic creatures such as Hedwig or the house-elves are mainly characterized by the – in both these cases: high – pitch of their voices. Other forms of magical presence, such as the sudden appearance of Ron's patronus, are – as they were in previous films in the series – defined by silent luminosity, just as acts of bodily transformation caused by the drinking of polyjuice potion are codified predominantly, if not exclusively on the level of a smooth and soundless visual change, highlighting the efficiency and pain-lessness of the process.

Figure 33. 'Disapparition shot' from *Harry Potter and the Deathy Hallows, Pt. 1*, dir. David Yates (Warner Bros., 2010).

In *Harry Potter and the Deathly Hallows, Part 1*, the full transformative or 'synesthetic' potential of simultaneous audiovisuality is unleashed only in those scenes where characters magically 'disapparate' from one place to another (Figures 33 and 34). These are also the scenes where most is made of the possibilities offered by digital surround sound to place and pan sounds across the whole 5.1-field of speakers. 'Disapparition', the neologism and 'one-word oxymoron' J. K. Rowling has found for this practice of magical teleportation, qualifies as a good example for a Wittgensteinian language-game. In the film, the 'disapparition shots' carry the same weight that Scott Bukatman has put on 'the archetypal kaleidoscopic (special) effects sequence', to which they – not incidentally – bear striking resemblance. Similar to the special effects sequences discussed by Bukatman, the 'disapparition sequences' in *Harry Potter* belong to a performative and 'presentational' rather than 'representational mode' and they equally work to 'redirect the spectator to the visual (and auditory and even kinesthetic) conditions of cinema and thus bring the principles of perception to the foreground of consciousness'; they are 'not so much journeys *to* other places or societies as flights *from* the strictures of instrumental reason'.[27] And if special effects sequences convey 'a hyperbole of the visible',[28]

27   Scott Bukatman, *Matters of Gravity: Special Effects and Supermen in the 20th Century* (Durham, NC, London: Duke University Press, 2003), 90–1, 117.

28   Ibid., 81.

the 'disapparition sequences' in the *Harry Potter* films suggest even more: the synesthetic, oxymoronic hyperbole of the audiovisual in the digital surround-sound 'art of world-making'. Or, put differently and in allusion to what Kurt Kroeber once identified as the literary genre's constitutive discursive trope and experiential mode: as figurations of the 'impossible possibility'[29] of cinematic fantasy, they capture the sensation of its magic.

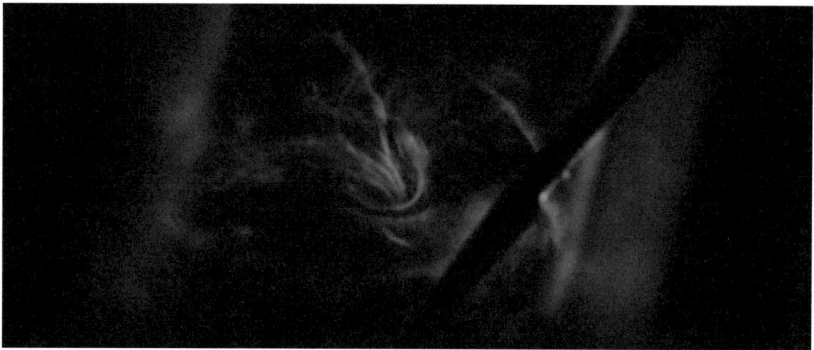

Figure 34. 'Disapparition shot' from *Harry Potter and the Deathy Hallows, Pt. 1*, dir. David Yates (Warner Bros., 2010).

As is often the case, there is one magic object which self-reflexively encapsulates this poetics of cinematic fantasy: the 'deluminator' left to Ron Weasley by Albus Dumbledore. In its oxymoronic denomination closely resembling its linguistic relative of 'disapparition', it is a device which, by command, absorbs and releases back into the surroundings all ambient light and sound. How exactly this process is meant to work remains as much in the dark as does the answer to the question what kind of mutual aggregate state the optical and the acoustical would have to enter for this remarkable modulation. But then again, it might not pertain to physicochemical laws at all, but rather stem from a mental and perceptual state sparked by the audiovisual magic of cinema.

29   Kurt Kroeber, *Romantic Fantasy and Science Fiction* (New Haven, CT, London: Yale University Press, 1988), 1.

Acknowledgement
In memory of Eileen Rositzka (1988–2021), to whom I am grateful for proof-reading this chapter.

Sarah Faber

The *Dragon Age* Series (2009–2014)

Introduction

Magic in games, and particularly digital games, represents an unusual facet of the discourse around magical practices and the supernatural. In most contexts, magic is loosely associated with a primal force, at least partly beyond human understanding and prone to being exerted in unforeseen and uncontrolled ways when the practitioner is in emotional distress. The very nature of games as a medium subverts these traits, however: being rule-regulated and typically aiming to provide equal chances to all players, games tend to express magic in predictable and quantifiable terms. Each spell has a clearly described effect, casting time and cost in terms of the caster's resources, and is performed reliably at the click of a button.

Bioware's popular *Dragon Age* series is a good example of this phenomenon: magic on the narrative level and the game mechanical level are widely at odds. The series' overarching plot addresses the dangers of magic and the limits of magic users' control quite extensively, but it is undercut by the necessarily reliable rules defining magic as a combat mechanism.

This chapter outlines the relationship between these different kinds of magic in the *Dragon Age* videogame series. A key theme in the narrative is the fragile balance between public safety and personal freedom, which, however, does not – and indeed, cannot – fully translate into the rules of the games, as the analysis will show. To explore this conflict further, I will touch on the narrative arcs of several companion characters, which negotiate questions of selfhood through the lens of demonic/spirit possession and call the storyworld's dominant narrative about magic into question, establishing a more nuanced middle ground.

Magic in *Dragon Age*'s Narrative

Thedas, the fictional world providing the setting for the series, paints a familiar picture of magic on a narrative level. We see magic as a volatile force and contested discipline, caught between art and science, religion and politics. Mages are portrayed as possessing an intuitive grasp of magic and an inherent connection to the Fade – the realm of spirits, demons and magic – but that connection needs to be tempered with logical reasoning and disciplined study, as well as closely monitored, as evidenced by the institution of the Circles. Each Circle of Magi is a school, home and prison to its mages, who spend their entire lives in the Circle Tower, under constant supervision from the Templars. The Templars form the military arm of the Chantry, one of Thedas's dominant religious institutions, that is, the familiar paradigm of religion as controlling and opposing magic and demons is reiterated. Free mages are labelled 'apostates' and considered so heavily at risk of demonic possession or using 'blood magic' as a last resort – a form of spellcasting that derives power from hurting living beings – that they pose a serious threat to society at large and must be (re)captured or killed.

Overall, the narrative conceptualization of magic as dangerous and related to temptation is made abundantly clear. However, the companions the player meets in the course of the series bring up some questions as to the nuances of this concept, making the player wonder whether the Chantry's narrative is the whole truth. One of these characters is Wynne from *Dragon Age: Origins*. Possessed mages – who turn into demonic hosts simply referred to as 'abominations' – regularly appear as enemies throughout the games, but Wynne turns out to have been saved from certain death by a friendly spirit and is now kept alive by that entity, which has 'bonded' to her.[1] Wynne is a kind, wise older lady and her being host to a spirit at no point becomes a danger to anyone; on the contrary, Wynne even gains a helpful spell called 'Vessel of the Spirit' after she reveals her condition. She reflects on the nature of her connection

---

1   BioWare, *Dragon Age: Origins* (Electronic Arts, 2009), Wynne's camp dialogue. (As games do not have page numbers, all videogame references in this chapter cite the quest or situation containing the relevant information/quotation.)

to the spirit and states that she has 'begun to wonder ... if a mage could be so possessed and still retain their sanity. Their humanity',[2] thus questioning the Chantry's dogma that all possessed mages are abominations. On the other hand, she is a firm believer in the institution of the Circles and their rules, and is convinced that '[e]very mage is vulnerable [to demons], no matter how accomplished or powerful'.[3] Wynne herself is thus an encapsulation of the storyworld's conflicting views on magic, and the many finer nuances of a phenomenon which that world's institutions unhelpfully subsume under the umbrella of 'possession'.

Anders is a more difficult case. Initially, in *Dragon Age: Origins – Awakening*, he just wants to escape the Circle, but his conversations with a spirit of Justice make him consider not only his personal freedom, but the larger, structural issue of the oppression of mages. In *Dragon Age II*, it turns out that Anders has now (willingly) become possessed by Justice. The spirit needed a host to survive outside the Fade, and Anders agreed to help him and work towards their common goal – freedom for all mages. Anders explains: 'He's part of me. [...] I feel his thoughts as my own. Not even the greatest scholar could tell you where I end and he begins.'[4] To further complicate the situation, Anders' anger about the mages' suffering has warped the spirit: 'He is no longer my friend Justice. He is a force of vengeance.'[5] Justice/Vengeance is frequently seen taking control of Anders, signified by a deep, distorted voice and glowing eyes, showing much clearer parallels to possession than Wynne. He describes it as 'a madness, a frenzy. I only find out after what I might have done.'[6] Anders' efforts to free the Circle mages escalate when he forces a violent confrontation between Templars and mages and destroys the local Chantry building, killing everyone inside.[7] Thus, Anders' story confirms that pacts with denizens of the Fade are dangerous and can be a slippery slope, but the question how heavily his decisions are influenced by Justice/Vengeance

---

2   Ibid.
3   Ibid.
4   BioWare, *Dragon Age II* (Electronic Arts, 2011), 'Tranquility'.
5   Ibid.
6   Ibid.
7   Ibid., 'The Last Straw'.

remains open, same as the question whether using violence in order to end a greater evil is justified.

Dorian, an ally in *Dragon Age: Inquisition*, is a mage from Tevinter, where mages are not only free, but run the country as a 'magocracy'. He raises the question whether allowing mages to self-regulate would not be a better alternative, and how much regulation is needed to prevent them from using blood magic and riding roughshod over the rest of the population – that, not possession, is the main concern in his eyes. Several other companions (especially Morrigan, Merrill, Cole, Vivienne and Solas) add further nuances to the games' reflections on magic, but analysing all of them would unfortunately go too far at this point.

Overall, the narrative of the *Dragon Age* games paints magic as a complex issue, fraught with moral dilemmas and ambiguities. Secular law and religious dogma are often insufficient to fully and fairly grasp the individual situations of the mages the player encounters.

Magic as a Game Mechanism

This narrative complexity is mirrored in some, but far from all aspects of magic as a game mechanism in the series. Certainly, there are many different spells and magic specializations available for the player to choose from, as well as symbiotic effects – such as frozen targets becoming brittle and thus more vulnerable to physical damage – which give magic a certain complexity from a strategic and tactical point of view. However, the issues which the narrative focuses so heavily on – the risk of possession, the potential danger represented by free mages and the evils of blood magic – are all but ignored on a mechanical level.

In *Dragon Age: Origins*, the player can choose the Spirit Healer specialization for all playable mages (including the main character). Given that the bond with a spirit is established as a life-changing event for Wynne, it seems strange and jarring that the same path can be selected for other characters and nothing changes except their available spells. There is no cut scene, no journey into the Fade to find a suitable spirit – the player simply selects the specialization on the skill menu and that is it. There are no long-term narrative consequences. This begins to make some sense when you consider that Spirit Healers are the only characters with access to healing abilities in the entire game. Especially if the player character is also a mage, having Wynne in the party at all times can be impractical, so choosing the Spirit Healer profession for the main character may become a strategic necessity, even though the player may chafe against the narrative implications. This discomfort is eased somewhat by the game treating the two as separate issues and behaving as if the player's strategic choices have little to do with the narrative about magic.

Similarly, players who choose the Blood Mage specialization face no greater consequences than an extra line of dialogue here and there. A scene in which Wynne confronts the player about being a blood mage[8] was removed from the final release. It still exists in the game's files, but this dialogue now only occurs if the player chooses to activate it via a fan-made patch.[9] This scene, in which a blood mage protagonist might have ended up having to kill crucial allies, was apparently considered a disproportionate effect for what at first seems like a mainly mechanical choice. At this point, it becomes evident that the disconnect between magic on a narrative and mechanical level is so deep and prevalent that it has reverberations and ends up re-entrenching itself.

The Blood Mage and Spirit Healer specializations are still present and similarly necessary on a strategic level, but insignificant on a narrative level in *Dragon Age II*. Only in *Inquisition*, the third instalment of the series, is the specialization system finally overhauled completely; several of the new specializations are individual to specific characters and thus tie in much more neatly with their respective narrative arcs, and the main character can no longer select specializations that do not make any narrative sense for them.

However, none of the games address the narratively very important risk of possession on a mechanical level – indeed, they cannot realistically do that without making the game pointlessly annoying. If there were, say, a small percentile of a chance of possession with every spell a mage casts, that would introduce a random event that basically derails the whole gaming experience.

---

8   BioWare, *Dragon Age: Origins*, 'Broken Circle'.

9   Cf. Avaraen, 'Dialogue Tweaks', Nexus Mods (2009), <https://www.nexusmods.com/dragonage/mods/336>, accessed 9 September 2020.

Such random 'sudden death' mechanisms are difficult to reconcile with the basic workings of goals in games: while 'factors outside our control may conspire against our reaching [a] goal' in real life, 'games appeal [...] by creating systems in which these goals are explicitly stated and specifically *designed to be attainable*'.[10] The game abruptly ending in the main character's death due to a random and inevitable consequence of that character doing what they are meant to do in the game – that is, for mages, casting spells – goes entirely against the basic principle of attainable goals, because it makes the very basic goal of 'don't lose' randomly unattainable due to no fault of the player's. The only type of game for which this principle does not apply is purely luck-based gambling or 'alea',[11] which role-playing games like the *Dragon Age* series clearly are not. Thus, the narrative of magic as volatile and risky is almost inevitably at odds with magic as a game mechanism.

Another problem with mirroring the narratively omnipresent risk of demonic possession in the game's rules is that possession is an all-or-nothing scenario in *Dragon Age*: the narrative posits a mage's becoming an abomination as a point of no return. Although some more forward-thinking characters wonder if there might be a cure,[12] such a cure is not exactly known or easily attainable. Thus, a playable character becoming randomly possessed would prompt one of three possible scenarios, none of which is conducive to a rewarding gaming experience: (1) possession might effectively result in 'game over', forcing the player to reload; (2) possession might cause the other characters to embark on an epic quest to find a cure, but the player might have to do that without actually controlling their primary player character, and it might happen at a time when it ties in very poorly with the overarching plot of the game; or (3) a cure would become part of a routinely accessible game mechanism, thus

---

10   Gordon Calleja, *In-Game: From Immersion to Incorporation* (Cambridge, MA, London: MIT Press, 2011), 150, emphasis added. On the same principle, cf. also: Tracy Fullerton, *Game Design Workshop: A Playcentric Approach to Creating Innovative Games*, 3rd edn (Burlington: Morgan Kaufmann, 2014), 99–100; Jesse Schell, *The Art of Game Design: A Book of Lenses*, 2nd edn (Boca Raton, London, New York: CRC Press, 2015), 179, 198–9.

11   Cf. Roger Callois, *Man, Play and Games*, trans. Meyer Barash (Urbana and Chicago: University of Illinois Press, 2001 [1958]), 17.

12   E. g. BioWare, *Dragon Age: Origins*, Wynne's camp dialogue.

entirely devaluing the dramatic conflict between the mages and Templars. As this range of options shows, there really is no way to translate this random high-stakes risk into a game mechanism, because it would either turn the narrative nonsensical, or produce an intensely frustrating gaming experience.

Conclusion

As has been shown in this chapter, magic as a game mechanism in the *Dragon Age* series often directly contradicts or undermines the games' narrative about magic. Some of this conflict is caused by the specialization system in the first two instalments of the series, in which becoming a Spirit Healer or Blood Mage should have narrative repercussions but does not; this problem is resolved when the specialization system is changed significantly. However, part of the opposition between magic in the games' narrative and as a game mechanism stems from deeper causes, which make it impossible to reconcile the two: a random chance of possession would counteract the basic tenets of attainable goals and rewarding gameplay, and a narrative in which possession is portrayed as irreversible makes it untenable to integrate a random chance of it occurring into the flow of the game.

That there are nevertheless some options for including a more truly volatile type of magic into games without destroying the gaming experience is proven by a few outliers. Tabletop role-playing games (TRPGs) in the *Warhammer 40k* universe use random outcome tables to embody the unreliability of psychic powers in the game's rules,[13] and *Baldur's Gate II* – an older game by the same development studio as *Dragon Age* – portrays a protagonist undergoing short spells of possession during which they turn into a mythical beast that the player has no control over. Both of these games make compromises to achieve that goal, however. *Warhammer 40k* accepts the small chance of entirely ruining the game for a player whose character might be killed by a

13   Ross Watson et al., *Rogue Trader – Roleplaying in the Grim Darkness of the 41st Millenium – Core Rulebook* (Roseville, MN: Fantasy Flight Games, 2009), 160–1.

catastrophically bad succession of dice results, though most of the random outcomes are non-lethal. However, TRPGs leave the final interpretation of the rules to the discretion of the game master, who is free to bend certain rules in order to create an experience that will fit their group of players – some of whom might accept their character's death and move on, while others might be extremely put off by such developments, in which case the game master is free to perhaps turn the character's death into a less severe misfortune, or create a quest for the rest of the group to save that character. Additionally, as a group endeavour, TRPGs usually allow players whose character is killed to re-enter the game by creating a new character and re-joining the group, which is less disruptive than the death of the main character in a single-player game.

In contrast, *Baldur's Gate II* carefully constructs a narrative in which the player character's possession poses a temporal and individual problem, but not an irreversible transformation or common problem that has shaped the political and religious systems of entire nations. Furthermore, possession in *Baldur's Gate II* is not a general part of the game's rules that can trigger whenever a mage casts a spell, but is limited to a tightly controlled, relatively short episode when it narratively makes sense for the main character to be particularly vulnerable.

Overall, while the successful incorporation of volatile magic into a game's rules is certainly possible, it requires careful balancing of the consequences and the narrative framework, and it may simply not be possible for all types of games and all types of stories.

Part V

Magic and the Body

Hannah Segrave

Salvator Rosa's *La Strega* (1647–1650)

In the twenty-first-century Western imagination, the word 'witch' conjures a variety of figures, from the Puritans of Salem, to Snow White's transforming evil stepmother, to the seductive temptresses of 1970s B-films. For the early modern European, the idea of a witch was similarly varied – corroborated by the numerous and diverging pictures and descriptions that crop up in demonological texts, mythological narratives, court documents and images of artistic fantasy. In this milieu, the notoriously audacious Neapolitan artist Salvator Rosa (1615–73), famed for his sublime landscapes and esoteric philosophical subjects, fashioned a specific stereotype of witches in his paintings of black magic. Made during the 1640s and 1650s between Florence and Rome, Rosa's pictures drew on a wide variety of sources, including popular superstitions, literary characters, demonological treatises and the rich visual tradition crafted by Renaissance artists.[1]

No picture captures the qualities of the 'Rosian witch' as explicitly as the painting *La Strega* (ca. 1647–50, Figure 35). Towering over two metres tall, it features a naked witch thrashing alone in the middle of a shadowy, cavernous space.[2] While the painting is atypical of Rosa's approach to depicting witchcraft (in that it is both structurally simple and physically large), it nevertheless foregrounds Rosa's paradigmatic witch. This 'hideous hag' is an explicitly old, naked woman – a *grotesque* character. I purposefully employ the term

---

1 This essay is derived from the second chapter of my doctoral dissertation, 'Conjuring Genius: Salvator Rosa and the Dark Arts of Witchcraft' (University of Delaware, 2020), which investigates Rosa's entire body of witchcraft imagery, as well as his interest in witchcraft in relation to his larger goals of self-fashioning and theories of picture-making.

2 *La Strega* is catalogue number 158 in Caterina Volpi, *Salvator Rosa (1615–1673): pittore famoso* (Rome: Ugo Bozzi editore), 477.

'grotesque' in order to lay bare the inherent misogynistic intentions behind creating this character and in her reception by an early modern audience, as well as to relate this witch directly to the Bakhtinian concept of the grotesque body – open, excessive and tangibly debased.[3] But rather than dismissing Rosa's witch as simply stereotypical or sexist, investigating her attributes and sources reveals how Rosa created a terrifying, electrifying and ambitious character. In so doing, he cemented stereotypes of the witch that share a direct line to the ideas of witches – and women – today.

Filling up the centre of a dark and ambiguous space, the solitary witch of *La Strega* shrieks as she brandishes a flaming branch in her proper right hand. With her left hand she clutches an orb-shaped vial, on top of which emerges a demon-sprite, a personification of the evil spirits invoked by the witch's rites. An array of still-life objects that were common to both witchcraft and *vanitas* imagery surround the writhing hag: a glass jug, coins, a mirror, bones, a skull and a sheet with esoteric, alchemical symbols (on which Rosa signed his monograph '*SR*'). But the most gruesome detail of her malevolent ritual is the infant engulfed in shadow behind her; swaddled tightly, lying on the floor, the child appears dead (or at least will be soon). The notion that witches tapped babies for their blood to create satanic unguents was popularized in early modern demonology and literature, especially the misogynist treatise *Malleus Maleficarum* (Speyer, 1487) by Heinrich Kramer and Jacob Sprenger, as well as Gianfrancesco Pico della Mirandola's *La Strega, ovvero, degli inganni de' demoni* (Bologna, 1523). Rosa had alluded to this disturbing practice in other paintings, such as the *Witches at their Incantations* (ca. 1646, London, National Gallery) where an infant is offered to a skeletal demon by a topless hag;[4] but *La Strega's* bleak atmosphere and foregrounded torment turn the bordering-burlesque qualities of the London painting into a terrifying nightmare.

During the fifteenth and sixteenth centuries, the visual culture of witchcraft flourished throughout Europe alongside the witch-hunts themselves. While specific beliefs about witchcraft were fluid and changed across regions and countries, in general witches were accused of renouncing their Christian

---

3   See Mikhail Bakhtin, *Rabelais and His World*, trans. Hélène Iswolsky (Bloomington: Indiana University Press, 1984).

4   Inventory number NH6491, see cat. no. 157 in Volpi, *Salvator Rosa*, 476.

Figure 35. Salvator Rosa: *La Strega*, c. 1647–50, oil on canvas, 212 cm × 147 cm.
New York, private collection. Reproduced with permission from the owner.

faith and entering into a sexual and submissive pact with the devil.[5] They would consummate this relationship at the Sabbath, the nightly gatherings where they performed their *maleficium*, dark magic. Coming to a climax between 1560 and 1640, these ideas of the so-called 'witch craze' circulated throughout the European continent through a steady stream of demonological treatises that justified and instructed the hunting of witches, as well as pamphlets, broadsheets and artworks that illustrated the demonologists' worst fears. Artists in Northern Europe in particular produced a wealth of prints that circulated widely to cement stereotypes of grotesque witches upending the rational, male world.

In Italy, however, images of black magic were less common, and in some cases dangerous: in Naples, just before Rosa was born, the Dutch artist Jacob van Swanenburg was brought before the Inquisition for his pictures of witches' Sabbaths.[6] The few seventeenth-century artists who did picture witches often depicted beguiling beauties, such as the ornately dressed, youthful sorceresses produced by Angelo Caroselli in the 1620s. Even more popular were subjects of mythological and literary witches, including Circe and Medea from classical myths as well as the sorceresses from Renaissance epic poetry, like Armida from Torquato Tasso's *Gerusalemme Liberata* (1581). Seventeenth-century Genoa, in particular, saw a surge of pictures of Circe, inspired by the lush and exoticized examples by Giovanni Battista Castiglione.[7] The velvety etching of *Circe Changing the Companions of Ulysses into Beasts* (1650–1, Figure 36) figures the witch who transfigured as alluring and melancholic, dangerous on account

5   These beliefs refer to major parts of the 'cumulative concept' of witchcraft, first discussed in Joseph Hansen, *Zauberwahn, Inquisition und Hexenprozess im Mittelalter und die Entstehung der großen Hexenverfolgung* (Munich: Scientia Verlag Aalen, 1964). For a warning against relying too heavily on this as a definitive construct, see Richard Kieckhefer, 'Mythologies of Witchcraft in the Fifteenth Century', *Magic, Ritual, and Witchcraft* 1/1 (2006), 79–108.

6   The record of van Swanenburg's trial was published in Luigi Amabile, *Il santo officio della inquisizione in Napoli: narrazione con molti documenti inediti* (Città di Castello: S Lapi, 1892). In reality, the 'witch craze', as it has been termed, in Italy was never as severe as it was in other countries, see Tamar Herzig, 'Witchcraft Prosecutions in Italy', in Brian P. Levack, ed., *The Oxford Handbook of Witchcraft in Early Modern Europe and Colonial America* (Oxford: Oxford University Press, 2013), 249–67.

7   Bertina Suida Manning, 'The Transformation of Circe: The Significance of the Sorceress as Subject in 17th Century Genoese Painting', *Scritti di storia dell'arte in onore di Federico Zeri* 2 (1984), 689–708.

Figure 36. Giovanni Benedetto Castiglione (Il Grechetto): *Circe Changing the Companions of Ulysses into Beasts*, 1650–1. Metropolitan Museum of Art. Public domain.

of her beauty. While these fictional witches were certainly used to justify the veracity of witchcraft (and thus the necessity for the Inquisition), the type of witchcraft they performed was fundamentally different from contemporary witches who practised diabolical, Satanic rituals.

Unlike those of his Italian contemporaries, Rosa's witches take on the characteristics of *Invidia,* the personification of Envy: half-naked with wild hair, a crooked nose and sagging breasts.[8] *La Strega* is shockingly naked, her genitals barely covered by the few leaves of a dark green ivy garland. Ivy, a symbol of Bacchus and the desires he could incite, mockingly reminds the viewer that witches were

8   Cesare Ripa, whose book of emblems was an most important source for early modern allegories, described 'Invidia' as 'Donna vecchia, magra, brutta, di color livido, haurà la mammella sinistra nuda' [An old woman who is thin, ugly, of a pale colour, and with her left breast nude]. All translations are my own unless otherwise noted. See Cesare Ripa, *Iconologia [Padua, 161]* (New York: Garland Pub, 1976), 261–3, 261.

envious of the passions and fertility of youth. This allegorical connection correlates to Lyndal Roper's thesis that older women were more vulnerable to persecution because the early modern age valued fertility; thus, post-menopausal women were assumed to be jealous of reproductive ability, envious of both younger women and their children.[9] The grotesqueness of *La Strega*'s slumping torso and exposed female genitalia juxtaposes against her taut and muscled arms, creating an androgyny that underscores the witch as a failed or unnatural female.

This type of abject witch drew directly from prints made by Northern European artists in the sixteenth and early seventeenth centuries from Albrecht Dürer to Jacques de Gheyn.[10] These prints were collected passionately by noble families in Florence, including the Medici, for whom Rosa worked during the 1640s when he made the majority of his witchcraft images. Hans Baldung Grien's *Witches Sabbath* (1510, Figure 37) is perhaps the most iconic and widespread depiction of witches, one that Rosa himself copied throughout his career.[11] The innovative chiaroscuro woodcut illustrates a Sabbath, with three central naked hags brewing potions while others fly through the air backwards on goats (the animal form of the Devil himself). Drawing on the precedents of his teacher, Albrecht Dürer, Baldung portrays the witch as women, splayed open, who work collectively for Satanic ends; they are both sexually available and repulsive, a dichotomy at the heart of patriarchal fears over black magic.[12] The one major

9   Lyndal Roper, *Oedipus and the Devil: Witchcraft, Sexuality, and Religion in Early Modern Europe* (London: Routledge, 1994). In particular, see 'Witchcraft and Fantasy in Early Modern Germany', 199–225.

10 For Rosa's use of Northern European imagery in his witchcraft images, see Stefania Macioce, and Tania De Nile, 'Influssi nordici nelle Stregonerie de Salvator Rosa', in Sybille Ebert-Schifferer Helen Langdon and Caterina Volpi, eds, *Salvator Rosa e il suo tempo 1615–1673* (Rome: Campisano, 2010), 139–58. See also Alessandro Campoli, 'Le Stregonerie di Salvator Rosa', in Stefania Macioce, ed., *L'incantesimo di Circe: Temi di magia nella pittura da Dosso Dossi a Salvator Rosa* (Rome: Logart Press, 2004), 158–80.

11 Rosa adapted the pose of the central witches in several of his paintings, such as the London *Witches at the Incantations*, and directly copies them in a late sketch from the 1660s, the *Sheet of studies with a sketch for 'The Death of Empedocles'*, now in the National Gallery of Victoria, Australia (Accession Number 1278.733-3).

12 See Charles Zika, *The Appearance of Witchcraft: Print and Visual Culture in Sixteenth-Century Europe* (London: Routledge, 2007) and Linda C. Hults, *The Witch As Muse: Art, Gender, and Power in Early Modern Europe* (Philadelphia: University of Pennsylvania, 2005).

Italian example of this *Invidia*-inspired witch is the female at the centre of the engraving known as *Lo Stregozzo* (ca. 1520), a diabolical yet *all'antica* procession that captures the theatricality Rosa translated into his paintings.

Figure 37. Hans Baldung (called Hans Baldung Grien): *The Witches*, 1510.
Metropolitan Museum of Art. Public domain.

While he clearly drew on these examples to create his 'hideous hag', Rosa was unique in the way that he took pains to remove traces of his witches' sexuality, focusing instead on the bodily horror of the witch. Like his teacher Jusepe de Ribera (1591–1652), Rosa seemed to take pleasure in painting the desiccated flesh of the hoary wild woman, describing the folds of her skin in long, quavering brushstrokes. With her horrifying expression and thrashing body pressed against the picture-plane – as if she is threatening to burst forth into the viewer's space at any moment – the painting is almost as if a portrait, like a 'speaking likeness' popularized by Gian Lorenzo Bernini's oratorical sculptural busts.

In focusing on the physical monstrosity of the witch, Rosa actually heightens the intellectual seriousness of his picture by moving beyond the visual and demonological to reference the infamous witches created by ancient imperial Roman poets, specifically Lucan's Erichtho and Horace's Canidia. Both witches practise diabolical rather than mythical magic, and both authors describe their features in grotesque detail; their lasting impression on Italian literature is seen in the evil hag-witch Falsirena from Giambattisto Marino's spectacular baroque epic *L'Adone* (1623). Erichtho appears in Lucan's *Pharsalia* (61–5 CE) as a witch from Thessaly, a renowned locus of magic, who uses her teeth to rip apart dead bodies, and sacrifices children. Similarly, 'savage Canidia', with her dishevelled hair and wild teeth, appears in several of Horace's *Satires* and *Epodes*, committing vile crimes from corpse desecration to murder. Rosa himself also wrote satires deeply influenced by Horace, and the Neapolitan artist's poem 'La Strega' (ca. 1645) reads like a reimagination of Canidia's night-time evils.[13] In *La Strega*'s shrieking countenance, you can almost hear her scream Canidia's curse: 'Diana, that queen of silence, / where our secret rites are performed, / now, aid me now, now, turn your anger and power / against the houses of my foes!'[14]

Creating this specific type of character, and employing her so often, allowed Rosa to explore witchcraft imagery in a way that was both immediately recognizable to his early modern audience and yet unique in *seicento* Italy. Linda Hults has convincingly argued that male artists capitalized on depicting female witches as a way to assert their (masculine) artistic genius through the virtuosic depictions of the female body; an idea at the heart of Rosa's witches.[15] The hideous hag – with her complex compilation of diverse ideas, which were extremely rare (or unheard of) in Rosa's time – exemplified Rosa's desire to only paint subjects that, in his own words, 'have never been treated before

13   Rosa's poem has been published several times, most recently in Daniela De Liso, *Salvator Rosa tra pennelli e versi* (Firenze: Franco Cesati editore, 2018).

14   '... Diana, quae silentium regis, / arcana cum fiunt sacra / nunc, nuc adeste, nunc in hostilis domos / iram atque numen uertite' in Epode V, lines 51–4, see Horace, and David Mankin, ed., *Epodes* (Cambridge: Cambridge University Press, 1995), 32–5.

15   See Hults, *The Witch as Muse*, especially 1–26.

by anyone'.[16] Thus, the diabolical hag was not only synonymous with Rosa's images of black magic themselves; she also embodied Rosa's conception of, and interest in, witchcraft; through the visceral depiction of grotesque witches Rosa could showcase the erudite, complex and exhilarating imaginings that he alone was creating.

The Witch's Body

---

16   'né tocchi mai da nessuno' is a quote from Rosa's 29 July 1662 letter to Giovan Battista
      Ricciardi. Translation from Hoare, Letter no. 281, in *Letters of Salvator Rosa*, 594–5.

Anna Grebe

Disability in Magic Performances

The heyday of stage magic in the late nineteenth century coincides with the boom of the so-called 'sideshow' or 'freak show', a 'formally organized exhibition of people with alleged and real physical, mental or behavioural anomalies for amusement and profit'.[1] In the course of these shows, people with disabilities were exhibited on stages for paying audiences, and their special features were accentuated by means of clothing, postures, stories or optical or mechanical tricks. People of short stature ('dwarfs'), people with microcephaly (advertised as 'missing links' in human evolution), women and men with aberrant hair growth ('the bearded lady') or people with physical deformities such as the world-famous 'armless man', Charles Tripp, were marketed by entrepreneurs, such as the US American Phineas Taylor Barnum for their travelling fairs and circuses as acts in stage shows.[2] The performers of the freak shows were marvelled at for their mainly physical deviations from any kind of normality, often objectified as 'wonders of nature' and rarely imbued with real agency. These shows achieved immense international success, so much so that culturally and historically the freak show has probably become the most famous *dispositif* of disability on stage. This success also discursively brought disability close to stage magic, since P. T. Barnum also had magicians perform in his shows and elements of the freak show were combined with the techniques and practices of magic. Tricks like the 'Sawing a Woman in Half' were staged with the help of

1 Robert Bogdan, 'The Social Construction of Freaks', in Rosemarie Garland Thomson, ed., *Freakery. Cultural Spectacles of the Extraordinary Body* (New York: New York University Press, 1996), 23–37, 23.

2 Rachel Adams, *Sideshow USA. Freaks and the American Cultural Imagination* (Chicago: Chicago University Press, 2001).

people with special physical characteristics or gave the stage illusion the status of healing magic which could make damaged bodies whole again.[3]

However, if one does not understand disability as an ontological-essentialist characteristic as it was popularly attributed to the performers of the freak shows, but rather as a restriction of a temporary nature, which is only produced in certain *dispositifs*, then another connection between magic and disability becomes apparent. As Karen Dearborn points out, disability, as disabling practices, becomes the starting point for many magic tricks of stage magic, because the able-bodied magician deliberately puts himself in a situation of restriction (e.g. by tying himself up or locking himself in a cage), from which he has to free himself in the course of the trick through his 'extraordinary cleverness' – or just through magic – and thus overcome his loss of agency.[4] Disability is produced as an obstacle and at the same time dissolved again by the liberation or transformation; it disappears because it was part of a planned illusion. The visual rhetoric with which disability is staged in both stage magic and freak show alike can be described as 'wondrous', and thus leads to a scopic or visual regime in which the audience is left in disbelief and amazement in the face of the performance on stage.[5] But what happens if the

3   A reversed example for involving people with a disability in magic shows by using them as mere props is a magic trick known as 'pulling a woman apart at the waist'. Criss Angel, an American magician, illusionist and musician, collaborated with Rose Siggins, an actress with sacral agenesis and thus amputated legs, to perform an illusion for his television programme *Mindfreak* on A&E in 2006: 'Purportedly a man in a park has a woman lie down on a bench. He enlists two other women to pull on her feet and arms in opposite directions. After he taps on her belly, the other two women pull apart the woman lying on the bench. It appears the torso crawls away and the legs sit up on the bench.' Snopes, <https://www.snopes.com/fact-check/pulled-apart/>, accessed 1 December 2020. Nevertheless, Angel does not assign any kind of agency to Siggins, she is staged as a nameless object to enable him to realize this performance in front of a live audience in a public park.

4   Karen Dearborn, 'Intersecting Illusions. Performing Magic, Disability, and Gender', in Francesca Coppa, Lawrence Hass, and James Peck, eds, *Performing Magic on the Western Stage: From the Eighteenth Century to the Present* (New York: Palgrave Macmillan, 2008), 177–96, 177.

5   Rosemarie Garland Thomson, 'Seeing the Disabled. Visual Rhetorics of Disability in Popular Photography', in Paul K. Longmore and Lauri Umansky, eds, *The New*

magician himself has a permanent physical limitation, a physical disability? What makes the audience marvel: the illusion or the body of the illusionist?[6]

Disabled historical figures like the German prestidigitator Matthias Buchinger, born in the seventeenth century with tetra-amelia syndrome (absence of all four limbs), or Eliaser Bamberg from the famous Bamberg Dynasty who in the eighteenth century hid items in his wooden leg, appear to be self-determined in exercising their abilities as magicians. Bamberg utilized his disability as a means of achieving this purpose; Buchinger was a magician despite his disability. In Buchinger's case, his physical handicap is perceived as a limitation that has to be overcome and compensated for, while in Bamberg's case his prosthesis served as a feature of his natural body which procures for him advantages in his performance. Both of them were equally admired for their extraordinary capabilities as magicians and inspired numerous able-bodied, as well as disabled, magicians in their following.

The link and interrelation between self-determination/agency and the respective visual regime, which is already apparent here, produces three essential (operationalizable) and closely linked narratives in the case of magicians with a disability that is innate or acquired over the course of life: firstly, the narrative of adaptation, secondly, the narrative of overcoming and thirdly, the narrative of inspiration. The self-presentation as well as the external perception of physically disabled magicians moves in the relationship of these three narratives and thus allows a reading of disability according to the cultural model of Disability Studies, which perceives of dis/ability in the light of the

---

Disability History. American Perspectives (New York: New York University Press, 2001), 335–74, 339.

6   An example I won't be able to discuss within this essay is the work of blind(folded) mentalists or psychics. For an overview about mentalism and telepathy in magic shows please see Katharina Rein, *Techniken der Täuschung. Eine Kultur- und Mediengeschichte der Bühnenzauberkunst im späten neunzehnten Jahrhundert* (Marburg: Büchner Verlag, 2020), 313–50 and Katharina Rein, 'Mind Reading in Stage Magic: The "Second Sight" Illusion, Media, and Mediums', *communication +1* 4/1 (2015), Article 8, <https://scholarworks.umass.edu/cpo/vol4/iss1/8>, DOI: 10.7275/R50C4SPB, accessed 25 February 2021.

interdependencies of normality and abnormality in historical, social, cultural, but also media dependence.[7]

The narrative of 'adaptation' can be understood in at least two ways: disability becomes an indispensable factor of the performance – or it is the disability that first produces the clever enchantment of the audience. The aforementioned Eliaser Bamberg was already a magician in the second generation of his family.[8] After he lost his leg in an explosion, he began to actively incorporate his wooden leg into his magic tricks and to use it for the illusion of the magical disappearance and reappearance of small objects such as coins and the like. From a supposed disadvantage an advantage arose – Bamberg adapted himself and his tricks to his new physical conditions. Another, albeit contemporary, magician also reinvented close-up magic according to his needs: the Argentinean René Lavand, who became famous in the USA through numerous TV appearances, had lost his right hand in a car accident at the age of 9. As his interest in magic began to develop, René had to adapt the tricks to his individual situation and changed them so that he could perform them with one hand. It was not apparent to the audience, however, during a large part of his performances that Lavand actually had only one physical hand, as he kept his right arm in his trouser pocket and sometimes only pulled his arm out of the pocket at the end of his tricks. In doing so, during the performance he made it clear that he basically had extraordinary skills – and subsequently that these special skills were based on the essential adaptation of two-handed magic tricks to his individual situation.[9]

The narrative of the 'overcoming' of disability by the affected people themselves is based on the concept of disability as an individual and mostly

---

7   For an introduction to Disability Studies see Lennard J. Davis, 'Crips Strike Back: The Rise of Disability Studies', *American Literary History* 11/3 (1999), 500–12; Paul K. Longmore, and Lauri Umansky, eds, *The New Disability History. American Perspectives* (New York: New York University Press, 2001); Colin Barnes, and Geof Mercer, eds, *Implementing the Social Model of Disability. Theory and Research* (Leeds: Disability Press, 2004).

8   'Bamberg Magical Dynasty', QAZ Wiki, <https://de.qaz.wiki/wiki/Bamberg_Magical_Dynasty>, accessed 30 November 2020.

9   For an excellent analysis of Lavand's work as a male disabled magician and an intersectional approach to Lavand in the light of Disability and Gender Studies see Dearborn, 'Intersecting Illusions'.

physical problem, which positions them outside a 'normal majority' to which they have to adapt through special effort and which, at best, at least exceeds this normality. The disabled person is initially marked as weak or disadvantaged because of their disability, but through hard training of their own skills and willpower they can obtain the recognition of 'normal society' for something they achieve 'despite' their disability.[10] Matthias Buchinger was one of the most famous showmen of the early eighteenth century; he played more than half a dozen musical instruments, was a master pistol marksman and an outstanding calligrapher – at a size of 84 cm. He became famous as a magician by developing his own technical device to make a bullet disappear – a trick that gained him entrance in magic textbooks under his name and as 'The Greatest German Living'.[11] Buchinger travelled all over Europe and was very popular at royal courts, not as a fool or as the property of a non-handicapped master, but out of his own desire and drive, precisely 'despite' his handicap. Contemporary magicians too accept this task of adaptation and overcoming, which is assigned to them by 'normal society' and win agency back through this attribution by using it for both economic and educational purposes. 'The Amazing Jeffo' has for many years been offering so-called 'Disability Awareness Shows', which he uses to demonstrate his abilities as a blind magician to his audience on the one hand, while on the other he uses these abilities as a motivational speaker to draw attention to the fact that people with disabilities have other, special abilities that normal society only needs to recognize. Jeff Smith, who performs under the stage name 'The Amazing Jeffo', does not see his blindness as an impairment but as a way to show that 'the most disabling thing in our lives is the thing we can do the most about: our attitude'.[12] Nevertheless, only the recognition of one's own disability as an alteration or special case becomes the starting point for his own narrative of adaptation and overcoming, on which the performance as a magician is then built.

10   The narrative of 'overcoming disability' is frequently used within the context of the depiction of disabled athletes, see: David P. Howe, 'Cyborg and Supercrip: The Paralympic Technology and the (Dis)empowerment of Disabled Athletes', *Sociology* 45/5 (2011), 868–82; Anna Grebe, and Beate Ochsner, 'Vom Supercrip zum Superhuman oder: Figuration der Überwindung', *Kritische Berichte* 1 (2013), 47–59.

11   Jay Ricky, *Matthias Buchinger: The Greatest German Living* (New York: Siglio, 2016).

12   Amazing Jeffo, <https://amazingjeffo.com/>, accessed 30 November 2020.

The narrative of 'inspiration' in the sense of artistic inspiration is in turn based on a moral exaggeration of the disabled person by the spectator. We encounter it nowadays especially in the form of videos on clickbait websites, in which disabled people display skills that impress the non-disabled spectator, because the challenges that the disabled person has to master 'despite' their disability seem almost unbelievable. The viewer not only feels amazed, but also challenged to take an example from the willpower and discipline of the disabled person. Disability activist Stella Young assigns the term 'inspiration porn' to this narrative: 'Like actual pornography, Inspiration Porn provides kind of superficial pleasure and gratification for the viewer, while objectifying, often harming the mostly passive subjects being looked at.'[13] However, when artists use this narrative to regain the power of interpretation over themselves, like The Amazing Jeffo or Ricky D. Boone,[14] the stage magician and founder of 'The Vanishing Wheelchair' with Morgagni's Syndrome, they determine for themselves in what way they want to be perceived as inspiration.

The media representation of Mahdi Gilbert, the magician born in Toronto, Canada in 1989 with malformations of the arms and legs, unites the three narratives adaptation – overcoming – inspiration in the interplay between self-designation and the expectations held by non-disabled people of people with disabilities. On his website <www.mahdigilbert.com> he not only promotes his work as a magician, as a teacher for aspiring magicians, but also as a motivational coach. According to his own statement, his qualification for this job is based on his ability to overcome 'some of life's most harsh conditions' and 'the extreme challenges of being born without hands and feet'. Through 'massive personal growth and achievement', but also by adapting magic tricks to his physical abilities, he is now able to 'inspire you to break through your limitations and shape your destiny.'[15] At the same time, he refers directly to the already mentioned Matthias Buchinger, though primarily because of the

---

13   Andrew Pulrang, 'How to Avoid "Inspiration Porn"', *Forbes* (29 November 2019), <https://www.forbes.com/sites/andrewpulrang/2019/11/29/how-to-avoid-inspirat ion-porn/>, accessed 1 December 2020.

14   The Vanishing Wheelchair, <http://www.vanishingwheelchair.org/>, accessed 1 December 2020.

15   Mahdi the Magician, <https://www.mahdithemagician.com/inspirational-speaker>, accessed 26 April 2022.

similar physical characteristics: 'Mahdi Gilbert is the only magician in the world without hands and feet since the renowned 17th century conjuror, Matthias Buchinger.'[16]

These examples of magicians make it clear that the dual nature or function of their disability can be used to support their core business ('the magician's stock-in-trade'): disability becomes one of many practices of making them invisible and visible to create illusions, which in turn are embedded in narratives and, as Karen Dearborn concludes: 'Magically, they display agency to shape their own identity outside societal constructs of bodily variation as disabling.'[17]

---

16   Mahdi the Magician, <https://www.mahdigilbert.com>, accessed 1 December 2020.
17   Dearborn, 'Intersecting Illusions', 194.

Jasmin Kathöfer and Jens Schröter

Disney Films

Many Disney animated films live on magic or contain magical elements. People can fly, objects are brought to life, good and evil magicians appear. It is striking that one motif in particular – namely that magic is used to make labour faster or easier – is used in a large number of these films. The good fairy tailors a ball gown for *Cinderella*.[1] Staff transformed into household objects prepare a wonderful dinner for Belle (*Beauty and the Beast*[2]). In *The Princess and the Frog*,[3] prince Naveen makes a pact with the voodoo witch Doctor Facilier so that he doesn't have to work after his parents cut him off. Is it a coincidence that labour and magic seem to be interwoven here or is there a specific reason behind it? In this short text we would like to explore this question with the help of two examples.

Our first example, the ballad *The Sorcerer's Apprentice* also translated as *The Pupil in Magic*,[4] written in the so-called *Balladenjahr* 1797 by Johann Wolfgang von Goethe and still very popular as subject material, was realized by Disney in 1940 in the animated film *Fantasia*,[5] with recourse to the symphonic

---

1   Dir. Clyde Geronimi et al. (Walt Disney Productions/Walt Disney Animation Studios, 1950).

2   Dir. Gary Trousdale, Kirk Wise (Walt Disney Pictures/Walt Disney Animation Studios, 1991).

3   Dir. Ron Clements, John Musker (Walt Disney Pictures/Walt Disney Animation Studios, 2009)

4   Edgar Alfred Bowring, trans., The Poems of Goethe, 2nd ed. (New York: Hurst, 1874); also known as "The Sorcerer's Apprentice." Published in German as "Der Zauberlehrling," in Friedrich Schiller, ed., *Musen-Almanach für das Jahr 1798* (Tübingen: J. G. Cotta, 1798).

5   Dir. Samuel Armstrong et al. (Walt Disney Productions/Walt Disney Animation Studios, 1940).

staging by the French composer Paul Dukas from 1897. Even though Goethe's text is not part of the animated film, it is nevertheless taken up in great detail.

In short, the film is about a sorcerer's apprentice (here embodied by Mickey Mouse) who, on the one hand cocky, but on the other hand recklessly assumes that he can easily control the magical power of his master. One day, when the sorcerer leaves the house and gives his apprentice the annoying task of fetching water, the latter is reluctant to perform the task. Without further ado, he bewitches a broom, which from now on is to carry the water for him.[6]

At first the spell works very well, but at some point, the tub is full and the broom, which stubbornly obeys its command, does not stop fetching water. To make matters worse, the apprentice has forgotten the spell for the retransformation of the broom and panic overcomes him.[7] As a last resort he chops the broom in two, whereupon both parts start to carry water (see Figure 38).[8] The apprentice threatens to drown and, in the end, only his master can save him and sort out the situation.

6   Johann Wolfgang von Goethe, *The Pupil in Magic*, lines 1-8: 'I am now,—what joy to hear it!— Of the old magician rid; / And henceforth shall ev'ry spirit / Do whate'er by me is bid; / I have watch'd with rigour All he used to do, / And will now with vigour Work my wonders too. / [...] And now come, thou well-worn broom, / And thy wretched form bestir; / Thou hast ever served as groom, / So fulfill my pleasure, sir! / On two legs now stand, / With a head on top; / Water pail in hand, / Haste, and do not stop!' Zipes, Jack, ed., *The Sorcerer's Apprentice. An Anthology of Magical Tales* (Princeton University Press: Princeton & Oxford, 2017), 97–100.

7   Goethe, *The Pupil in Magic*, lines 37-41: 'Stop, for, lo! / All the measure / Of thy treasure / Now is right!— / Ah, I see it! / Woe, oh woe! / I forget the word of might. / Ah, the word whose sound can straight / Make him what he was before!' and lines 58-61: 'Wilt thou not obey, / Oh, thou broom accurs'd? / Be thou still I pray, / As thou wert at first!'

8   Goethe, *The Pupil in Magic*, lines 76-81: 'Woe, oh woe! Both the parts, / Quick as darts, / Stand on end, / Servants of my dreaded foe! / Oh, ye gods protection send!'

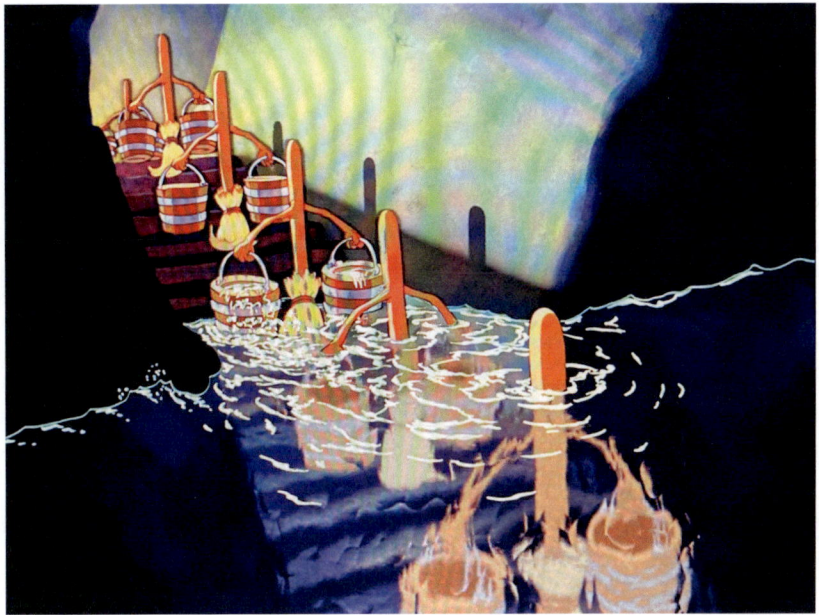

Figure 38. Enchanted broomsticks carrying water in *Fantasia*, dir. Samuel Armstrong et al. (Walt Disney Productions/Walt Disney Animation Studios, 1940).

What this first example clearly shows is the automation of work through using magic. But the viewer also witnesses that this automation fails because it is performed by an authority that does not (yet) have the necessary know-how to keep control of the situation in the long run. Ballad and cartoon can be read as a reminder to respect authorities and to assess one's own abilities in the right measure. However, the reference to the topic of automation of labour also allows another reading: the broom can be read as a magically driven robot created to do annoying work and, in turn, the sorcerer's apprentice is becoming dependent on the robot and thus also dependent on a type of magic that he does not understand. If it works differently or not at all, he is doomed. Finally, the magically moving broom can also be understood as a symptomatic figuration of the self-movement of things in capitalism, famously describes as 'fetishism' by Marx. Things develop a life on their own, estranging and threatening human subjects.[9]

The ballad *The Sorcerer's Apprentice* is reminiscent of the story about the *Golem of Prague*, which is about a man-made creature that functions as a worker. The main character in the legend is Rabbi Loew, who was very well versed in the arts and sciences and was thus able to bring figures made of clay or wood to life. They then did everything they were told to do, but without ever having to eat, sleep or drink, nor did they ask for any remuneration (as robots do today[10]). The animation of the figures was achieved by means of a Schem – a kind of magic formula – which was placed in the mouth of the figure. This golem took over all tasks in the house for the whole week except on the Sabbath, because on that day he had to rest. For this purpose, the Schem was taken out of his mouth. But once the rabbi forgot it and the golem devastated the entire city. In retrospect, the legend of the golem is explained in such a way that Rabbi Loew was a skilled mechanic who made an automaton – the very golem – that did the work for him.[11]

The second example deals with a scene[12] from the Disney movie *The Sword in the Stone*[13] from 1963, in which the magician Merlin is seeking his student Wart, later to become King Arthur, who lives as an orphan with Sir Ector. Wart was given the task to wash the dirty dishes of the whole castle. But Merlin – who prepared a completely different lesson for Wart – bewitches the dishes so that they clean themselves (see Figure 39). Merlin comments on the situation of washing dishes by hand as a medieval model that he wants to modernize. And when Wart remarks that he should wash the dishes after all, the magician replies that the dishes do not show being washed magically, and that 'no one will

---

9   See on this Jane Bennett, *The Enchantment of Modern Life. Attachments, Crossings and Ethics* (Princeton, NJ, Oxford: Princeton University Press, 2001), 117.

10   The word *robot* is actually a loan word from the Czech, which means something like artificial human or automaton, goes back to Karel Čapek. He first used the term 'robot' (Czech) in his drama *R.U.R.* (Rossum's Universal Robots) in 1921.

11   See Harald Salfellner, ed., *Der Prager Golem. Jüdische Sagen aus dem Ghetto* (Prague: Vitalis, 2007).

12   *The Sword in the Stone*, Enchantment of the Dishes, YouTube, <https://www.youtube.com/watch?v=dMwo1muyIfo>, accessed 1 September 2020.

13   Dir. Wolfgang Reitherman (Walt Disney Productions/Walt Disney Animation Studios).

care when the work is done'. It is interesting and problematic that the examples of labour substituted by magic are most often types of labour associated with 'female housework' – this might be seen as an ideological implication of these discourses on magic, especially since the production of these films was based on lots of badly paid female work.[14] According to Bennett's formulation, that '[c]ommodity fetishism [...] animates artifacts and then obscures the source of that animation',[15] the obscured source of the Disney animation movies, the female work, is erased a second time on the level of content.

Figure 39. Enchanted dishes cleaning themselves in *The Sword in the Stone*, dir. Wolfgang Reitherman (Walt Disney Productions/Walt Disney Animation Studios, 1963).

14   See Nathalia Holt, *The Queens of Animation. The Untold Story of the Women Who Transformed the World of Disney and Made Cinematic History* (New York, Boston, London: Little, Brown and Company, 2019) and Patricia Zohn, 'Coloring the Kingdom', *Vanity Fair* (5 February 2010), <https://www.vanityfair.com/culture/2010/03/disney-animation-girls-201003>, accessed 20 June 2021.

15   Bennett, *Enchantment*, 117.

Now Merlin enchants the kitchen and automates the cleaning of plates, pots and pans and both – the magician and Wart – devote themselves to another task. Meanwhile, the cook notices what is going on in the kitchen and alarms Sir Ector and his son Kay. They try to strike down this 'Black magic of a kind' with swords and are then attacked by the dishes.[16]

In contrast to the first example, magic fails not because of the magician's overestimation of himself, but because of the narrow-mindedness of other people. Without the intervention of Sir Ector and his son, the automation would probably have worked very well. Wart – who is punished for Merlin's magic – comments on Ector's fear of using magic with the following words: 'His magic is good. Just because you can't understand something, it doesn't mean it's wrong.'[17]

Both examples show that the representations of magic are often deeply intertwined with the question of the avoidance of labour. This tradition already starts in *The Bible*. In Genesis 3, 17–19 God curses Adam, after he and Eve ate from the forbidden fruit:

> Cursed is the ground because of you; through painful toil you will eat food from it all the days of your life. It will produce thorns and thistles for you, and you will eat the plants of the field. By the sweat of your brow you will eat your food.[18]

The curse simply means that being expelled from paradise means the necessity to work and from the very beginning work is marked as something painful. But also in the Greek tradition we can find similar statements: the following can be read in Aristotle:

> [I]f every tool could perform its own work when ordered, or by seeing what to do in advance, like the statues of Daedalus in the story, or the tripods of Hephaestus which the poet says 'enter self-moved the company divine,' – if thus shuttles wove and quills played harps of themselves, master-craftsmen would have no need of assistants and masters no need of slaves.[19]

16   *The Sword in the Stone*, Attack of the Dishes, YouTube, <https://www.youtube.com/watch?v=HJnaXaNzEVg>, accessed 1 September 2020.

17   Ibid.

18   *The Bible, New International Version*, <https://biblehub.com/niv/genesis/3.htm>, accessed 1 September 2020.

19   Aristotle, *Politics*, with an English translation by H. Rackham (London: Heinemann, Cambridge, MA: Harvard University Press, 1998), 1253b, 17.

Magic and Labour

This passage suggests two ways in which labour can be avoided: the magic one, in which tools do the work by being 'ordered' (with a spell presumably) or the technological one, suggested by the 'shuttles' weaving by itself (a technology which would really begin to exist in 1785, when Edmond Cartwright constructed the first power loom). Technology and magic can be seen as two answers to the problem of labour – and therefore it is not surprising that Arthur C. Clarke once stated: 'Any sufficiently advanced technology is indistinguishable from magic.'[20]

Since the industrial revolution the potentials of technology to erase work evolved and produced lots of fears if a society based on work can survive in the future or what it means that technology may substitute work.[21] This might explain the ambivalence of the magic substitution of labour in our examples: in all the above examples, the automation of labour by magic has a negative effect: the broom almost drowns the sorcerer's apprentice, the golem destroys houses and wreaks havoc, third parties are afraid of magic and punish Wart, and even get attacked. The question is: why? Why is the magical automation of work put in such a bad light? We can see now why this is the case: the magic substitution of labour is, on the one hand, a relief from painful work (see *The Bible* and Aristotle); on the other hand, it threatens modern society which is based on it[22] – even modern man as such might be defined by work as Arendt and Foucault have analysed.[23]

20   See Arthur C. Clarke, *Profiles of the Future. An Inquiry into the Limits of the Possible* (London: Gollancz, 2013, ebook). See also the role of magic in relation to technology in Gilbert Simondon, *On the Existence of Technical Objects* (Washington, DC: Univocal, 2017), especially 106, 108, 111 and 176–82 on the 'primitive magical unity'.

21   See for the US especially Amy Sue Bix, *Inventing Ourselves out of Jobs? America's Debate over Technological Unemployment 1929–1981* (Baltimore, MD, London: John Hopkins University Press, 2000).

22   See Gregory R. Woirol, *The Technological and Structural Unemployment Debates* (Westport, CT, London: Greenwood Press, 1996). Other authors have embraced the Aristotelian promise of liberation from labour through advanced technologies, that could eventually lead to new post-capitalist forms of society, see (among many others): Nick Srnicek, and Alex Williams, *Inventing the Future: Postcapitalism and a World without Work* (London: Verso, 2015).

23   See Hannah Arendt, *The Human Condition* (Chicago: University of Chicago Press, 1958) and Michel Foucault, *The Order of Things. An Archaeology of the Human Sciences* (London, New York: Routledge, 2002), especially chapter 8.

The ambivalence between magic and labour (or technology) is also shown in a further example that is not from Disney but should be mentioned, because it presents our topic in a unique way: *The Prestige* by Christopher Nolan (2006).[24] This movie is about two rival magicians, or more precisely: two people who professionally perform magic tricks in front of an audience. The central point of the plot is the trick of 'The Transported Man' – a trick that one of them does better than the other, whereupon the latter seeks out the inventor Nicola Tesla. Tesla is supposed to build a machine for the purpose of performing 'The Transported Man' better than his rival. He succeeds, but at a horrible price. The machine Tesla built doubles the object or person inside it, so that an identical clone is created.

In the movie this is shown on the one hand in a scene in which a mountain slope is full of hats (see Figure 40). And it is always the same hat, doubled by the machine. Even though this may not be the intention, the motif of (identical) industrial mass production is used here. On the other hand, the machine is used to perform a magical trick to transport a person from A to B, or at least for the eyes of the audience. But here too, an identical twin is created: the man who disappears and the man who reappears. But one of them has to die every time the machine is used.

Figure 40. Reproduced top hats in *The Prestige*, dir. Christopher Nolan (Touchstone Pictures et al., 2006).

24   *The Prestige*, dir. Christopher Nolan (Touchstone Pictures et al., 2006).

This example also underlines the closeness between magic and technology – this time relating to serial mass production. While the one magician 'really' does the trick in collaborating with his twin brother, the other does it by technologically cloning himself: again, this can be read as the conflict between human labour and its technological substitution. But in *The Prestige*, in the end, the magician who does it with human work wins over that magician who does the trick with advanced technology. This might even be read as a reflexive critique of illusionist technologies, like the cinema, which made the work of magicians in a way obsolete, due to their immersive and illusionistic possibilities. In *The Prestige* we are reminded of the role of human imagination, even sacrifice that is necessary to produce good illusions. Magic can be hard labour itself. But what the movie also does is to raise the question of original and copy in the motif of serial mass production. A question that runs through the entire film – thus, also calling up Benjamin's analysis of the age of technical reproducibility and the loss of aura.[25] By copying himself technologically the 'bad magician' disrupts the aura of the magic trick. As all these examples show: magic is in many ways interwoven with the question of labour, as is technology.

---

25   See Walter Benjamin, *The Work of Art in the Age of Mechanical Reproduction* (London: Penguin, 2008).

Stephanie Weber

Ray Bradbury's 'The Illustrated Man' (1950)

The history of tattoos and tattooing in a Western context is still associated with 'the other', with eighteenth-century voyages of discovery as well as lower classes and subcultures like sailors, criminals, circus performers, or prostitutes. The practice of altering and adorning the body, however, dates back to ancient times and cultures. While it is possible that tattooing was also considered an act of beautification, the reason for pricking, poking, or stitching the skin was very often a spiritual, religious, or even medical one. Tattoos and their motifs were used to ward off evil spirits and enemies, protect their wearers and anchor their souls to their bodies, establish a connection to ancestors, heal the sick body from ailments, and mark a transitional time or rite of passage.[1] Nowadays, tattoos and body modifications have entered fashion and left their mark on popular culture, yet there is still something magical about them. Fictional narrations of tattoos being inscribed onto bodies as magical symbols not only showcase how characters can be turned into living books of magic, but also demonstrate how the tattoos themselves are treated like magical tokens or talismans that may even come to life to protect or warn their wearers. In some cases, however, their agential power is linked to black magic. In these cases, the tattoos become a curse, since they do not only act independently, but uncontrollably, eventually overpowering

---

1   Lars Krutak, *Spiritual Skin: Magical Tattoos and Scarification. Wisdom, Healing, Shamanic Power, Protection* (Aschaffenburg: Edition Reuss, 2012); Margo DeMello, *Bodies of Inscription* (Durham, NC: Duke University Press, 2000), 146.

the wearer.[2] Ray Bradbury's short story 'The Illustrated Man' (1950) is such a case of magical tattooing which turns fatal. William Philippus Phelps, the protagonist, decides to become a tattooed man after he loses his job at a carnival and learns of a special tattoo artist. This artist, an old, blind woman, tattoos his skin with monsters and animals, placing two special tattoos on his chest and back. These tattoos, she explains, are to be finished by his own sweat and thoughts, and must not be looked at until the time is right, since they will reveal his future. The tattoo on his chest, which is the first one to be publicly revealed as Mr Phelps steps in front of an audience in his new role as an illustrated man, shows how he murders his wife. After fulfilling the first tattoo's prophecy, he is chased out of town and beaten to death by the other circus performers, a scene which becomes visible in his back tattoo as it is posthumously revealed.

In this chapter, I will look at the history and tradition of magical tattooing, as well as the ability that tattoos have to tell stories and alter the identity of their wearer, in order to analyse Bradbury's 'Illustrated Man' and his indelibly inked magic.

How Tattoos Tell Stories

Getting tattooed is considered a very personal choice and the reason behind modifying the body varies from signs of resistance to signs of community, from honouring loved ones to honouring memorable events. It is not surprising, then, that tattoos are often compared to diary entries written on the body. Together, these individual marks, each telling a small story, are plotted into the story of the wearer's life.[3] Tattoos help to mark and maintain memory

---

2   Stephanie Weber, ' "So Much Magic on Your Flesh": The Ma(r)king of Selves in the TV Series Salem', in Sinah Theres Kloß, ed., *Tattoo Histories. Transcultural Perspectives on the Narratives, Practices, and Representations of Tattooing* (New York, London: Routledge, 2020), 118–35.

3   Atte Oksanen, and Jussi Turtiainen, 'A Life Told in Ink: Tattoo Narratives and the Problem of the Self in Late Modern Society', *Auto/Biography* 13/2 (2005), 111–30, 114.

and raise awareness of the corporeality of existence.[4] This makes them not only powerful as a site of discourse,[5] but, like all forms of body modification, they can have a therapeutic character. According to Enid Schildkrout, tattooing, branding and piercing 'inevitably involve subjects who experience pain, pass through various kinds of ritual death and rebirth, and redefine the relationship between self and society through the skin'.[6] This narrative quality of real-life tattoos and the way they tell stories is turned literal in fictional accounts of tattooing and tattoos, especially in speculative fiction featuring magical tattoos. Not only does Bradbury rewrite these tattoo narratives, he also distinguishes between ordinary tattoos and magical 'Skin Illustrations' by giving the latter an active role in the production of the story, along with the ability to change form and shape.[7] The difference between a tattooed man and an illustrated man lies on the one hand in the quality of the tattoos – the Illustrated Man's body art is announced as being 'greater than Michelangelo'[8] – and on the other, in the origin of the word 'illustration' itself, meaning 'manifestation', 'spiritual illumination', or making something clear by help of an image.[9] Skin, our outer appearance, is not only the place of the first contact with the outer world and the boundary of self, it is also, as Terence Turner suggests, the symbolic stage for the drama of socialization; its marking becoming the language through which this drama is staged.[10] Tattoos allow one to 'write oneself' and to 'be read by others'.[11] This dramatization is picked up in fiction. As Peter Brooks argues, modern

4   Mary Kosut, 'Tattoo Narratives: The Intersection of the Body, Self-Identity and Society', *Visual Sociology* 15/1 (2000), 79–100, 94, 97.

5   DeMello, *Bodies of Inscription*, 12.

6   Enid Schildkrout, 'Inscribing the Body', *Annual Review of Anthropology* 33/1 (2004), 319–44, 320.

7   Bradbury also writes about Skin Illustrations and illustrated characters in his short story collection *The Illustrated Man* and the novel *Something Wicked This Way Comes*.

8   Ray Bradbury, 'The Illustrated Man', *Esquire* (1950), <https://classic.esquire.com/article/1950/7/1/the-illustrated-man>, accessed 15 August 2020.

9   'illustration (n.)', *Online Etymology Dictionary*, <https://www.etymonline.com/word/illustration>, accessed 9 September 2020.

10   Terence Turner, 'The Social Skin', *HAU: Journal of Ethnographic Theory* 2/2 (2012), 486–504, 486.

11   DeMello, *Bodies of Inscription*, 12.

narratives take place more and more on the body as a site and locus of meaning. The body is then no longer simply a participant but 'it carries the burden of significance of a story'.[12] In the case of magical tattooing in 'The Illustrated Man', however, this process of 'writing oneself' is counteracted, as the tattoos illustrate someone else's magical capabilities and are thus not a sign of the protagonist's self-expression.

Magical Tattoos

The art of magical tattooing was (and still is) practised by nearly all indigenous people,[13] and even the Greeks and Romans tattooed for spiritual and mythical reasons.[14] Archaeological findings even suggest that tattooing as a form of sympathetic magic dates back to the Bronze Age, where symbols were applied to injured or diseased body parts in order to cure their wearers of their ailments.[15] The basis of magical tattooing, argues Lars Krutak, often lies upon the belief in a fundamental spiritual essence and life force, which is shared by humans, animals and all objects in the universe alike.[16] Tattoos were viewed as 'magical mediators between this world and the next that are capable of channelling powerful cosmic forces that transcend nature, the mind, body, and soul'.[17] The magical tattoos were themselves charged with

12   Peter Brook, *Body Work* (Cambridge, MA: Harvard University Press, 1993), 38, 54.

13   Krutak, *Spiritual Skin*, 8; Lars Krutak, 'Shamanic Skin: The Art of Magical Tattoos', *Lars Krutak. Tattoo Anthropologist* (2013), <http://www.larskrutak.com/shamanic-skin-the-art-of-magical-tattoos>, accessed 15 August 2020.

14   John A. Rush, *Spiritual Tattoos. A Cultural History of Tattooing, Piercing, Scarification, Branding, and Implants* (Berkeley, CA: Frog Ltd, 2005), 37.

15   Natalia I. Shishlina, E. V. Belkevich, and A. N. Usachuk, 'Bronze Age Tattoos: Sympathetic Magic or Decoration?', in Philippe Della Casa and Constanze Witt, eds, *Tattoos and Body Modification in Antiquity. Proceedings of the Sessions at the EAA Annual Meeting on The Hague and Oslo, 2010/11* (Zürich: Chronos Verlag, 2013), 67–74, 71.

16   Krutak, *Spiritual Skin*, 8.

17   Ibid., 12.

Magical Tattoos

supernatural power, and the sympathetic magic of the inked symbols was thus embodied and turned corporeal. They were believed to assist their wearer in hunting, in combat, provide protection, heal or even function as love charms.[18] Human life and destiny could be influenced through the tattoos. The tattooists often either held a religious position themselves or were assisted by a religious or spiritual practitioner like a shaman, priest, or monk, or guided by spirits or patron deities.[19] Bradbury's Illustrated Man is tattooed by a woman who holds magical powers, and who imbues the tattoos with her powers as well. She is, however, not a practitioner of pagan, natural spirituality, but of black magic, and resembles a fairy-tale witch. She alters the bodies and possibly the souls of the people she marks. Historically speaking, the connection between tattoos or skin markings and dark forces is not an arbitrary one: during the times of the witch trials in the Western World, witches were recognized through a 'witch mark' or 'devil's mark' and it was even believed that the devil himself 'tattooed' this mark onto his servants' bodies.[20] The woman who tattoos Mr Phelps is not only ancient, but all of her senses and sensory organs, except for her mouth, are stitched and sealed shut. Even though she cannot see him, she knows who he is and tells him she has been expecting him for fifty years. As proof, she shows him his portrait tattooed on her hand. Her knowledge and her magical powers manifest on her skin, and this seemingly impossible ink helps her to convince Mr Phelps to let her tattoo him, claiming the act will transfer her knowledge onto his flesh as well.

> 'I know the Deep Past and the Clear Present and the even Deeper Future', she whispered, eyes knotted into blindness, face lifted to this unseen man. 'It is on my flesh. I will paint it on yours, too. You will be the only *real* Illustrated Man in the universe. I'll give you special pictures you will never forget. Pictures of the Future on your skin.'[21]

18   Ibid., 8, 70.
19   Ibid., 8.
20   S. W. McDonald, 'The Devil's Mark and the Witch-Prickers of Scotland', *Journal of the Royal Society of Medicine* 90/9 (1997), 507–11, 508; Wilfrid Dyson Hambly, *The History of Tattooing* (Mineola, NY: Dover Publications, 2009), 45, 77; Margaret Murray, *The Witch-Cult in Western Europe* (Oxford: At the Clarendon Press, 1921), 79.
21   Bradbury, 'The Illustrated Man' (italics in original).

She covers his entire body with animals and mythical creatures, a process described as 'being bitten by a silver snake'.[22] It thus seems like the tattooist's hands are guided by a higher power, enabling her to see while being blind, and to control forces Mr Phelps is neither able to understand nor to rule. He is covered by tattoos that seem to come to life, yet the real magic is poked into his skin on his back and chest with the two special, unfinished tattoos he is not yet allowed to look at.

> Later, you may look. The Future is in these pictures. You can't look now or it may spoil them. They are not quite finished. I put ink on your flesh and the sweat of you forms the rest of the picture, the Future – your sweat and your thought.[23]

In magical, pagan, or spiritual tattooing, the use of secret ingredients, incantations, prayers or spells is a common practice.[24] The secret ingredient in this case seemingly comes from within himself. While spiritual tattoos relate to and are influenced by the wearer's inner life and spirit, and create spiritual armour,[25] they do not guard the Illustrated Man. His deepest, darkest desires will be revealed and seal his fate. During a fight, in which he later kills his wife, he is suddenly unsure if the old woman or if he himself formed the tattoo. He becomes uncertain of his own intentions: 'Do I really want her dead? No! And yet ...'[26] While indigenous tattooing as initiation rites or for medical purposes aimed to anchor someone's soul to their body,[27] the Skin Illustrations of the Illustrated Man led to a loss of his soul to dark forces. No real artist/client or master/student connection is established between himself and the tattooist, and since Mr Phelps does not know how to control his tattoos and their powers, the tattooist's magical abilities are not passed onto him. On the contrary, the act serves the purpose of demonstrating her powers and wit, which she accepts as payment from Mr Phelps:

22   Ibid.
23   Ibid.
24   Krutak, *Spiritual Skin*, 12, 14, 16.
25   Maureen Trudelle Schwarz, 'Native American Tattoos: Identity and Spirituality in Contemporary America', *Visual Anthropology* 19/3–4 (2006), 223–54, 224, 228.
26   Bradbury, 'The Illustrated Man' (italics in original).
27   Krutak, *Spiritual Skin*, 140–2; Krutak, 'Shamanic Skin'.

If you walk with these pictures on you, I will be repaid with my own satisfaction. I will sit here for the next two weeks and think how clever my pictures are, for I make them to fit each man himself and what is inside him. Now, walk out of this house and never come back. Good-by.[28]

The tattoos even transcend the body of the Illustrated Man, as they influence not only his life and story, but blend into the fate of the people who look at them. After the first disastrous unveiling of the chest tattoo, which leaves the audience shocked, the ringmaster takes off the adhesive on the back prematurely and what he sees is only a patch of naked skin. The magical illustrations are too clever to reveal their secret before they want to. Only when Mr Phelps is dead, and the mob who killed him removes the cover, does the tattoo become visible, showing a group of artists bending over a dead, obese man with a tattoo on his back, depicting the scene over and over in an uncanny mise en abyme. The tattoo shows their fate as much as it does its wearer's. The tattooist's magical powers in the end control not only the people she tattoos, but all aspects of their lives and stories. The ritual death and rebirth, symbolized in the tattooing process, leads Mr Phelps onto a dark path which inevitably ends in physical death. Instead of marking a transitional time in his life and assisting in developing and controlling a coherent identity, his identity is magically generated, violently altered and stolen by the tattooing 'witch'. The drama which is acted out on his body by the Skin Illustrations overpowers him, and he is nothing but a blank canvas for her rituals and magic. Bradbury's short story thus rewrites the narrative function and corporeal magic of tattoos as signs of self-augmentation by transferring them into the domain of witchcraft and black magic.

28   Bradbury, 'The Illustrated Man'.

Dunja Haufe

Charles Foster's *Being a Beast* (2016)

The shapeshifter[1] takes a middle position on the human-animal continuum, which commonly defines humanness and the human being 'as what is *not* animal'.[2] Modern stances on human-animal relationships, however, call this rigid division into question, especially after the 'animal turn' and the emergence of animal studies in recent years. The shapeshifter, a being that 'belongs both to the world of humans and of beasts,'[3] can be considered a link between animals and humans. Shapeshifters not only oscillate between human and animal, but also between culture and nature, the natural and the supernatural, the known and the unknown. It is due to this liminality and consequent unpredictability that shapeshifters are often perceived as a threat: they undermine the normative assumptions of rigid species categories, they 'contest cultural categories of "normality" '[4] and emphasize the instability of the supposedly fixed body. By challenging the status quo, however, they also represent a chance to gain a new and better understanding of the animal other. This article aims to analyse how the figure of the shapeshifter can be utilized to explore the relationship

---

1   This article will only analyse the shapeshifter as a being that oscillates between a human and an animal form.

2   Margo DeMello, *Animals and Society: An Introduction to Human-Animal Studies* (New York: Columbia University Press, 2012), 15.

3   Miranda Aldhouse-Green, and Stephen Aldhouse-Green, *The Quest for the Shaman: Shape-Shifters, Sorcerers and Spirit-Healers of Ancient Europe* (London: Thames & Hudson, 2005), 172.

4   Dana Oswald, *Monsters, Gender and Sexuality in Medieval English Literature* (Woodbridge: D. S. Brewer, 2010), 7.

between animals and humans by drawing on Charles Foster's work *Being a Beast*.

Foster, a veterinarian-turned-author, attempts to answer the question of what it would be like to be a badger, a fox, an otter, a deer, or a swift, by adopting the lifestyle of the respective animal. Breaking with the tradition of restricting the supernatural to genres such as fantasy and sci-fi, Foster chooses to move shapeshifting to the real world and to experience such transformative modes of magic for himself. In his unconventional non-fictional approach, he takes the argument that 'biologically speaking, humans *are* animals,'[5] for example, in terms of a shared method of data transmission – 'the buzzing of our neurones'[6] – as the base to his endeavour. Foster concludes that '[t]he animals and I speak a shared language [... which] I can slowly learn.'[7] This 'shared language' can also be interpreted in more abstract terms as a deeper connection to or understanding of one's environment. An example for such a worldview can be found in shamanic societies and the figure of the shaman in particular. Foster picks up on this and combines the shamans' role as 'intermediaries between the human and [the] non-human'[8] with scientific perspectives, as well as a specific shapeshifter identity. I will argue that by doing so, he extends the traditional, purely physical, notion of the shapeshifter, which eventually results in a (partial) deconstruction of the human-animal dichotomy.

Traditionally, shapeshifters are defined as beings that can transform their physical form. Foster's desire to understand the animal other, however, goes beyond this purely body-oriented definition, since 'understanding another mind [...] mean[s] seeing with another's eyes [... thus it] implie[s] experience, and individualized experience at that.'[9] This form of becoming an animal cannot be achieved through a mere physical change. In fact, it exposes the traditional

5   DeMello, *Animals and Society*, 15.
6   Charles Foster, *Being a Beast* (London: Profile Books, 2016), 18. From here on called '*Beast*'.
7   Foster, *Beast*, 18–19.
8   James Endredy, *Shamanism: For Beginners: Walking with the World's Healers of Earth and Sky* (Woodbury: Llewellyn Publications, 2009), 5.
9   Lorraine Daston, 'Intelligences: Angelic, Animal, Human', in Lorraine Daston and Gregg Mitman, eds, *Thinking with Animals: New Perspectives on Anthropomorphism* (New York: Columbia University Press, 2005), 37–58, 53.

notion of the shapeshifter as being incomplete because it neglects the possibility of a mental transformation. Foster deduces that 'you don't start with an
idea. In the beginning was the deed. [...] You've got to scratch, scratch, scratch
the world with the same paw or wing movements as the creatures you long to
know.'[10] Thus, in order to 'scratch the world', he puts unprecedented emphasis
on the concept of identity to gain direct experiences of what it is like to be an
animal. This combination of physical and mental elements of shapeshifting
allows Foster to accomplish what Daston and Mitman call thinking with animals, that is, 'thinking about what it would *be* like to be that animal'.[11] As the
major source material for such a mental framework and the consequent specific
liminal identity, Foster employs shamanism and basic shamanic ontological
systems. In fact, during his experiment, he adopts the role of the shaman and
their concomitant in-between position. Only afterwards does he attempt to
transform and become a shapeshifter.

Shamanism has been a part of human societies around the globe for centuries and can be loosely defined as 'a set of practices and understandings concerning the cosmos, spirits, and human needs.'[12] Here, a careful connection
to magic is suggested – a delicate subject, especially in Western discourses,
since in the past, this link has been used to devalue shamanism as a religious
denomination. The significant changes this view underwent in the last decades can partially be traced back to a more positive attitude towards magic in
general, which is now '[a]ny attempt to control or affect the physical world
or the human psyche that does not conform to modern scientific principles'.[13]
It is a manipulation of 'supernatural or natural forces by anything other than
direct, physical means, [... thus, even] religion may better be conceived as a
subcategory of magic'.[14] This definition equips magic with a more neutral
connotation and abolishes its previous position as evidence for the supposed

---

10   Foster, *Beast*, 204.

11   Lorraine Daston, and Gregg Mitman, 'Introduction', in Lorraine Daston and Gregg
     Mitman, eds, *Thinking with Animals*, 1–14, 10.

12   Thomas DuBois, *An Introduction to Shamanism* (Cambridge: Cambridge University
     Press, 2009), 6.

13   Michael D. Bailey, *Magic and Superstition in Europe: A Concise History from Antiquity
     to the Present* (Lanham, MD: Rowman & Littlefield Publishers, 2007), 2.

14   Ibid., 12.

falseness of a minority religion such as shamanism. It must be noted further that shamanism should be considered an umbrella term for multiple concepts and practices rather than one consistent and absolute idea, since '[n]o pure version of shamanic practice [...] exists. Searches for a "First Shaman" [...] are equally unproductive.'[15] Nonetheless, there are some common aspects that can be traced in most communities that practise shamanism.[16]

One key feature is the idea of interconnectivity. Within the animist conception of shamanism, everything, from living beings to stones and even the elements, is infused with spirits whose interactions with each other make the world function. The shaman uses their position as intermediary to exert (scientifically unexplainable) power over this (super)natural environment. In fact, navigating this system of interdependency and negotiating with spirits is a '[basic] responsibilit[y] associated with traditional shamanism'.[17] Foster picks up on this system, for example, when he runs through the woods attempting to escape a dog that is hunting him: 'The wood was still maddeningly leisurely, but it wasn't out to get me. Everything seemed to have a voice, and now the voices were, by and large, sympathetic.'[18] Here, not only is nature anthropomorphized through attributes such as sympathetic, leisurely and non-aggressive, but also the 'voices', or the spirits, of the surrounding flora become comprehensible, and even seem to offer their help to Foster, who takes on the role of a shaman.

Probably the best-known shamanic element is the spirit helper, who acts as a shaman's supernatural guide and/or guardian. Such spirits can assume many different forms, frequently also those of animals. One straightforward example for spirit animals in Foster's case are the urban foxes, whom the veterinarian, 'still blind, deaf and anosmic, [... starts to follow]. Eventually they

---

15   Marjorie   Mandelstam   Balzer,   *Shamans,   Spirituality,   and   Cultural Revitalization: Explorations in Siberia and Beyond* (Basingstoke: Palgrave Macmillan, 2011), 218.

16   It must be noted that the features discussed here form only a short list intended to facilitate working with the general concept of shapeshifting and that are applicable to Foster's work. This list should by no means be taken as representative for a complete analysis of shamanism.

17   Aldhouse-Green, *The Quest for the Shaman*, 173.

18   Foster, *Beast*, 157.

t[ake] [his] collar between their teeth and sw[i]m with [him] to four islands.'[19] Once again, Foster adopts the position of a shaman who is guided by his animal spirits to magical locations that seem to exist outside of the ordinary human world since they can only be seen with one's nose and from a lowered position.

The presence of guiding or helping spirits implies another important aspect of shamanic cosmology: the existence of other (spirit) worlds, which the shaman can access. This act of travelling, of crossing the border between worlds, highlights the shaman's position as a 'crucial mediating figure [... who] bridges the gulf between [...] the generally known and the largely unknown,'[20] between the natural and the magical. Moreover, the shaman's affiliation with spirits and, in turn, the spirits' association with animals, then identifies the shaman not only as a mediator between the human and the spiritual, but also between the human and the animal realm. Foster, for instance, realizes that '[t]hose foxes have the ability to connect to me, and I to them.'[21]

Shamans are also able to transform themselves: some accounts tell of physical/bodily shapeshifting, others refer to shaman doubles. The latter represents a transformation into an animal that takes place on the level of the soul, meaning that the shaman's soul either enters the body of an animal in the real world – thus effectively merging with it and becoming the animal in question – or their soul enters the spirit realm in which it takes on the form of the shaman's spirit animal and travels in this shape through the other world. When the beliefs refer to the former, to physical/bodily shapeshifting, the shaman's transformation is often connected to the usage of animal parts such as skins, horns, or antlers. With them, the shaman carries out what Judith Butler calls performativity and performs the animal identity to the point that they *become* the animal. Performativity, according to Butler, is constitutive of (gender) identities that, as social constructs, can either support or disrupt cultural norms and assumptions. Similarly, the shaman, by wearing pelts and horns of their chosen animal and performing its identity, challenges presumed natural boundaries; only it is the category species (human/animal) instead of gender (male/female) that is destabilized. By adopting the animal's identity through repetitive, deliberate and ritualistic performances, some shamans (partially)

---

19   Ibid., 125.
20   DuBois, *An Introduction to Shamanism*, 82.
21   Foster, *Beast*, 122.

cross the seemingly rigid species line and ultimately *become* the animal itself on a physical level as well: they shapeshift.

The notion of performing an identity to trigger a physical change goes hand in hand with Foster's conviction that for successful shapeshifting, direct experiences of what it means to be the other is indispensable. He describes the process of (shamanic) shapeshifting as follows:

> [Y]ou had to insist [...] on the reality of shared ancestry. You had to dance to the drum around a fire until you were so dehydrated that blood spouted out of your ruptured nasal capillaries, or stand in an icy river and chant until you could feel your soul rising like vomit into your mouth [...]. Then you could pass through the thin membrane that separates this world from others, and your species from other species. [...] From it you emerged as a wolf or a wildebeest.[22]

The auditory experience of hearing 'the drum', the haptic experience of feeling the 'icy river', and the simultaneous, continuous 'chant' accompanying and heightening these experiences – all these are required, according to Foster, to ultimately transform and 'emerge' as an animal. To put it simply, Foster first takes on the role of a shaman by, for instance, listening to the surrounding flora's voices and following the guidance of foxes, that is, by accepting and enacting a general ontological system of shamanism. Afterwards, Foster starts performing the animal's identity by immersing himself in a new environment and adopting said animal's behaviour pattern until his performance becomes automatic and naturalized. In some cases of his experiment, this leads to his successful act of shapeshifting. To become another being, to shift one's form, therefore entails more than the purely physical transformation of the body. It includes what Daston and Mitman term an 'extreme form of thinking with animals [... which expresses the] irresistible desire to jump out of one's own skin, exchange one's brain, [and] plunge into another way of being.'[23]

Foster, for instance, practises this extreme form of thinking with animals when he lives as a badger in the forest and gets 'callouses where it [is] good to get them; [and his] legs lear[n] to stretch to slide easily over a fallen beech'[24] due to his animalistic locomotion. In other words, his physical change is a

---

22   Ibid., 3.
23   Daston, and Mitman, 'Introduction', 8.
24   Foster, *Beast*, 65.

direct result of him moving like a badger and performing the animal's identity. A second example takes place during Foster's time as a fox in London, when he comes across small areas where he encounters specific scents through the 'eyes, ears, noses and feet' of the foxes.[25] However, this sensory experience is not so much due to a shared ancestry between foxes and humans, but rather a result of Foster behaving similarly to his guiding spirit. The 'fox islands' are not 'visible from more than two feet above the ground [... and can] be seen only with the nose';[26] therefore, the experiences described by Foster can only happen because he enacts the role of a fox and smells the ground. It is his successful performance of the badger and fox identities that leads to his physical enhancement and ultimately allows him to gain experiences that he would not have been able to undergo otherwise. In other words, the result of this performance is an act of shapeshifting that expands the traditional conception of a purely physical change.

Throughout his project to examine the liminal position of the shapeshifter, Foster also takes shapeshifting identities into account, which can lead to a more thorough understanding of the animal other. To achieve the liminality of the shapeshifter's identity, Foster performs this identity on a bodily/sensual as well as on a mental level. Here, the shaman's position as a mediator between human and (magical) non-human worlds and entities is employed as an intermediate stage in Foster's approach towards the animal other. In addition to the introduction of a new definition of shapeshifters, Foster also manages to provide a framework for their in-depth analysis that combines scientifically and culturally based methods. As a result, he not only sheds new light on this (supposedly) fantastic cultural figure that is still 'a source of ongoing controversy regarding the question of establishing valid distinctions between people and animals',[27] but also partially breaks down the binary of magic and science, thus questioning one fundamental pillar of our perception of reality. In this regard, Foster's experiment is vital as a helpful tool to continue the exploration of the shapeshifter as well as the topic of magic as it is understood in our modern world.

25   Ibid., 126.
26   Ibid.
27   Elizabeth Lawrence, 'Werewolves in Psyche and Cinema: Man-Beast Transformation and Paradox', *Journal of American Culture* 19/3 (1996), 103–12, 111.

Part VI

Magic and Resistance

Marie Barras

J. W. Waterhouse's *The Magic Circle* (1886)

Painted in 1886 by John William Waterhouse, *The Magic Circle* (see Figure 41) is one artwork amongst many others which shows that, although witch-hunts were long gone in Europe by then, the production of representations of sorceresses did not stop. Scholars have only mentioned the existence of these paintings without thoroughly analysing them as a complex corpus through the prism of their context. This lack of comprehensive analysis results in a void in our knowledge of both the late Victorian era and the iconography of sorcery. The following study of *The Magic Circle* seeks to answer two broad questions: what social interrogations do the representations of sorceresses address? And how do these images enlighten the dynamics of gender and power in the Victorian era? A theoretical framework using interdisciplinary tools is thus necessary, considering the artwork as a discourse employed 'not only for the replication of established social forms [...], but more broadly also for the construction, deconstruction of society itself'.[1] Moreover, using Michael Baxandall's period eye methodology,[2] this study will identify some of the cognitive tools that allowed the Victorian[3] to recognize the magicians as such. Indeed, when confronted with an artwork representing a sorceress,

1   Bruce Lincoln, *Discourse and the Construction of Society: Comparative Studies of Myth, Ritual, and Classification* (New York: Oxford University Press, 2014), 1.

2   Michael Baxandall, *Painting and Experience in Fifteenth Century Italy: A Primer in the Social History of Pictorial Style* (Oxford: Clarendon, 1988 [1972]).

3   The majority of the Royal Academy's public was masculine, as shown in William Powell Frith's *A Private View at the Royal Academy 1881* (1883): the women either accompany a man, are seated and passive or are watched by or looking at one of them. Consequently, the artworks in general are calibrated to appeal to the ruling class, namely the educated man.

the spectator had to replace in his 'cognitive style'[4] the two elements implicitly contained in the word *sorceress*, that is to say *woman* and *magic*.

The iconography of witchcraft emerged mainly during the witch-hunts, responding to contemporary fears. The representations[5] are closely linked with the devil, depicting horrifying Sabbath scenes. However, in the nineteenth century, magicians were no longer painted with the use of the same Christian intertext. After the last execution for the crime of witchcraft in Europe (Anna Göldi in 1782), the belief in witchcraft slowly faded away. In the second half of the nineteenth century, magic was romanticized, thanks in particular to Jules Michelet's writings in *La Sorcière* (1862). The witch-hunts were progressively seen as persecutions against women. As the suffragette Matilda Joslyn Gage wrote in 1893: 'When for "witches" we read "women", we gain fuller comprehension of the cruelties inflicted by the church upon this portion of humanity.'[6] These examples are part of a paradigm shift in the reception of the figure of the witch, which is also observable in the visual arts: young and powerful sorceresses gradually invest the territory until then reserved for old satanic witches.

In the Victorian era, witches' pyres were part of the past. However, magic persisted, manifesting itself through pictorial representations of sorceresses, such as Frederick Sandys' *Medea* (1866–8), Edward Burne-Jones' *The Beguiling of Merlin* (1872–7), John Collier's *An Incantation* (1887) or Evelyn De Morgan's *The Love Potion* (1903). These representations of magicians show powerful and subversive women embodying a femininity that defies the prevailing ideal, particularly in their personification of a radical otherness in relation to the dominant class – the English educated white man. These representations were subversive both because of their ambiguous character and the discourses they conveyed, which are linked to two contemporary phenomena: the birth of anthropology and the questioning of the feminine ideal. The figure of the magician embodied thus a double otherness: colonial and gendered.

4   According to Baxandall, the visual perception depends both on the context and on one's cognitive style, defined as 'the interpreting skills one happens to possess, the categories, the model patterns and the habits of inference and analogy'. Baxandall, *Painting and Experience in Fifteenth Century Italy*, 29–30.

5   To read more about the representations created at the time of the witch-hunts, see Hannah Segrave's contribution to this volume.

6   Matilda Joslyn Gage, *Woman, Church and State* (New York: Prometheus Books, 2002 [1893]), 278.

Figure 41. J. W. Waterhouse, *The Magic Circle*, 1886. Reproduced with permission from Tate Britain, London.

At the centre of *The Magic Circle*, a young woman gazes at the smoke produced by the cauldron, as if she were expecting to see forms appear in the fumes. Her hand traces an incandescent circle around her, as she seems to be chanting an obscure incantation. Her thick black hair rests on her shoulders and her forehead, shadowing her eyes. Calm and curious, six crows and a green toad observe her, all remaining outside of the circle. The magician's waist is girded by an ochre belt, in which a flower bouquet is slipped, and the bottom of her light blue dress is decorated with antique figures. Behind her, ancient ruins stand on barren cliffs, at the foot of which a cave shelters three figures dimly lit by the flame of a lamp. The sorceress stands tall, in a dynamic and assured movement, certain of the efficiency of her powers. Shortly after his election as Associate Member of the Royal Academy, Waterhouse's participation to the Summer Exhibition in 1886 was significant for the launch of his career. Although the *Magazine of Art* noted that 'the Royal Academy is at its worst', Waterhouse received particularly positive feedback: 'Mr. Waterhouse, in "The Magic Circle", is still at his best – is still original in conception and pictorial in his results.'[7] Moreover, the artwork was directly bought by the Chantrey Bequest[8] in 1886 for the huge sum of 650£, underlining the fact that *The Magic Circle* was one of the most popular pictures.

The late Victorian era witnessed a spiritual renewal,[9] manifested both in a certain puritanism justified by the Christian religion and in heterogeneous research, seeking to combine spirituality and modern rationality. Strong personalities like Aleister Crowley or Helena Blavatsky occupied the centre of attention, whereas 'women's involvement with spiritualism was at one level all about gender expectations, sexual politics, and the subversion of existing power relations between men and women'.[10] This 'esoteric'

7   Anonymous, 'Current Art I', *The Magazine of Art* 9 (June 1886), 345–6.
8   As mentioned on the online notice of the Tate Gallery, <https://www.tate.org.uk/art/artworks/waterhouse-the-magic-circle-n01572>, accessed 2 September 2020. The Chantrey Bequest is administered by the Royal Academy, <https://www.royalacademy.org.uk/art-artists/organisation/chantrey-bequest>, accessed 2 September 2020.
9   Nevill Drury, *Stealing Fire from Heaven: The Rise of Modern Western Magic* (Oxford: Oxford University Press, 2011).
10 Alex Owen, 'Introduction', in *The Darkened Room. Women, Power, and Spiritualism in late Nineteenth Century England* (London: Virago Press, 1989), not paginated.

vogue emerges concurrently with the questions raised by the first feminist movements and the exhibition of pictorial representations of magicians. Given its context of production, it is tempting to qualify *The Magic Circle* as 'occult' or 'mystic', therefore deducing a proximity between its painter and 'esoteric' circles.

A. Lys Baldry in 1895 and Rose Esther Sketchley in 1909 each wrote a monographic article about Waterhouse. Both highlighted his alleged interest in 'mysticism'[11] or 'occultism',[12] but these two concepts are particularly difficult to define precisely. As contemporaries, they might have been able to discuss it directly with him, but neither clearly mentioned it. Moreover, remarkably little documentation remains on the painter himself.[13] Therefore, one can only observe a rapprochement between *The Magic Circle* and a romanticized idea of certain 'occult' practices; it is also reasonable to assume that Waterhouse read the specialized press featuring the latest scientific discoveries and that he had surely heard of certain 'esoteric' practices or spiritualist circles, particularly popular at the time. In the absence of evidence, one must settle for a contemporaneity between an unprecedented spiritual renewal and the production of images representing magicians.

From the 1860s, there arose a new field dedicated to the scientific study of religious practices, aiming to 'treat religion purely as an element in human cultures. This new field was both a response to and a reflection of the sense of religious crisis that troubled so many Victorians.'[14] Indeed, British imperialism led to confrontation with the colonial other. Anthropologists sought to put words on these cultural shocks, using new analytical categories. Non-European cultures were seen as a conservatory of the past: not all have progressed at the same pace, some had remained behind and still practised magic (the 'savages') while the 'civilized', after going through a religious phase, had already reached the upper stage defined by science.

11   A. Lys Baldry, 'J.W. Waterhouse and His Work', *Studio* IV (January 1895), III, 115.

12   Rose Esther Dorothea Sketchley, 'The Art of J.W. Waterhouse, R.A.', Christmas number, *The Art Journal* (1909), 11–15.

13   Peter Trippi, *J.W. Waterhouse* (London: Phaidon, 2002), 4.

14   Marjorie Wheeler-Barclay, *The Science of Religion in Britain, 1860–1915* (Charlottesville: University of Virginia Press, 2010), 2.

Thus, if *The Magic Circle* were to be analysed with anthropological categories, it would show an undeveloped stage. The magician would be absorbed in practices belonging to a primitive state of evolution. As Edward Burnett Tylor argued in 1871: 'Witchcraft is part and parcel of savage life.'[15] Furthermore, the sorceress embodies in Tylor's system a 'survival' defined as: 'processes, customs, opinions, and so forth, which have been carried on [...] into a new state of society [...], and they thus remain as proofs and examples of an older condition of culture'.[16] Here, the magician is represented in the middle of a very minimalist setting – a plain with some cliffs in the background. This locates her in an undetermined area: the sorceress could draw her circle on either side of the ocean, amongst the 'savages' as well as in a British valley, far in the depths of Scotland. The magician is both distant and, on the contrary, strangely close. Moreover, she adopts a determined physical position, whereas if one follows the evolutionary logic, she belongs to a dominated social group whose humility is a central characteristic. She embodies an otherness which is both primitive and feminine, but shows itself in an unexpected, seductive, erudite and powerful way.

The Magic Circle shows an independent woman, with subversive potential, in direct opposition to the Victorian feminine ideal of the turn of the century, often characterized as *The Angel in the House*, according to the title of the poem by Coventry Patmore (1854). During the Victorian era, women were the subject of an ambivalent gaze, between adoration and male domination.[17] A home run by its domestic angel appears as a shelter in the face of adverse social forces. Amongst them, debates on women's rights or the increase of prostitution stirred up public opinion. To guarantee the survival of Victorian society, everyone must therefore fulfil their specific role in the sphere assigned to them. The woman devoutly maintained peace at home; caring for others was her mission. She was the guardian of a serene family life, not seeking identity

---

15   Edward Burnett Tylor, *Primitive Culture*, vol. 1, 2nd edn (London: John Murray, 1873 [1871]), 138.

16   Tylor, *Primitive Culture*, 16.

17   About the separated spheres ideology and women's social roles, see, for example, Lynda Nead, *Myths of Sexuality. Representations of Women in Victorian Britain* (Oxford, New York: Basil Blackwell, 1988).

beyond that of daughter, wife or mother.[18] The man acts in the public sphere, working outside and fulfilling his civic duties.

In the Victorian era, women were subaltern to men and placed their resources at their disposal, just like colonized populations. Moreover, according to Randall Styers, 'Europe was configured as the locus of appropriate forms of masculine autonomy and authority; other racial and cultural groups were portrayed as feminine and denatured'.[19] Simultaneously, evolutionist theories described indigenous people as inferior, thus justifying resource plunder and enslavement. According to Silvia Federici, the feminine and masculine archetypes were increasingly differentiated – each living in his/her own separated sphere – while 'it was established that women were inherently inferior to men [...] and had to be placed under male control'. Federici adds: 'None of the tactics deployed against European women and colonial subjects would have succeeded, had they not been sustained by a campaign of terror'[20] – namely the early modern accusation of witchcraft for women and the threat of extermination and slavery for the natives.

Thus, the figure of the magician is opposed in every way to the Victorian feminine ideal while also echoing an anthropological otherness. Neither mother, sister, daughter, wife, lover, nor prostitute, the sorceress is not defined by any man. She resides mostly outdoors, a territory traditionally reserved to men or 'savages'. She is nulliparous, violating what constitutes the essence of the Victorian ideal – the care of others and the perpetuation of the husband's lineage. She embodies independence, the ability to make her own choices and act on her own behalf, two things impossible for a Victorian woman. Moreover, her hair is loose, far from the 'acceptable' and trendy hairstyles at the time.[21] When she is not walking naked, she is wearing soft dresses, the drapes

---

18   For a striking visual example of the Victorian feminine ideal, see George Elgar Hick's triptych *Woman's Mission*: *Guide of Childhood* (Dunedin Public Art Gallery), *Companion of Manhood* and *Comfort of Old Age* (both in Tate London), 1862–3.

19   Randall G. Styers, *Making Magic: Religion, Magic and Science in the Modern World* (Oxford: Oxford University Press, 2004), 62.

20   Silvia Federici, *Caliban and the Witch: Women, the Body and Primitive Accumulation*, 3rd edn (New York: Autonomedia, 2009 [2004]), 100–2.

21   Galia Ofek, *Representations of Hair in Victorian Literature and Culture* (London: Routledge, 2009).

emphasizing her curves without constraining them[22] – no crinoline or corset, inevitable in Victorian women's clothing. Seductive and fascinating, she can be dangerous too, linking her partially with the *femme fatale* archetype, but 'a *femme* cannot be *fatale* without a male being present',[23] whereas the magician is independent. This emancipation was threatening for the dominant male status, all the more so in view of the emergence of the first feminist movements. Radically opposed to the idealistic *Angel in the House,* the sorceress incarnates a 'demon on the outside'. Her magical powers allow this emancipation; even more since she is dissociated from the Christian intertexts at work during the witch-hunts. She no longer flies to Sabbaths or devours newborn babies. Instead, she stands tall, casting mysterious spells.

Outside of the main mental categories mobilized by the Victorian man to give meaning to an image, *The Magic Circle* neither allows the viewer to summon an intertext to replace the episode in a narration or to simply understand the image independently. The spectator is out of his comfort zone, but he is reassured by the pictorial style in line with the Royal Academy values. Marginal, the magician rises to the edge of categories, instilling a diffuse malaise while directly addressing Victorian societal issues around power relationships and, specifically, the determination of gender roles.

Metaphorically, Victorian paintings of sorceresses are caught in the middle of a spider-web, where every detail can trigger a vibration through a semantic thread, awakening a larger issue. Perhaps a little anecdotal at first glance, stylistically pleasant and conventional, *The Magic Circle* in fact addresses contemporary issues of burning actuality. Through their power of seduction and their knowledge, painted magicians transcend their condition as subordinates. Confusing, they stand at the crossroads and escape any definitive classification: they could gather each characteristic of a definition or show none. Existing at the interstice between categories, they subvert them at will: they are neither goddesses, nor completely human, blurring the boundaries between the

---

22   Rachel Weathers, 'The Pre-Raphaelite Movement and Nineteenth-Century Ladies' Dress: A Study in Victorian Views of the Female Body', in Watson Margaretta Frederick, ed., *Collecting the Pre-Raphaelites: The Anglo-American Enchantment* (Brookfield: Ashgate, 1997), 95–108.

23   Rebecca Stott, *The Fabrication of the Late-Victorian 'femme fatale': The Kiss of Death* (Basingstoke, London: Macmillan, 1994), viii, emphasis in original.

physical and spiritual worlds. Their image is painted at the end of the Victorian era, yet they appear timeless; once the witch-hunts ended, they were neither entirely real nor absolutely imaginary, neither good nor bad. Simultaneously, they are both witnesses and builders of their own context. Unpredictable, they transform themselves according to their epoch, echoing social issues, blazing controversies and crystallizing power relations.

The Sorceress and Victorian Gender Roles

Jessica Gossling

Arthur Machen's *The Hill of Dreams* (1907)

Decadence and alternative religions underwent a parallel revival at the end of the nineteenth century. This 'revolt against positivism', to use historian Henry Stuart Hughes' well-known phrase, was characterized by a fascination with spiritualism and the occult, a vogue for non-Western religions and art, and a turn to magic and neo-paganism.[1] These new-age religions and practices were particularly attractive to decadent writers who developed the Romantic idea of the poet as a mage or prophet, attuned to the occluded and interconnected secrets of the universe, into a more cosmopolitan figure of transgression and aesthetic refinement who finds magic and arcane knowledge in the ordinary world.

The intersection between decadence, magic and the occult is exemplified in many iconic decadent texts, such as Charles Baudelaire's *Les Fleurs du mal* [*The Flowers of Evil*] (1857), Joris-Karl Huysmans's *Là-bas* [*Down There*] (1891), Aleister Crowley's *White Stains* (1898), and Gustav Meyrink's *Das grüne Gesicht* [*The Green Face*] (1916). As well as developing the now stereotypical figure of the dandy occultist, more importantly these works examine the synthesis of the spiritual and the profane in everyday experiences. The correspondence between the supernatural and the mundane is a cornerstone of decadent writing and it is also a central component of the freer forms of magic and mysticism that emerged in the nineteenth century. As Arthur Symons writes in 'The Decadent Movement in Literature' (1893), decadence is not limited by a specific set of beliefs or practices, but is more of a feeling or a spiritual tradition: 'To fix the last fine shade, the quintessence of things; to fix it fleetingly; to be a disembodied voice, and yet the voice of a human soul: that

---

1   Henry Stuart Hughes, *Consciousness and Society: The Reorientation of European Social Thought, 1890–1930* (New York: Random House, 1958), 39.

is the ideal of Decadence.'[2] Symons's definition, which draws on mystical beliefs, indicates the interrelationship of decadence and magic – one does not seem to be able to exist without the other.

Arthur Machen's *The Hill of Dreams* (written between 1895–7 and published in 1907) is an example of this symbiosis. Although there has been a resurgence of interest in Machen in recent years, he is not typically considered decadent and is often considered alongside other proponents of 'weird fiction', such as H. P. Lovecraft and Algernon Blackwood. However, as critics such as Dennis Denisoff have argued, 'Machen's utterly original contribution to British decadence' should not be overlooked.[3] This becomes especially clear in *The Hill of Dreams,* a semi-autobiographical work which follows the development of the protagonist Lucian Taylor, an aspiring writer loosely based on Machen, as he is seduced into an aesthetic magical realm of supernatural creatures, sadomasochistic rituals and bibliophilia. Lucian dedicates his life to the pursuit of beauty through his otherworldly visions, literature, and, finally, a nameless drug.

Machen labelled his novel a '*Robinson Crusoe* of the soul'[4] and his intention was to explore the mystical workings of the mind – its dreams, desires and downfalls. Magical practices and occult rituals become a method of decadent self-expression for Lucian, and his search for more exquisite sensations takes him away from nature and mundane quotidian experiences towards artificiality and the preternatural. 'Magic' and 'decadence' have both been used as pejorative terms, but in Machen's novel they become synonymous with artistic rebellion and revolt against secular authority.

2   Arthur Symons, 'The Decadent Movement in Literature', *Harper's New Monthly Magazine* 87 (November 1893), 858–67; 862.
3   Dennis Denisoff, 'Introduction: Arthur Machen's Chamber of Decadence', in Dennis Denisoff, ed., *Arthur Machen: Decadent and Occult Works* (Cambridge: MHRA, 2018), 1–28; 1.
4   Arthur Machen quoted in Aidan Reynolds and William Charlton, *Arthur Machen* (Oxford: Caermaen Books, 1988), 55.

The Hill of Dreams

Arthur Llewellyn Jones-Machen was born in 1863 in Caerleon, on the outskirts of Newport, South Wales. The beautiful landscape of Gwent, with its associations with Celtic, Roman and medieval history, made a powerful impression on the young Machen and the landscape of his childhood is central to many of his works. In *Far off Things,* an autobiographical work published in 1922, Machen wrote:

> I shall always esteem it as the greatest piece of fortune that has fallen to me, that I was born in that noble, fallen Caerleon-on-Usk. [...] For the older I grow the more firmly am I convinced that anything which I may have accomplished in literature is due to the fact that when my eyes were first opened in earliest childhood they had before them the vision of an enchanted land.[5]

For a child growing up in rural Wales at the end of the nineteenth century, Machen's literary tastes were unusually eclectic and refined. Alongside 'solitude and woods and deep lanes and wonder', books were also a dominant element of his early life.[6] Early Machen scholars, such as Fred Hando, have traced his use of pagan, supernatural and occult themes back to his early reading. When he was 8, for example, Machen was particularly interested by a volume of Charles Dickens's magazine, *Household Words*, in his father's rectory library, which contained a short series of papers on alchemy.[7] In Machen's works, as in his life, it is the amalgamation of landscape and literature that provides an insight into unknown realms and metaphysical experiences.

Underpinning the magical outlook in *The Hill of Dreams* is the idea that the world contains hidden mysteries that are obscured to the uninitiated. For Machen, these mysteries are most closely tied to physical places. Of the seven chapters of the novel, four are set in a semi-fictionalized Caerleon (the border town of Caermaen) and the surrounding countryside, and three in West London. London is perceived as cosmopolitan and contemporary, while Wales

---

5   Arthur Machen, *Far Off Things* (London: Martin Secker, 1922), 8.
6   Ibid., 33.
7   See Fred Hando, *The Pleasant Land of Gwent* (Newport: R. H. Johns Limited, 1949).

is old, sacred and spiritual. It is a pagan place which reveals the hidden powers of the natural world to Lucian on his meditational walks through the countryside. As he describes in the opening chapter, it is an 'occult territory' that has the power to inspire awe as well as terror and horror.[8] The most notable place Lucian encounters is the 'hill of dreams' itself, modelled on the Roman hillfort of Twyn Barlwm (known locally as the 'pimple' or the 'nipple'). It is a place with sensual and sexual connotations. On his first visit, he is lured by a strange fascination and compulsion to the hill, where he removes his clothes and lies naked in a hollow:

> His eyes were fixed and fascinated by the simulacra of the wood, and could not see his hands, and so at last, and suddenly, it seemed, he lay in the sunlight, beautiful with his olive skin, dark haired, dark eyed, the gleaming bodily vision of a strayed faun.
>
> Quick flames now quivered in the substance of his nerves, hints of mysteries, secrets of life passed trembling through his brain, unknown desires stung him.[9]

This is his first real experience of the hidden powers of the natural world outside of his books, and he is both ecstatic and frightened by his experiences. In the Welsh apparitions, Machen conjures up a vision of the beauty of nature in all its horror. Paradoxical states and in-between spaces recur in decadent literature, as spaces that hover on the threshold between one world and the next are creative and uncontained zones that challenge and subvert the notion of borders and boundaries. However, *The Hill of Dreams* evokes liminal spaces in a deeper, more pagan sense. The hill exists on the threshold between real and supernatural plains. It is a magical place, and magic is a liminal practice – an attempt to use the physical body and mind to tune in the unknown world. Also, Lucian is in a liminal situation – not quite a novice but not yet an initiate.

It is in the shadow of this magical hill that Lucian has his erotic encounter with the otherworldly Annie, falling to his knees at her feet while she whispers 'beautiful, wonderful words, that soothed him as a song'.[10] He has no idea what

---

8   Arthur Machen, *The Hill of Dreams*, in Dennis Denisoff, ed., *Arthur Machen: Decadent and Occult Works* (Cambridge: MHRA, 2018), 110–250; 111.

9   Ibid., 120.

10   Ibid., 146.

these words mean but, like an incantation, they bewitch him and inspire the arcane devotional practices described in Chapter 3. Annie is transformed by Lucian into 'the symbol of all mystic womanhood' and his secret vigils verge on occult practices.[11] The female body becomes his religion and her corporeality is imbued in his magical book of carefully illuminated text. This book is a reliquary for his desires and the focus of his devotional self-abasement. He describes himself prostrate before it, 'rejoicing as a Templar before the image of Baphomet', a pagan idol who was adopted and popularized as a figure of Satanic worship by Aleister Crowley.[12] In this part of the novel a crossover is suggested – from natural pagan worship to decadent occult rituals.

That Terrible Manuscript

Books are an obsession for Lucian, as they were for Machen, and like a sorcerer's apprentice in the occult tradition, he develops his magical practice through literature. Bibliophila is not a new obsession in decadent writing. Notably, in Huysmans's quintessential decadent novel *À rebours* [*Against Nature*] (1884), Duc Jean Des Esseintes surrounds himself with an extensive collection of arcane and occult texts, and in Oscar Wilde's *The Picture of Dorian Gray* (1890–1) it is the receipt of the 'yellow book' from Lord Henry that prompts Dorian's moral and spiritual downfall. In Machen's novel, however, the magical book is more than a collectors' curio or a source of inspiration for depravity. Writing, for Lucian, is a form of spell-making.

Through the creation of his devotional text to Annie in the third chapter of the novel, Lucian develops his magical practice and expresses his decadent tastes. Writing is torturous and intolerable, yet also an exciting and titillating process, and this is amplified into a sadomasochistic act when Lucian creates a book that becomes, literally, a fetish.

11   Ibid., 235.
12   Ibid., 159.

[T]aking off his nightgown, [he] gently lay himself down on the bed of thorns and spines. Lying on his face, with the candle and the book before him, he would softly and tenderly repeat the praises of his dear, dear Annie, and as he turned over page after page, and saw the raised gold of the majuscules glow and flame in the candle-light, he pressed the thorns into his flesh. At such moments he tasted in all its acute savour the joy of physical pain; and after two or three experiences of such delights he altered his book, making a curious sign in vermilion on the margin of the passages where he was to inflict on himself this sweet torture.[13]

This description of Lucian's 'nightly devotions' clearly contains some of the key tropes of decadent writing, such as the perverse beauty of the book with its golden lettering marked with blood and the intersensory relationship between taste, touch and sight. However, his secret ritual is also an example of ceremonial magic, in which ritual tools are used as an extension of the body.[14] Each tool has its own symbolic significance and particular use, and in this novel the book is the object through which Lucian makes manifest his decadent desire to both create and be consumed by beauty. Later in the novel, when he moves to London and finds himself 'strengthened by the change from the hills to the streets',[15] the overtly sexual aspects of his devotion to writing decline but his quest for 'magic [...] that quality that gives to words something beyond their sound and beyond their meaning' remains.[16]

Machen outlines his ideas about the relationship between magic and literature in his essay 'The Literature of Occultism' (1899). While there is a magical quality to all 'fine literature', he argues, there is a particular type of writing 'which is occult in a more special sense, which either undertakes to explain and comment on the secrets of a man's life. Or is explicitly founded on mysterious beliefs of one kind or another.'[17] In *The Hill of Dreams* Machen makes a conscious effort to develop this new prose style, but like Lucian's

---

13   Ibid., 194.
14   For more details about the use of tools in magical ceremonies and rituals, see Arthur Edward Waite, *The Book of Ceremonial Magic: Including the Rites and Mysteries of Goetic Theurgy, Sorcery, and Infernal Necromancy* (Eastford, CT: Martino Fine Books, 2011 [1911]).
15   Machen, *The Hill of Dreams*, 196.
16   Ibid., 198.
17   Arthur Machen, 'The Literature of Occultism' (1899), in *Arthur Machen: Decadent and Occult Works*, 276–83; 276.

attempts, it was something that he found very difficult to do. Years after the novel was published, he gave a detailed description of the mental anguish he suffered when writing the book. He reflects that in this new style, 'I found I was halting, uncertain, harsh, tautological'.[18] The novel expresses this suffering and confusion. In places it becomes a tortured text that reflects through its prose style the mental suffering of both the protagonist and the author.[19] As Denisoff writes, 'a reaction against literature as a rigid form, language as a corpse' is central to decadence and is a cornerstone of Machen's literary style.[20] In a similar way to the attraction to freer forms of spiritual belief that characterized the occult revival, the novel's indulgence in its own style and highly self-conscious prose can be interpreted as an attempt to capture ideas and experiences that are hidden, or 'occluded', from general knowledge.

At the conclusion of the novel, 'the scattered heap of that terrible manuscript', discovered by Lucian's landlord after his drug overdose, is perceived as the ravings of a mad man – 'all covered with illegible hopeless scribblings; only here and there it was possible to recognise a word'.[21] This is perhaps the only true moment of horror in the novel, as every writer's fear that their life's work is nothing but indecipherable nonsense becomes realized. However, through the lens of decadent magic this ending is more ambiguous. The manuscript emerged from the 'dreadful nonsense'[22] of which Lucian used to talk, and like the novel we have just read, is perhaps indecipherable to the ordinary public neither attuned to decadent style nor open to the spiritual experiences described in the narrative. To the uninitiated, even the most powerful grimoire would appear to be a book of nonsense.

18   Machen, 'Introduction to *The Hill of Dreams* (1907)', quoted in Henry Danielson, *Arthur Machen: A Bibliography* (Folcroft: Folcroft Library Editions, 1973), 38–42; 39.

19   For an insight into Machen's writing process, see *Arthur Machen's 1890s Notebooks*, ed. The Friends of Arthur Machen (Leyburn: Tartarus Press, 2016) which contains 'notes and suggestions' for *The Hill of Dreams* and his contemplation and abandonment of various ideas for the novel, including one page dedicated to writing out 'the hill of dreams' in different fonts; 240.

20   Denisoff, 'Introduction', 9.

21   Machen, *The Hill of Dreams*, 250, 249.

22   Ibid., 249.

Magic and Decadence

Conclusion

The Hill of Dreams follows a similar trajectory to many other decadent literary works. It charts a solitary quest for beauty through literature, dreaming and, finally, escapism through drug use. In essence, like *À rebours*, it is a study of mental collapse. In a comparable way to Des Esseintes' experience with his collections of books, perfumes and hothouse flowers, what begins as an appreciation of strange and natural/unnatural beauty turns into a terrifying nightmare. Lucian's lucidity at the beginning of the novel is replaced with obsessive thoughts, confusion and disconnection from reality. Central to this initial imaginative flurry and subsequent decline are Lucian's magical practices and the novel provides the reader with an insight into how esoteric ideas and iconography become subverted and developed in the decadent imagination. Lucian's despairing search for the divine begins on the hill and ends in the book.

Implicit in Machen's novel is the idea that there is a difference between the stale tastes of the public and the refined ideas of the decadent artist. The idea of the *hypocrite lecteur*, to use Baudelaire's phrase, is a recurrent concern in decadent texts, and Machen's dedication to high artistic and decadent styles, especially in the wake of the Wilde trials in 1895, made *The Hill of Dreams* unpublishable when it was written. Even when the novel was eventually published at the beginning of the high-Modernist period in 1907, it was read as either a piece of *fin-de-siècle* nostalgia or a titillating piece of salacious genre fiction. As Kirsten MacLeod argues, *The Hill of Dreams* was more than just badly received. It was the 'swan song' that marked the end of decadence.[23] As a result, like the spaces and experiences in the novel, Machen has become somewhat of a liminal figure – publishing outside of the English Decadence of the 1890s and at the same time writing fiction that did not fit in with the newly emerging literary style of the early twentieth century. The lingering legacy of *The Hill of Dreams*, however, illustrates that decadence, like magic, is not something that can be contained by temporality. Rather it seeps between the cracks in

---

23   See Kirsten MacLeod, *Fictions of British Decadence: High Art, Popular Writing and the Fin de Siècle* (Basingstoke: Palgrave, 2006), 135–7.

cultural history, re-emerging at times of crisis and change. As the ending of the novel attests, what may appear to be a conclusion could equally be a new beginning: '[T]he flaring light shone through the dead eyes into the dying brain, and there was a glow within, as if great furnace doors were opened.'[24]

24   Machen, *The Hill of Dreams*, 250.

Hayes Hampton

Coil's LP *Scatology* (1984) as a Queer Grimoire

Magic against Homophobia

Coil's 1984 album *Scatology* is an important work of industrial and electronic pop and a milestone in queer culture. *Scatology*'s overarching metaphor is the alchemical process: the transformation of base matter and impulses into the 'gold' of spiritual insight and cognitive freedom. Coil's occult influences were central to their work; lyricist and singer John Balance (né Geff Rushton) was steeped in Western esoteric writers like Aleister Crowley, Kenneth Grant and Austin Osman Spare, and said the band's mission was to create 'sacred music'.[1] Peter Christopherson, Coil's other core member, was previously in Throbbing Gristle, a band heavily influenced by both Crowley and the electronic occultism of William S. Burroughs. Burroughs's experiments with textual and sound sampling were an important influence on Throbbing Gristle and Coil.

In its kaleidoscopic portrayal of sexuality, fetishism, pollution and transgression, *Scatology* follows the structure of grimoires going back to the Renaissance, in particular the ritual pattern set forth by Crowley in *Magick in Theory and Practice* (1929), a book quoted on the album sleeve. Crowley distilled his analysis of ritual from dozens of grimoires and from scholarly sources such as William James's *The Varieties of Religious Experience* (1902) and James Frazer's *The Golden Bough* (1890).[2] *Magick in Theory and Practice* and other

1   John Everall, 'Obscure Mechanics', *Brainwashed*, <https://brainwashed.com/common/htdocs/publications/coil-1995-the_wire-obscure_mechanics.php?site=coil08>, accessed 25 August 2020.
2   Aleister Crowley, *Magick in Theory and Practice* (Edison, NJ: Castle Books, 1991), 210–11.

grimoires typically guide the adept through a process of evoking and banishing incorporeal forces in order to learn, profit and gain power from them. Crowley makes it clear that these forces, while they may have been understood as spirits in past centuries, are equally well understood as psychological and social forces. Released as HIV diagnoses crested in the UK, *Scatology* evokes, in turn, the gay sexual body, delirium and hallucination, occultism and pollution, while conjuring their shadows: the socially constructed, heteronormative body, reason, religion and codes of purity. Through this dialectic, the album banishes homophobic attitudes and symbol systems in favour of liberating ones.

Typically, grimoires are understood as 'books of conjurations and charms' that 'arm people against evil spirits [...] heal their illnesses, fulfill their sexual desires, divine and alter their destiny, and much else besides'.[3] One formative influence on Coil, Burroughs, extended 'conjurations and charms' to recorded sound. Burroughs describes his own experiments with manipulated tape recordings, claiming that 'by playing back [...] recordings' of a location 'when I want and with any changes I wish to make [...] I become God for this locale'.[4] As in traditional grimoires, but using electronic means, Burroughs presents techniques for fighting malign influences; for him, the latter ranged from rude coffee shop employees to Scientologists to politicians.[5] Balance recognized Burroughs as an occult mentor in a 1986 interview: 'Burroughs is a "Brujo" – a shaman in literary clothing'.[6]

Perhaps the most important link joining Coil, Burroughs and Crowley is their shared aim of changing reality via alteration of consciousness. In the sleeve notes to *Scatology*, this project is called 'performing surgery on yourself – psychic surgery – in order to restore the whole being, complete with the aspects that sanitised society attempts to wrench from your existence'.[7] In

---

3   Owen Davies, *Grimoires: A History of Magical Books* (Oxford: Oxford University Press, 2009), 1.

4   Daniel Odier, *The Job: Interviews with William S. Burroughs* (New York: Penguin Books, 1989), 19.

5   Ibid., 17–19.

6   John Balance, 'COIL – Interview from 1986 Plus Introduction', *Datacide* (2009), <https://datacide-magazine.com/coil-interview-from-1986-plus-introduction/>, accessed 30 November 2013.

7   Coil, *Scatology* (Force & Form, K.422, 1984).

different ways, Burroughs and Crowley, the primary influences on *Scatology*, advocated queer liberation; Crowley incorporated homosexual rites into his magical system, while Burroughs's writings more directly confronted Christian morals and heteronormativity – themes important on *Scatology*.

The sleeve notes are the logical place to start when considering *Scatology*'s resemblance to a grimoire, for they reproduce textual features and a central image from works by Crowley. The black sun glyph on the album's cover is taken from Crowley's *Liber Arcanorum* (1912), which contains the sigils of spirits presiding over paths in the Kabbalistic Tree of Life (see Figure 42). Significantly, Crowley's black sun also resembles an anus, reinforcing the album's exploration of gay sexuality and the tension between matter and spirit. In the initial pressing of *Scatology*, the black sun image was pasted over with a photo of a spiral staircase in St Paul's Cathedral, an image later used again on Coil's EP *The Anal Staircase* (1986). This image, like the black sun, mingles profane and sacred, matter and spirit.

Figure 42. Black sun from Aleister Crowley's *Liber Arcanorum* (1912). Reproduced with permission from William Breeze, Ordo Templi Orientis.

Unusually for its era, *Scatology*'s album art is almost exclusively text-orientated. Columns of text occupy almost all of the front and back sleeve, resembling the columns and capital letter headings in *777* (1909), Crowley's compendium of occult correspondences. Balance owned this book by 1983[8] and

---

8　Phil Legard, personal communication, 7 January 2016. All my information about John Balance's book collection comes from Legard's excellent work. See 'For Learning, Not for Show: Esoteric Books from the Coil Estate', in Phil Barrington, ed., *The Golden*

frequently consulted it to help him 'see [Coil's] music in ritualistic terms' and to 'find [...] parameters' for music and lyrics.[9] *Scatology*'s sleeve (see Figure 43) both describes how songs were created and provides quotations and allusions about their subject matter, combining the typical grimoire's 'how-to' instructions with that genre's allusiveness and apophasis in the face of ineffable spiritual experience. A quotation from Salvador Dalí equating shit with gold serves as epigraph for the album's alchemical theme.

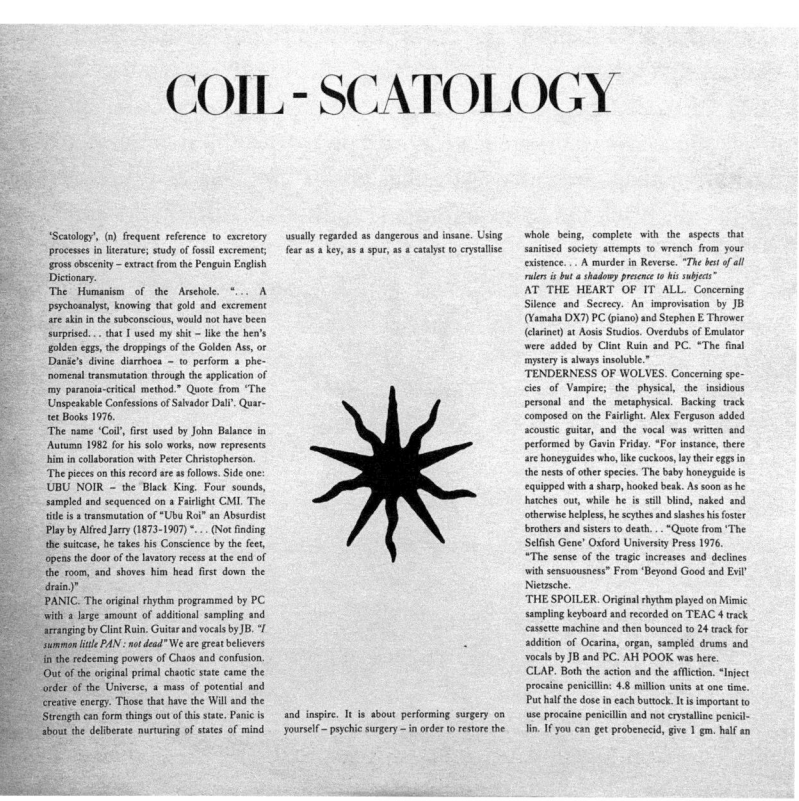

Figure 43. Coil, *Scatology* LP, front cover (1984). Photo by Hayes Hampton.

Age of Bloodsports: The Collected Words, Lyrics and Performed Songs of Jhonn Balance (Barrington Arts, 2015), 319–22.

9   David Keenan, *England's Hidden Reverse* (London: Strange Attractor, 2016), 166.

Scatology begins with the song 'Ubu Noir', a 'conjuration', to use Crowley's term,[10] of Alfred Jarry's grotesque antihero. The lyric sheet reproduces a woodcut by Jarry, an illustration for the play *Guignol* (1891), the first appearance of the Ubu character. The final scene of *Guignol* depicts the 'Apotheosis' of Ubu, at which a chorus sings a hymn identifying excrement with death, night and darkness,[11] similar to correspondences noted throughout *Scatology*. Jarry's woodcut of Ubu shows him floating above the chorus, adorned with a black spiral reminiscent of *Scatology*'s black sun design.

'Ubu Noir' is followed by another invocatory song, 'Panic', whose illustration on the lyric sheet – the god Pan fondling a youth – makes clear the homoerotic, pagan subtext of the song's somewhat indirect lyrics. Pan, in Crowley's system, symbolizes not only rampant phallic sexuality but is associated with the colour black and with death;[12] 'Pan', Crowley writes, 'has the power of destroying all positive manifestation'.[13] Pan and Ubu symbolize what Christianity and mainstream society seek to repress: darkness, death, excrement, sexuality. Ubu, portrayed as the Antichrist in Jarry's *César-Antéchrist* (1895), and Pan, a phallic pagan god, are appropriate 'spirits' to invoke at the beginning of an album that, in its final songs, attacks Christian morality and mythology as homophobic and sex-averse.

Having invoked these twin figures of transgression, *Scatology* offers a third invocation, the improvised instrumental 'At the Heart of It All', marked on the lyric sheet with an Egyptian Eye of Horus. Central to Crowley's magical system, Horus is 'Lord of the Aeon', the 'Crowned and Conquering Child' who abolishes the old Abrahamic codes.[14] Crowley also used the term 'Eye of Horus' to refer to the anus in *The Book of Lies* (1912), from which this song's title also comes.[15] Like the songs before it, 'At the Heart of It All', through its

---

10   Crowley, *Magick in Theory and Practice*, 68.

11   Alfred Jarry, *Les Minutes de Sable: Mémorial* (Paris: Édition du Mercure de France, 1894), 53–4.

12   Aleister Crowley, *777* (York Beach, ME: Weiser, 1986), 7–11.

13   Ibid., 84.

14   Aleister Crowley, 'One Star in Sight', in Israel Regardie, ed., *Gems from the Equinox* (Phoenix, AZ: Falcon Press, 1986), 13–30.

15   Aleister Crowley, *The Book of Lies* (York Beach, ME: Weiser, 1986), 132.

combination of sexual and pagan imagery, sets up the album's banishing, on Side 2, of oppressive Christian social norms.

'At the Heart of It All' begins a suite of songs about gay sexuality ('Tenderness of Wolves', 'The Spoiler', 'Clap'). The songs' sound evolves along an arc of increasing harshness, and the accompanying words and images on the lyric sheet likewise trace this arc, which in Crowley's system corresponds to 'the Bloody Sacrifice' and 'Purification' phases of the ritual. 'Sacrifice' in Crowley's system is a coded term for the spilling and consumption of sexual fluids – a politically as well as magically charged act in the AIDS era. The predatory, parasitic, diseased imagery in this series of songs suggests the constraints placed on gay relationships by 'A moral mean majority / Who'd / "Kill a queer for Christ"'.[16] 'Clap', while an instrumental, is accompanied by sleeve notes quoting the guerrilla medical book *Where There Is No Doctor* (1970), perhaps a reference to gay men's estrangement from the mainstream medical system. An ironic nod to 'Purification', this quotation explains how to cure bacterial STIs.

On Side 2, *Scatology* shifts to triumphant and even more transgressive imagery as the album's sound grows elegiac, portentous. The side begins with 'Solar Lodge', whose title refers to an offshoot of Crowley's magical organization Ordo Templi Orientis that attained notoriety in the late 1960s for allegedly disciplining a child by keeping him chained in a crate. The notes for the song quote Charles Manson's testimony at his 1970 murder trial (the Solar Lodge was spuriously associated with Manson in Ed Sanders's book *The Family* (1971)). The lyric 'See the Black Sun rise / From the Solar Lodge', when read alongside Manson's words about youth rebellion, the story of the confined child, and *Scatology*'s use of the black sun as symbol of queer, liberatory energy, implies that, as Side 2 begins, a new phase of the ritual has begun. This phase resembles what Crowley calls 'Consecration': 'inflame the Will to the proper pitch', he instructs, to form a 'Magical Link' between one's desire and a symbol of that desire.[17] Thus, album cover's black sun is now charged as a talisman. The boy in the box, symbolic of gay men in a society of compulsory heterosexuality, has been set free.

16   Coil, 'Godhead <=> Deathead', *Scatology* (Force & Form, K.422, 1984).
17   Crowley, *Magick in Theory and Practice*, 116.

The remainder of *Scatology* closes the ritual with a 'Eucharist' and then the 'Constraints and Curses' Crowley recommends for binding malign spirits.[18] Crowley's discussion of the 'Eucharist' is heavily informed by alchemy and sexual symbolism, as is *Scatology*, though the latter's 'Eucharist' seems, at first, like a sensational excursion into extreme fetishism. 'The Sewage Worker's Birthday Party', according to Balance, contains 'Sounds of [...] people shitting into each other's mouths',[19] and its sleeve notes contain a lengthy excerpt from a work of similarly themed BDSM erotica. Part of the lovely, elegiac instrumental's alchemical intent lies in the act of turning unmusical sounds into music, or 'making good things from what is perceived as being bad things' as Balance puts it.[20] Another part of the alchemical symbolism may originate from an act of coprophagy performed by Crowley to demonstrate his magical attainment; his account of this event uses the language and symbolism of 'Eucharist' and transubstantiation.[21]

After his ordeal, Crowley proclaims, 'I am indeed High Priest.'[22] After 'The Sewage Worker's Birthday Party', *Scatology* adopts a similarly triumphant tone. The final songs are sonic versions of Crowley's advice about adverse symbols and talismans: 'By destroying these sacred symbols, you can overcome magically the people who adore them.'[23] The 'sacred symbols' in question come from Christian mythology; the song 'Godhead <=> Deathead' assails the Trinity, the virgin birth and the New Jerusalem. Underscoring this assault are the song's martial beat and the quote from Crowley's *The Book of the Law* (1909) in the song's sleeve notes: 'The word of Sin is Restriction.' This quote is juxtaposed with the Book of John's 'In the beginning was the Word', a pairing whose significance becomes clear in the final song, 'Cathedral In Flames'.

18   Ibid., xxvii.

19   John Balance, and Peter Christopherson, 'Coil: *Melody Maker*, 1992', <https://www.brainwashed.com/common/htdocs/publications/coil-1992-melody_maker.php?site=coil08>, accessed 4 May 2015.

20   John Balance, 'Coil: An Interview with John Balance', *Compulsion* (1992), <http://www.compulsiononline.com/interview_coil.htm>, accessed 8 September 2020.

21   Aleister Crowley, *The Magical Record of the Beast 666*, ed. John Symonds and Kenneth Grant (London: Duckworth, 1972), 235.

22   Ibid.

23   Crowley, *Magick in Theory and Practice*, 137.

The burning cathedral is couched in the sleeve notes as 'a vision' had by the Marquis de Sade, who fantasized a world free of the constraints of morality. The song's (and album's) closing line, 'Paradise stands in the shadow of swords', a quotation from the Hadith, is probably adapted from Idries Shah's (writing as 'Arkon Daraul') *A History of Secret Societies* (1962), a book owned by Balance. Shah's book quotes this saying in a chapter on Hassan-i Sabbah, whom Shah claims 'asked' his followers 'to meditate upon' the saying as kind of *kōan*.[24] Sabbah is also written about extensively by Burroughs, who credits him with the insight that social mores are a form of mind control, an opinion reiterated in the work of Throbbing Gristle and Psychic TV, the band that Balance and Christopherson were members of before Coil. Burroughs's use of 'the Word', like Coil's, is pejorative: 'What scared you all into time? Into body? Into shit? I will tell you: *"the word."* [...] I Hassan i Sabbah *rub out the word forever*.'[25] As Balance said shortly before the release of *Scatology*, 'god structure is a macro version of [...] social hierarchy [...] it all leads to ... manipulation of guilt, fear of god, hell and imposed moral structure'.[26]

Thus, the final two songs enact a fiery expulsion of what Balance, echoing Crowley, calls 'an old god' whose 'power is dying' yet whose mythology still 'affects us at school – on television – in the courts of Law – in morality and accepted codes of behaviour. In the very conditioning of our personality.'[27] This ritual expulsion is made necessary by codes of Christian morality authorizing homophobia and its association of gay men with shit, as in the infamous remarks by Manchester Chief Constable James Anderton, who in 1986 'told a conference on Aids [sic] that gay men "were swirling about in a human cesspit of their own making"'.[28] By invoking gods like Pan, adapting the methods of Crowley and Burroughs and confronting the moral codes encouraging homophobia, *Scatology*'s intent is to empower listeners to 'Help bring down the old order [...] to speed on the advent of the New,'[29] and give

24   Arkon Daraul, *The History of Secret Societies* (New York: Citadel Press, 1962), 29.
25   William S. Burroughs, *Nova Express* (New York: Grove Press, 1964), 12, emphasis in original.
26   John Balance, interview, *They're Coming to Take Me Away Ha Ha* (1984), 11–18.
27   John Balance, 'A Letter Interview with John Balance (Coil)', *The Feverish* 4 (1985), 24.
28   Richard Smith, 'Behind the Story – Section 28,' *Gay Times* (2008), <http://www.gayti mes.co.uk/Magazine/InThisIssue-sectionid-650.html>, accessed 1 September 2012.
29   Balance, 'A Letter Interview with John Balance (Coil)', 24.

them the cognitive tools for doing so: a new mythology and a method of 'psychic surgery' rooted in creating and using powerful symbols 'to perform a phenomenal transmutation'.[30]

Acknowledgement
In writing this article I received invaluable assistance from William Breeze, Brian Conniffe, Phil Legard and Terje Øverås. The expertise is theirs; any errors or misreadings are mine.

Magic against Homophobia

---

30   Coil, *Scatology* (Force & Form, K.422, 1984).

Luce deLire

Queer Feminist Witchcraft and Embodied Reason

Figure 44. Alyk Blue, *Mushroom Witches*, 2020. Reproduced with courtesy of the artist.

Introduction

In contemporary queer-feminist culture and politics, the witch is a stock figure of global resistance.[1] 'The reality is that this figure symbolises insubordination and the transgression of normality, and she pays dearly for her alterity.'[2] 'In it are incorporated elements of historical and social fantasy which are sensitive to the underground existence of forbidden images: it is anarchical and rebellious in its rejection of chronology and historical accuracy'[3] (illustrated in Figure 44). This image of the witch motivated her re-entry into the political vernacular of the 1970s in heterosexual feminist circles,[4] and in 'gay and lesbian liberation movements'.[5] This post-68 revival 'is only part and parcel of a larger trend, namely, the vogue of the occult and the esoteric [...],'[6] frequently peppered with exoticism, cultural appropriation and neoliberal exploitation. Contemporary queer feminist witchcraft sets out to sidestep this problematic heritage in manifold ways.

In this essay, I argue that queer feminist witchcraft is historically illuminating and politically empowering. Its main political struggle is against

---

1   On the witch as a symbol of resistance see also the chapter by Daniela Lazoroska in this volume.

2   Anna Colin, 'Introduction', in Anna Colin, ed., *Witches – Hunted, Appropriated, Empowered, Queered* (Paris: Maison Populaire, 2013), 9.

3   Silvia Bovenschen, 'The Contemporary Witch, the Historical Witch and the Witch Myth', *New German Critique* 15 (Autumn 1978), 82–119, 84.

4   Silvia Federici, interviewed by Anna Colin, 'Primitive Accumulation and Witchhunts: Past and Present', in Colin, *Witches*, 25.

5   Colin, 'Introduction', 17; see also 'The introduction to the twentieth anniversary edition' in Starhawk, *The Spiral Dance – A Rebirth of the Ancient Religion of the Great Goddess* (New York: Harper and Row, 1999 [1979]).

6   Mircea Eliade, *Occultism, Witchcraft and Cultural Fashion* (Chicago: University of Chicago Press, 1976), 69. See exemplarily Peter Manseau, 'Fifty Years Ago, a Rag-Tag Group of Acid-Dropping Activists Tried to "Levitate" the Pentagon', *SmithonianMag.com* (20 October 2017), <https://www.smithsonianmag.com/smithsonian-institution/how-rag-tag-group-acid-dropping-activists-tried-levitate-pentagon-180965338/>, accessed 20 October 2020.
     Starhawk, *The Spiral Dance* should be mentioned as a crucial work in the revival of feminist witchcraft.

a violently enforced split between soulless bodies and incorporeal minds. However, practitioners tend to omit philosophical traditions of *Embodied Reason*. This omission re-inscribes the division queer feminist witchcraft aims to overcome. *Embodied Reason* is the way forward – and it is already present in queer feminist witchcraft today.

A Very Short History of European Witchcraft

> The battle against magic has always accompanied the development of capitalism, to this very day.[7]

In the European Early Modern period, labour had become expensive. Years of war and diseases had thinned out the population so that everybody's labour did count. The poor put their power to use: they went on strike, they went for the better offer, they even went to war. The *peasant wars* were essentially a response to the process now known as *original accumulation*: what used to be common property was meant to become private property. Land was fenced in, peasants expropriated, populations re-located, chased into cities. Here, they would sell their labour power cheaply, bereft of the land that had secured their sustenance of centuries. The peasants, however, responded with violence. They took down the fences, threatened their rulers, sometimes they even proclaimed short-lived independence. The ruling classes fought back by extending the playing field.

In order to fight the enemy within, European rulers decided to export the war, colonize and enslave non-European peoples, devalue labour in Europe and acquire resources to end the conflict at home.[8] This, however, was not enough. Besides the devaluation of labour by way of colonial conquest and slavery, capitalism invented its first industrial machine: an army of soulless bodies, severed from their disembodied minds.[9] This process of submission

---

7   Silvia Federici, *Caliban and The Witch* (New York: Autonomedia, 2004), 208.
8   Ibid., 123.
9   Anonymous, *baeden – a queer journal of heresy* (Seattle, WA: Self-Published, 2014), 87.

and disciplining entailed rendering the colony the body of the empire, the proletariat the body of the ruling class and women* the body, men* the mind. The European witch-hunt is part of this overall process.[10] Magic stood in for a world that had to give way so as to enable the intensification of power, the maximization of production, the orientation of life towards the accumulation of capital instead of communal sustenance and the prohibition of 'the non-professional knowledge of the multitude, [...] as it was traditionally practiced by women, colonized peoples, and non-authorized sorcerers'[11] (a process illustrated in Figure 46).

Fluid and Mechanical Bodies

[T]he elimination of wild diversity is never total. The newly internalized divergence often re-emerges in the form of heresy.[12]

Contemporary queer feminist witches mostly understand themselves as 'individuals on the edges of normative culture'[13] and political heirs of these aforementioned struggles.[14] Many are involved in social activism,[15] often on social media. The political traction originates in opposition to the industrialized,

---

10   Federici, *Caliban and The Witch*, 169.

11   Paul Preciado, *Testo Junkie – Sex, Drugs, and Biopolitics in the Pharmacopornographic Era* (New York: The Feminist Press, 2013), 152.

12   Anonymous, *baeden*, 75.

13   Lee Harrington, and Tai Fenix Kulystin, 'Introduction', in Lee Harrington and Tai Fenix Kulystin, eds, *Queer Magic, Power Beyond Boundaries* (Anchorage: Mystic Production Press, 2018), 19; see also Introduction to this text.

14   See, for example, Preciado, *Testo Junkie*, 275–6; Maranda Elizabeth, 'Trash-Magic: Signs & Rituals for the Unwanted', in Katie West and Jasmine Elliot, eds, *Becoming Dangerous* (Newburyport, MA: Weiser Books, 2019), 36; Anonymous, *baeden*, 70; Peter Gray, 'The Manifesto of Apocalyptic Witchcraft', in Breanne Fahs, ed., *Burn It Down! – Feminist Manifestos for the Revolution* (London, New York: Verso, 2020), 286, §§ 1–4, § 8, § 10; W.IT.C.H, 'W.I.T.C.H. Manifesto', in Fahs, *Burn It Down!*, 287.

15   See Deb Chachra, 'The Future Is Coming for You', in West and Elliot, *Becoming Dangerous*, 111 for a pointed example.

mindless machine body (illustrated in Figure 45) by way of reclaiming a fluid magical body (illustrated in Figures 44 and 46) – an opposition which we will now analyse in more detail.

History

In the European Early Modern period, '[t]he body is composed of various *humours,* each of which has different qualities (cold, warm, humid, dry) of variable perfection'.[16] A site of originary *permeability,* it appears open in all directions, constituted by flows and generally porous.[17] It is celebrated in theatrical performance, torture and punishment: while the insatiable fools cannot control their bodily needs,[18] the public execution has bodies broken open as a display of royal power.[19] It is a magical body, susceptible to its surroundings, the stars and invisible powers (illustrated in Figures 44 and 46). It is embedded in 'a dynamic rather than passively gendered society' that (occasionally at least) facilitates abortions, non-marital sex and same sex relations.[20] But 'Magic kills industry'.[21] In fact, '[...] the capitalist organization of work must refuse the

16   Elsa Dorlin, *La Matrice de la Race – Généalogie sexuelle et coloniale de la Nation française* (Paris: La Découverte, 2009), 23.

17   See, for example: Michail Bakhtin, *Rabelais und seine Welt* (Frankfurt Main: Suhrkamp, 1995) and Barbara Duden, *The Woman beneath the Skin: A Doctor's Patients in Eighteenth-Century Germany* (Cambridge, MA: Harvard University Press, 1998 [1987]).

18   Karen Jürs-Munby, 'Hanswurst and Herr Ich: Subjection and Abjection in Enlightenment Censorship of the Comic Figure', *New Theatre Quarterly* 23/2 (2007), 124–35; 131. Alexander Weigel, 'König, Polizist, Kasperle ... und Kleist', *Impulse* 4 (1984), 253–77; 261. Beatrix Muller-Kampel, *Hanswurst, Bernadon, Kasperl – Spaßtheater im 18. Jahrhundert* (Paderborn: Ferdinand Schöning, 2003), 36.

19   See, for example, Michel Foucault, *Discipline and Punish* (New York: Vintage Books, 1995 [1975]), 3.

20   Jonathan B. Durand, *Witchcraft, Gender and Society in Early Modern Germany* (Leiden, Boston, MA: Brill, 2007), xxv.

21   '[...] lamented Francis Bacon, admitting that nothing repelled him as much as the assumption that one could obtain results with a few idle expedients, rather than with the sweat of one's brow.' Federici, *Caliban and The Witch*, 170.

Magic and Queer Feminism

unpredictability implicit in the practice of magic, [...]. The world had to be "disenchanted" in order to be dominated.'[22]

The counter-paradigm is Descartes' mechanical philosophy[23] and its 'bodily machine'[24] (illustrated in Figure 45).

> [T]he heat in the heart is like the great spring or principle responsible for all the movements occurring in the machine. The veins are pipes which conduct the blood from all the parts of the body towards the heart, where it serves to fuel the heat there. The stomach and the intestines are another much larger pipe perforated with many little holes through which the juices from the food ingested run into the veins; [...][25] etc.

This picture became so successful that '[e]ven those who did not follow Descartes saw the body as a beast that had to be kept incessantly under control'[26] – a process applied in various degrees of brutality, bearing names such as 'civilizing mission', 'colonization' or '*Bildung*' (formative education).

> [T]he counterpart of the mechanization of the body is the development of Reason in its role as judge, inquisitor, manager, administrator. We find here the origins of bourgeois subjectivity as self-managements, self-ownership, law, responsibility, with its corollaries of memory and identity. [...][27]

22   Ibid., 208.
23   The mechanical philosophy 'recognise[s] no kind of "matter" in corporeal objects except that "matter" susceptible of every sort of division, shape, and motion, which geometers call quantity, and which they presuppose as the subject-matter of their proofs'. Rene Descartes, 'Principles of Philosophy', in *The Philosophical Writings of Descartes I* (Cambridge: Cambridge University Press, 1985), 247 [II.64].
24   René Descartes, 'Description of the Human Body', in *The Philosophical Writings of Descartes I*, AT XI, 226.
25   Ibid., AT XI, 226–7.
26   Federici, *Caliban and The Witch*, 183.
27   Ibid., 179.

Figure 45. Alyk Blue, *mxchine*, 2020. Reproduced with courtesy of the artist.

Magic and Queer Feminism

Present

This historical picture is mirrored by contemporary queer witch discourse. I will now lay out the general structure of that discourse along four basic elements:

1. The individual must be liberated from external constraints in the form of rationality, discipline, institutions, racism, sexism, transphobia, patriarchy, etc.[28] These 'social constructs strangle

---

28 Elisabeth von Samsonow, *The Scandal of the Autoplastic Mind*, public lecture at Saas Fee Summer Institute of Arts, 16 July 2019 at Spike Berlin; recording on file. Arguably, Starhawk, *The Spiral Dance* played a significant role in publicizing this view in Western discourse. See also Sady Dole, 'Monsters, Men and Magic: Why Feminists Turned to Witchcraft to Oppose Trump', *The Guardian* (07 August 2019), <https://www.theguardian.com/lifeandstyle/2019/aug/07/monsters-men-magic-trump-awoke-angry-feminist-witches>, accessed 21 September 2020; Gray, 'The Manifesto of Apocalyptic Witchcraft', 286, § 26.

individuality'.[29] One of the principle means of oppression is the machine body and its division between an incorporeal mind and a soulless body, which was an integral part of the submission of colonized peoples *and* Europeans. This shared legacy allows for solidarity in a collective struggle (in the West). 'The sex/gender dichotomy, but also the dichotomies of race are neatly mapped over the body/mind, and correspond to an unending set of disciplinary measures and techniques of the self designed to maintain binary conformity'.[30]

2. 'Healing' is liberation as individual self-expression of some inexplicable, a-rational inner force that may be summarized under the slogan[31]: '[D]are to look within yourself [...].'[32] In order to 'heal', we must 'find our own inner pulse, draw out its power,'[33] 'that *inexpressible* moment of queerness [...]. We *cannot comprehend* [it], but we can try to illustrate its contours.'[34] This is to be achieved by way of focusing on 'the relationship each individual has with their authentic self, and their authentic bodies, their ancestral lineage, as well as how their bodies and energies can connect with other physical and energetic bodies [...].'[35]

3. Healing ultimately aims at the erosion of violently enforced dichotomies to different degrees. 'What wonder it would be to take off the projections of others, like clothing, and to just be you,'[36] thriving in 'relations between individuals in their singularity, [...].'[37] Or 'a world

---

29   Orion Foxwood, 'Queer-Fire Witchery: The Rainbow-Flame That Melts the Soul-Cage', in Harrington and Kulystin, *Queer Magic*, 87; see also W.I.T.C.H., 'W.I.T.C.H. Manifesto', 287.

30   Anonymous, *baeden*, 85. See also Maisha Najuma Aza, 'Queering Tantra – A Queer Black Woman's Perspective', in Harrington and Kulystin, *Queer Magic*, 58.

31   See Luce deLire, 'The New Queer – Aesthetics of the Esoteric Left and Virtual Materialisms', *Public Seminar* (2019), <https://publicseminar.org/essays/the-new-queer>, accessed 28 September 2020.

32   W.I.T.C.H., 'W.I.T.C.H. Manifesto', 287.

33   Foxwood, 'Queer-Fire Witchery', 84; see also Gray, 'The Manifesto of Apocalyptic Witchcraft', 286, § 29.

34   Anonymous, *baeden*, 130, emphasis added.

35   Aza, 'Queering Tantra', 52.

36   Ibid., 56.

37   Anonymous, *baeden*, 113.

in which physical beauty is irrelevant to women's self-esteem and self-worth'.[38]

4. The individual must use all means to do so. 'There is one Witchcraft under many names'.[39] A certain eclecticism finds its expression in lists, associative concatenations.[40] Whether a practitioner performs tantra, sex magic, witchcraft or something else is at times a question of personal taste and historical association. Yet again, the individual is key:

> There are two kinds of rituals in the world. The first is to do something once, in a carefully specified way, with the goal of effecting change in the world. The second is to repeat something over and over again, in order to effect change in oneself.[41]

What turns these arbitrary actions into rituals is the intention behind them.[42]

Reclaiming Reason

Unhappy Affinities

It should, however, not be forgotten that witchcraft and magical practices (see 4 above) may be found in various political alignments. Firstly, National Socialism and its heirs show ties with magical practices and their mythologies,[43] which find their contemporary manifestations in Trumpism, QAnon, Corona-denial and

---

38   Laura Mandanas, 'Uncensoring My Ugliness', in West and Elliot, *Becoming Dangerous*, 52.

39   Gray, 'The Manifesto of Apocalyptic Witchcraft', 286, § 16.

40   For example Harrington, and Kulystin, 'Introduction', 19; Anonymous, *baeden*, 6, 20, 49, 62; Preciado, *Testo Junkie*, 27–6; Gray, 'The Manifesto of Apocalyptic Witchcraft', 286; W.I.T.C.H, 'W.I.T.C.H. Manifesto', 287.

41   Chachra, 'The Future Is Coming for You', 111.

42   Katie West, 'Introduction', in West and Elliot, *Becoming Dangerous*, 11.

43   Peter Levenda, *Unholy Alliance – A History of Nazi Involvement with the Occult* (London: Continuum, 2002); Stephen E. Flowers, *The Secret King – The Myth and Reality of Nazi Occultism* (Port Townsend, WA: Feral House, 2007).

other right-wing political religions.[44] All kinds of channels may function as semi-permeable membranes in this respect: 'It appears that several [QAnon related] conspiracies migrated from 4chan to Instagram via YouTube beauty and wellness influencers who used to share content about magic formulas, oils and crystals.'[45]

Secondly, contemporary neoliberal capitalism uses magical practices to increase surveillance,[46] optimize productivity and exploit employees.[47] The

44   For more on this, see: Southern Poverty Law Center, 'Neo-Volkisch', *splcenter.org*, <https://www.splcenter.org/fighting-hate/extremist-files/ideology/neo-volkisch>, accessed 5 October 2020. Jules Evan, 'Nazi Hippies: When the New Age and Far Right Overlap', *Medium* (2020) <https://gen.medium.com/nazi-hippies-when-the-new-age-and-far-right-overlap-d1a6ddcd7be4?gi=c81877a55285>, accessed 21 September 2020. Jan Friedmann, Ansgar Siemens, and Benjamin Schulz, „Keltische und germanische Werte" – Sie sollen Angriffe auf Polizisten und Asylsuchende geplant haben', *Spiegel* (25 January 2017), <https://www.spiegel.de/panorama/justiz/razzia-im-reichsbuerger-milieu-selbsternannter-druide-unter-den-verdaechtigen-a-1131739.html>, accessed 29 October 2020 and NoPeGiDa, 'Karl Burghard Bangert (Burgos von Buchonia) – Reichsbürger und Druide', *NoPeGiDa.Blogspot.com*, <https://nopegida.blogspot.com/2017/01/karl-burghard-bangert-burgos-von.html>, accessed 29 October 2020.

45   Mariel Padilla, 'The 19th Explains: The Spread of Conspiracies and Disinformation by Women on Social Media', *19ᵗʰnews* (19 October 2020), <https://19thnews.org/2020/10/19th-explains-women-disinformation-election-2020/>, accessed 29 October 2020. Cf. Charlotte Ward and Prof. David Voas, 'The Emergence of Conspirituality', Journal of Contemporary Religion 26/1 (2011), 103-121, <https://conspirituality.net/wp-content/uploads/2021/03/Ward-Voas-Conspirituality.pdf>, accessed 01 May 2022; Jules Evans, '"Conspirituality" - the overlap between the New Age and conspiracy beliefs', Medium (17 August 2020), <https://julesevans.medium.com/conspirituality-the-overlap-between-the-new-age-and-conspiracy-beliefs-c0305eb92185>, accessed 02 May 2022; Julian Feeld, Travis View, and Jake Rockatansky, 'Episode 94: The New Age to QAnon Pipeline', in: QAnon Anonymous Podcast, <https://podcasts.apple.com/gb/podcast/episode-94-the-new-age-to-qanon-pipeline/id1428209307?i=1000476575169>, accessed 01 May 2022.

46   See Zach Blas, *Metric Mysticism*, 2019, <https://vimeo.com/320505641> and <https://zachblas.info/works/metric-mysticism>, and Simon Denny, *Secret Power*, 2015, <http://www.simondennysecretpower.com>, Charlotte Higgins, 'Simon Denny, the Artist Who Did Reverse Espionage on the NSA', *The Guardian* (5 May 2015) <https://www.theguardian.com/artanddesign/2015/may/05/edward-snowden-nsa-art-venice-biennale-reverse-espionage>, all links accessed 21 September 2020.

47   Jessa Crispin, 'Thought Capitalism Couldn't Get Worse? Meet the Workplace "Spiritual Consultants"', *The Guardian* (6 September 2020),

systematicity of both affinities is hardly mentioned in queer outputs. However, despite the oppression of the magic body, magic practices themselves do not guarantee progressive politics. Proponents of instrumental rationality may well appropriate the matter. Despite its oppression, is there anything genuinely emancipatory in magic to begin with? This does not mean that rituals and witchcraft cannot alleviate the pain of the traumatized and disenfranchised, that they cannot encourage those facing the police or fascists or both in the streets or elsewhere. But it does mean that a more thorough analysis is in order. Here is a first step.

Embodied Reason

> 'Why did I make a book about rituals?' [...]
> 'Because everything else hasn't worked.'[48]

Surprisingly, the opponents of the Cartesian mechanistic body turn a blind eye on Descartes' natural enemy: Spinoza. The *enfant terrible* of European philosophy might seem like a strange ally for contemporary queer witches.[49] After all, to him, 'superstition' (entailing witchcraft) is the enemy of reason and based entirely on fear.[50] But what exactly does Spinoza mean by *reason*?

> Whereas Cartesianism has long been seen as objectionable by those feminists who seek to valorize the body as a site of knowledge and activity, Spinozism [...] conceptualize[s] bodies as inseparable from minds, [...] affirm[s] reason as 'an active emotion', and [...] understand[s] culture not as an imposition upon inert nature but as something that nature does.[51]

<https://www.theguardian.com/commentisfree/2020/sep/06/office-spiritual-consultants-capitalism>, accessed 21 September 2020.

48   West, 'Introduction', 12.

49   Opposition to Spinoza was a driving force of the European Enlightenment. The counter-enlightenment *and* its moderate counterparts strove to make themselves more agreeable by discrediting Spinoza and thus demonstrating their piety. See Israel, *Radical Enlightenment*, 22.

50   Baruch Spinoza, 'Theological Political Treatise', in Edwin Curley, ed., *The Collected Works of Spinoza, Volume 2* (Princeton, NJ: Princeton University Press, 2016), TTP III/5/25–35.

51   Hasana Sharp, 'Women in Philosophy: Why Spinoza and Feminism?', *APA Online* (13 March 2019), <https://blog.apaonline.org/2019/03/13/women-in-philosophy-why-spinoza-and-feminism>, accessed 8 October 2020.

To Spinoza, body and mind are aspects of the same thing,[52] which is why every conscious affect is the idea of a causal effect on the body.[53] Affects, then, are in no way merely irrational. Their suppression will remain futile.

Besides the disciplinary reason that proclaims war on witches and corporeality, there is thus another kind of reason – *Embodied Reason*. This is noticeable because the expropriation of reason from the body initiates the oppressive division at stake. Only once reason is denigrated into *disembodied* reason, institutions can domesticate it, render the unlearned unreasonable and academics stupid. But a disembodied reason is as powerless as an unreasonable body. Both are instruments of the disempowerment of each and everyone of us. Yet the tacit enmity against reason *in general* that shines through in contemporary queer witchcraft performatively re-inscribes this violent division, which allegedly it opposes.[54]

Cognitive knowledge, however, is embodied power already.[55] Unmistakably, contemporary queer feminist witchcraft echoes this:

> My rituals very much reflect my decision to become the ultimate danger: a white man, or rather, what the white man purports himself to be. What is so galling about these ludicrous attempts to reshape women, to reshape people of colour, to reshape Indigenous, trans, and queer people, is that the standards to which they are held can never be met by oppressors themselves. White men insist upon logic while dismissing emotion, only to irrationally lose their tempers when it is pointed out that anger, too, is an emotion. And in the midst of these demands for reason, they present weak, poorly formed arguments. They paint themselves as near portraits of perfection, while falling dramatically short of their own self-image.

52   Baruch Spinoza, 'Ethics', in Edwin Curley, ed., *The Collected Works of Spinoza, Volume 1* (Princeton, NJ: Princeton University Press, 1985), E2p7.

53   Ibid., E2p13. For a feminist Early Modern version of Embodied Reason that is still very much relevant, see Margaret Cavendish, *Observations Upon Experimental Philosophy* (Cambridge: Cambridge University Press, 2003). See also: Luce deLire, 'Erotics as First Philosophy - Metaphysics and/of Desire between Aristotle, Avicenna, Cavendish and Spinoza', in Ben Gook, ed., *Libidinal Economies of Crisis Times* (Bielefeld: Transcript, 2022).

54   This enmity comes in degrees. See Anonymous, *baeden*, 130, and Gray, 'The Manifesto of Apocalyptic Witchcraft', 286, § 29 for especially clear examples.

55   Compare Federici, *Caliban and The Witch*, 169 for an opposite view.

In an attempt to survive, before I knew that I'd done it, I became what they asked of me. I became soft-spoken; I became committed to reason; on most days, I became even-tempered in the face of conflict. I became the white ideal. And I am so satisfied to be the monster that they have created. I am so satisfied to see how much they pale in comparison. My quiet words only contrast their tendency to shout. My sharp rhetoric only highlights the softness of their foundation. My patience only provides them rope – rope with which they inevitably hang themselves. My rituals serve ultimately to expose their lack of dignity. My rituals serve to let them wither in adequacy. My rituals serve to remind them that nothing they own was deserved.[56]

Rather than leaving reason behind, here, Micheline *reclaims reason* in and through a body under attack, not by *rejecting* the disciplining force, but by appropriating it. Call it witchcraft, call it Spinozism: this *Embodied Reason*, embedded in a particular political context, striving to overcome internal as well as external restrictions, is the way forward.

Figure 46. Alyk Blue, *Manila Cross*, 2020. Reproduced with courtesy of the artist.

56   J. A. Micheline, 'Ritualizing My Humanity', in West and Elliot, *Becoming Dangerous*, 209.

Magic and Queer Feminism

Acknowledgement
Many thanks to Michelle Alexander, Saja Moon, Kyla Greenhalgh, Simon Kubisch, Marian Ochoa, Sophia Raphaeline, Andrea Roland-Rodríguez, Topshelf and Lene Vollhardt.

Daniela Lazoroska

#MagicResistance: Witchcraft on Social Media as Political Activism

Introduction: #MagicResistance

After Trump's 2016 election, the hashtags #BindTrump and #MagicResistance emerged, and a social movement formed. Witches across North America gather monthly and perform rituals to stop Trump from doing harm, which they then disseminate through social media. The witches are a heterogeneous group, but have prominent commonalities, such as leftist political orientation, political engagement and affiliations with nonbinary and queer identities.[1] This essay will explore the employment of magic under the banner of witchcraft as a political practice. As hexes are being performed collectively, filmed and transmitted through social media, protest and witchcraft are becoming intermingled and embody a ritualized modality of political activism. By viewing witchcraft as a political activity, we can understand what it is about witchcraft that has geared political struggles in a manner that party politics fails to. The essay is based on digital observations of social media groups and a literature review.

---

1   Julia Fine, '#MagicResistance: Anti-Trump Witchcraft as Register Circulation', *Journal of Linguistic Anthropology* 0/2 (2018), 1–18, 6.

Anthropological Approaches to Witchcraft and Its Presence on Social Media

Anthropology has had a long-standing engagement with witchcraft, with prominent examples dating to the early days of the discipline.[2] Witchcraft and sorcery are within the discipline used to describe how humans engage with magic, with the term 'witch' as a designation for people accused of practising prohibited forms of magic.[3] Despite the plenitude of anthropological research, the phenomenon is most frequently examined among non-Western peoples. This essay examines how witchcraft is practised in a Western context; in a predominantly Christian, richer, democratic and secular society, where it has been under-researched because it is usually considered to be part of the practices of the 'exotic other'.

While among non-Western peoples, 'witch' is frequently used as an accusation, in the contemporary and Western examples, subjects choose to identify as one. Furthermore, the existing research from Western societies postulates that practitioners can empower themselves as individuals through the practice.[4] This emphasis on self-empowerment ties into the popular representations of the figure of a witch, tending to take on the shape of a solitary and marginalized person, living and practising their craft on the outskirts of mainstream society.

There have been notable forerunners of the contemporary political witches that diverge from this solitary figure, such as W.I.T.C.H. (Women's International Terrorist Conspiracy from Hell), the independent feminist

---

2   Edward Evan Evans-Pritchard, *Witchcraft, Oracles and Magic Among the Azande* (Oxford: Oxford University Press, 1937); Bronislaw Malinowski, *Magic, Science, and Religion* (Garden City, NY: Doubleday, 1955).

3   Pamela A. Moro, 'Witchcraft, Sorcery, and Magic' (2018), in Hilary Callan, ed., *The International Encyclopaedia of Anthropology*, <https://onlinelibrary.wiley.com/doi/full/10.1002/9781118924396.wbiea1915>, accessed 23 September 2020.

4   Susan Greenwood, *Magic, Witchcraft and the Otherworld: An Anthropology* (London: Bloomsbury Academic, 2000); Tania Luhrmann, *Persuasions of the Witch's Craft: Ritual Magic in Contemporary England* (Cambridge, MA: Harvard University Press, 1989).

groups that arose from the women's liberation movement during the late 1960s. Witchcraft is a fluid phenomenon, changing to adjust to contemporary social, political and technological circumstances. Through social media, witches have gained a catalyst for self-expression and a platform for community and growth. Indeed, social media have long enabled the activism of disenfranchised groups.[5] The information age in general has allowed for access to obscure writings, imagery and social contexts in an unprecedented manner.[6] Consequently, contemporary witchcraft practice is characterized by its relative accessibility. Nonetheless, digital space is also filled with contradictions. Recent studies have started to focus on the complexity of social movements' engagement with social media and to examine the tensions that each particular movement materializes.[7] The resurfacing of 'political witchcraft' after the election of Trump links into the polarized debates about the role of the Internet for political engagement. On one hand, it is taken as a source of unprecedented possibilities for user engagement and cooperation[8] and on the other, as contributing to the political segmentation across the world and a movement away from public deliberation and society-wide engagement in democratic politics.[9] The phenomenon herein described offers a nuanced view, as I show how these political witches surpass the self-centred logic of social media and sustain their collective activism.

5 Veronica Barassi, *Activism on the Web: Everyday Struggles against Digital Capitalism* (New York: Routledge, 2013); Veronica Barassi, 'Ethnographic Cartographies: Social Movements, Alternative Media and the Spaces of Networks', *Social Movement Studies* 12/1 (2015), 48–62; Yarimar Bonilla, and Jonathan Rosa, '#Ferguson: Digital Protest, Hashtag Ethnography, and the Racial Politics of Social Media in the United States', *American Ethnologist* 42/1 (2015), 4–17; Aristea Fotopoulou, *Feminist Activism and Digital Network: Between Empowerment and Vulnerability*. Palgrave Studies in Communication for Social Change (London: Palgrave Macmillan, 2016).

6 Occult Humanities, 'About Occult Humanities' (2019), <https://occulthumanitie sconference.org/#about-section>, accessed 10 September 2020.

7 Barassi, *Activism on the Web*, 3.

8 Manuel Castells, *Communication Power* (Oxford: Oxford University Press, 2009); Clay Shirky, *Here Comes Everybody: The Power of Organizing without Organizations* (London: Penguin Group, 2008).

9 Evgeny Morozov, *The Net Delusion: How Not to Liberate the World* (New York: Public Affairs, 2011); Terje Rasmussen, 'Internet and the Political Public Sphere', *Sociology Compass* 8/12 (2014), 1315–29.

Magic against Trump

Witchcraft as a Form of Political Resistance

In 2017, author Michael M. Hughes conjured 'the largest magical working in history' through a spell, titled *A Spell to Bind Donald J. Trump and All Those Who Abet Him* and it started a social media movement with the hashtags #BindTrump and #MagicResistance. Hughes provided witches with an open-source spell to be conducted at midnight on every waning crescent moon. The spell is a binding spell, which has the purpose of stripping the subject of their power and capacity to act. The ingredients include the Tower Tarot card, an unflattering photo of President Trump, a feather, orange and white candles, a pin, water, salt, matches and an ashtray. The witches are instructed to write 'Donald K. Trump' on the orange candle with the pin, arrange the ritual items in a circle and lean the Tower card so that it's standing up and say a prayer for protection.[10] An excerpt of the ritual text follows: 'I call upon you / To bind / Donald J. Trump / So that his malignant works may fail utterly / That he may do no harm / To any human soul / Nor any tree / Animal / Rock / Stream / or Sea.'[11] The witches are further instructed to light the photo of Trump from the flame of the orange candle stub and to speak loudly and with increasing passion as the photo burns 'so mote it be!' One of the larger groups where the bindings are shared is 'Bind Trump (official)', which at the time of writing numbers more than 5,000 members. Members use this platform to share and comment on news related to the forthcoming presidential election; support each other in voting against Trump; discuss the 2020 protests instigated by the violent death of George Floyd; share imagery of their preparations for forthcoming rituals, as well as documentation of ones they have already conducted, et cetera.

The bindings play out in the privacy of homes, as well as publicly. They can be conducted by one person, as well as by groups that gather for the occasion. For example, a public group binding was conducted in front of Trump Tower

10   Michael M. Hughes, 'A Spell to Bind Donald Trump and All Those Who Abet Him: August 17th Mass Ritual', *ExtraNewsFeed* (17 February 2017), <https://extran ewsfeed.com/a-spell-to-bind-donald-trump-and-all-those-who-abet-him-february-24th-mass-ritual-51f3d94f62f4>, accessed 10 September 2020.

11   Hughes, 'A Spell to Bind Donald Trump and All Those Who Abet Him'.

in 2017. At midnight, a small group of people burned photos of Trump and orange candles. An event attendee stated that they hope that 'we collectively have the capacity with our bodies, with our spirits, with our minds to overcome what it is we've been given'.[12] The potential of the collective has also been accentuated by Hughes, who writes that the 'threat from Trump and his cabal is enormous, not just to individuals, but to the collective body and spirit. Be bold! Say the words with ferocious intensity and feel them!'[13] While witchcraft has been portrayed as being an individualist, or even anti-social practice, its socializing power comes to view as it is being employed to confront societal challenges. The actions of these political witches are oriented towards harnessing and changeling power on behalf of a community, rather than for the sake of individual empowerment. The community is achieved through the pursuit of 'ferocious intensity', or the affective engagement of subjects and their bodies in ritual practice. Affect is here understood as the forces that drive us towards movement, towards thought and extension.[14] Affect does not end with the rituals but keeps moving and extending through digital networks. Döveling, Harju and Sommer's work on digital affect cultures introduces a distinction between the levels that digital affect can be manifested, being the *micro*, *meso* and *macro* level.[15] Social media for personal use of these witches has grown into the meso level of groups of resonant individuals, to a wider, macro level landscape of political affiliation engaged in socio-political issues transcending the individual. The entanglement of the affective, the digital and the performative are central to the contemporary practice of political witchcraft in the USA and have spurred the growth and potential of the community.

The online and onsite rituals and public protests represent the witches' pursuit for a 'space of appearance',[16] which is 'the organization of the people as

12 'Watch Witches Cast a Spell at Trump Tower', *TIME* (27 February 2017), <https://time.com/4683033/protesters-cast-spell-trump-tower/>, accessed 10 September 2020.

13 Hughes, 'A Spell to Bind Donald Trump and All Those Who Abet Him'.

14 Melissa Gregg, and Gregory Seigworth, *The Affect Theory Reader* (Durham, NC: Duke University Press, 2010), 1.

15 Katrin Döveling, Anu Harju, and Denise Sommer, 'From Mediatized Emotion to Digital Affect Cultures: New Technologies and Global Flows of Emotion', *Social Media + Society* 4/1 (2018), 1–11.

16 Hannah Arendt, *The Human Condition* (Chicago: University of Chicago Press, 1958), 198.

it arises out of acting and speaking together', so that they can appear as political subjects. For politics to take place, according to Judith Butler, the body must appear.[17] Now, this does not disavow the digital actions of the witches as political. Action is invariably bodily, even in its virtual forms, according to Butler.[18] The rituals performed by the witches, as aforementioned, are inevitably material, demanding the performative engagement of the body and the senses with ritual objects. As Butler further argues, Twitter and other virtual technologies have not led to a disembodiment of the public sphere, as media requires bodies on the street to have an event, even as the street requires the media to exist in a global arena.[19] Following Butler, it can be gathered that the practices of the witches, both on- and offline, constitute the contemporary version of the public sphere. Furthermore, according to Bonila and Rosa, engaging in 'hashtag activism' can forge s shared political temporality,[20] as users that are displaced over space and time can feel united and experience 'public time', a counterpart to public space. Hashtag activism thus provides the witches to experience 'real-time' participation and community.[21]

While certain political scientists and media scholars could position political witchcraft as an index of the fragmentation of political engagement away from public deliberation and society-wide engagement in democratic politics,[22] I argue that it is, in fact, a battle cry for the reformation of these institutions. Issues of race, class, gender, generation, religion, sexuality and reproduction are the fault lines of mainstream political division and struggle in the USA.[23] The witches who have turned their attention towards the Trump administration aim at confronting patriarchy, white supremacy and colonialism. This positioning does not tally with Trump's policies concerning national autonomy, religious freedom, increased police and military spending,

17   Judith Butler, 'Bodies in Alliance and the Politics of the Street', *Transversal Texts* (2011), <https://transversal.at/transversal/1011/butler/en>, accessed 10 September 2020.
18   Ibid.
19   Ibid.
20   Bonila, and Rosa, '#Ferguson', 7.
21   Ibid.
22   Morozov, *The Net Delusion*; Rasmussen, 'Internet and the Political Public Sphere'.
23   Sarah Franklin, and Faye Ginsburg, 'Reproductive Politics in the Age of Trump and Brexit', *Cultural Anthropology* 34/1 (2019), 3.

racial profiling, border control and reproductive politics, which rearticulate a distinctly American legacy of white Christian nationalism.[24] According to Hughes, political witchcraft is

> less a replacement for calling your congressperson than a spiritual companion to that activism [...] A way to keep going, to keep the faith, as it were, in trying times [...] Any progressive social movement needs a spiritual aspect to keep from burning out and to keep people engaged.[25]

Through this prism, we can view the binding rituals as a platform for the expression and affirmation of collective experiences and identities of the engaged groups as well as an enhancement of their agency. Rather than perceiving political witchcraft as a threat to democratic participation, I follow Nancy Frazer's argument that in a democratic society, the public sphere must be characterized by conflictual counter-publics.[26]

Conclusion

The election of Donald Trump as the forty-fifth president of the USA stirred a vibrant modality of activism. Monthly binding rituals are conducted across the states by groups and individuals who aim to bind the president and strip him from his power. These rituals are widely shared online and can thus be positioned within the wider and ever-growing practices of collective mobilization and activism via social media. Witchcraft has enabled people to come together, speak, act and appear as political subjects. It has resurfaced as an appealing mode of political activism and mobilization due to its capacity to stir the affective. While the self-centred logic of social media can be

24 Ibid.
25 Emma Gray Ellis, 'Trump's Presidency Has Spawned a New Generation of Witches', *Wired* (30 October 2019), <https://www.wired.com/story/trump-witches>, accessed 10 September 2020.
26 Nancy Fraser, 'Rethinking the Public Sphere: A Contribution to the Critique of Actually Existing Democracy', *Social Text* 25/26 (1990), 56–80, 61.

challenging for the collectivist cultures of political activists,[27] engaging in bindings onsite as well as online has enabled the witches to partake in a contemporary version of the public sphere and experience a shared political temporality. While academic debates can represent such a phenomenon as a problem for democracy, I have tried to show here that it is, in fact, an essential part of it.[28]

27   Barassi, *Activism on the Web*, 3.
28   Fraser, 'Rethinking the Public Sphere'.

Notes on Contributors

ENRIQUE AJURIA IBARRA is Senior Assistant Professor at Universidad de las Américas Puebla (UDLAP) in Mexico. He has published widely on Mexican Gothic and Mexican Horror Cinema, and is the editor-in-chief of the peer-reviewed online journal *Studies in Gothic Fiction*.

KATARZYNA ANCUTA is a lecturer at the Faculty of Arts, Chulalongkorn University in Bangkok, Thailand. Her research interests oscillate around the interdisciplinary contexts of contemporary Gothic/Horror, currently with a strong Asian focus. Her recent publications include contributions to *B-Movie Gothic* (2018), *Twenty-first-century Gothic* (2019), *Gothic and the Arts* (2019), and *The New Urban Gothic* (2020). She also co-edited three special journal issues on Thai (2014) and Southeast Asian (2015) horror film, and *Tropical Gothic* (2019), and two collections on *Thai Cinema: The Complete Guide* (2018) and *South Asian Gothic* (2021).

BEATRICE ASHTON-LELLIOTT completed her PhD at the University of Portsmouth in 2021 on the autobiographies of nineteenth-century magicians and representations of conjuring in Victorian literature. She is the co-organizer of the Supernatural Cities IV: Magical Cities 2019 conference and recently completed a research placement contextualizing nineteenth-century playbills and periodical reviews at the British Library. Her other research interests include occulture, Romanticism and fantasy fiction.

MARIE BARRAS is an art historian whose research focuses on issues of cultural history, especially the dynamics of gender and power. In her recent work, she analysed the representations of witchcraft in Europe from antiquity until today. She specializes in how and where late Victorian art was exhibited and she studies its reception in various contexts, including Victorian anthropology. In 2021, she was a member of the curatorial team of the exhibition

To play to the gallery. Fashion and portrait at the Musée d'Art et d'Histoire in Geneva. Always looking for new challenges, she completed a Master of Advanced Studies in Cultural Heritage and Museology and a Certificate of Specialization in Digital Humanities at the University of Geneva. She is working as a research assistant at the same university.

ANTJE BOSSELMANN-RUICKBIE FRHistS studied Art History, Classical Archaeology and Christian Archaeology at the University of Bonn, Germany. After her MA in medieval architecture, she wrote a PhD thesis on jewellery, which won her two academic awards (*Byzantinischer Schmuck des 9. bis frühen 13. Jahrhunderts*, 2011). Antje was a member of the academic staff at Mainz University and is currently at Gießen University. She led a research project on Late Byzantine goldsmiths' works, funded by the Deutsche Forschungsgemeinschaft (German Research Fund). She is also joint manager of two international interdisciplinary research projects at the Römisch-Germanisches Zentralmuseum Mainz (RGZM). She has published extensively on medieval arts and crafts, cultural exchange in the middle ages, Byzantium and Heavy Metal, and magic and amulets.

NOEMI DAUGAARD, MA, is a film scholar whose research focuses on the emergence of early colour film technologies (1890–1940) and their interrelationship with cultural norms, discursive practices, and ideological currents, with a specific focus on the representation of human bodies in color film. She is currently working as a scientific research manager at the University of Zurich while writing her dissertation in the framework of the research project *Film Colors. Technologies, Cultures, Institutions,* funded by the Swiss National Science Foundation. She is the author of *Grauenvolle Atmosphären* (2018) and co-chairs the NECS work group 'Color in Film and Media'. Furthermore, she works in media relations, project management and programming for several Swiss film festivals and is on the editorial board of the film magazine *CINEMA – Das Schweizer Filmjahrbuch.*

JOSEPHINE DIECKE-is a postdoctoral researcher in film and media studies at Philipps-Universität Marburg and academic coordinator of the project *Digital Cinema-Hub (DiCi-Hub),* funded by the Volkswagen Foundation

(2021–2026). Her research interests include film and media historiography, media archaeology, moving image archiving and conservation practices and digital methods. After graduating in Film Studies from the Universities of Mainz and Frankfurt in Germany, she supervised and assisted in a number of film digitization projects in the framework of the research project *Film Colors. Technologies, Cultures, Institutions* at the University of Zurich and as film lab technician for German and Swiss service providers. In 2021 she received her PhD with a thesis on the discursive construction of the German color film process Agfacolor. Since 2019 she works as communications manager for the European Network of Cinema and Media Studies (NECS) and since 2021 as co-editor of the *Open Media Studies Blog*.

LUCE DELIRE is a ship with eight sails and she lays off the quay. A time traveller and collector of mediocre jokes by day, when night falls, she turns into a philosopher, performer and media theorist. She loves visual art, installations, video art, etc. She is working on and with treason, self-destruction, fascism and seduction – all in mixed media. For more, see: www.getaphilosopher. com

SARAH FABER's research focuses on games, the fantastic, and nineteenth-century British literature, united by an overarching interest in constructions of gender and identity. She holds a doctorate from Mainz University, where she was a research and teaching associate for five years, and is currently a fellow at Brandenburg University of Applied Sciences.

JESSICA GOSSLING is a fractional lecturer in the Department of English and Comparative Literature at Goldsmiths, where she teaches Victorian literature, decadence, modernism, poetry and literary theory. She is a member of the Decadence Research Unit and she completed her PhD on decadent threshold poetics in 2018. Jessica is co-editor, with Alice Condé, of *In Cynara's Shadow: Collected Essays on Ernest Dowson* (2019) and her chapter ' "Things worldly and things spiritual": Joris-Karl Huysmans's *À rebours* and the house at Fontenay' appears in *Decadence and the Senses* (2017). She has also contributed a chapter on "Decadence and Interior Design" to the *Oxford Handbook of Decadence* (2021). Jessica worked as Editorial Assistant for *Cambridge*

Critical Concepts: Decadence and Literature, ed. by Jane Desmarais and David Weir (2019) and is Assistant Editor for *The Literary Encyclopedia*. She is also Deputy Editor of the international Decadence journal *Volupté* and treasurer of the British Association of Decadence Studies (BADS).

ANNA GREBE graduated in literature, arts and media studies from the University of Konstanz and the Universidad Nacional de Córdoba/ Argentina in 2010. She also obtained her PhD at the University of Konstanz with a dissertation on the visual representation of disability in photography in 2015. Her research focuses on disability studies and visual culture, on youth participation and youth protection in the digital era and on politics of opinion forming and disinformation. She is also a university lecturer for media and gender studies in Berlin, Vienna, Braunschweig and Valparaíso/ Chile, and is currently working as a political consultant and independent researcher in Berlin.

HAYES HAMPTON is Professor of English at the University of South Carolina Sumter, where he teaches writing, American and African American literature, the history of spiritual autobiography, and rhetoric and popular culture. His research focuses on the intersections between religion, magic and popular culture. His most recent publications on Coil appear in the books *Sacred Lands and Spiritual Landscapes* (Tucson: ADF Publishing, 2014) and *Folk Horror Revival: Harvest Hymns* (2018).

DUNJA HAUFE holds a master's degree in British and North American cultural studies from the University of Freiburg, Germany, and is currently working on her PhD dissertation at the same institution. Her MA thesis, titled *Medieval Lays: The Representation of the Supernatural in the Lais of Marie de France*, won the Freiburg Alumni Prize in 2020. She has taught several undergraduate courses on various topics of English literature and her current research focuses on shapeshifters in medieval literature. She is also interested in magic and the supernatural, especially in medieval literatures and cultures, as well as narrative theory and cultural studies.

JASMIN KATHÖFER is working as the assistant to the director of the Institute of Media Studies of the Braunschweig University of Art. She holds a BA in literary, cultural and media studies and art history and an MA in media culture from the University of Siegen. From 2016 to 2019, she was a PhD student in the graduate programme Das fotografische Dispositiv (The Photographic Dispositive) at the Braunschweig University of Art; from 2016–18 a research fellow in the Project Society after Money (University of Bonn). In English, she recently published (together with the project group of the same title) *Society after Money. A Dialog* (Bloomsbury) and 'When loud Weather buffeted Naoshima. A Sensory Walk', in: *Walking, Academic Quarter*, vol. 18/2019.

FRANK KESSLER is Professor of Media History at Utrecht University, The Netherlands, and one of the founders and editors of *KINtop: Jahrbuch zur Erforschung des frühen Films*. He is a former president of Domitor, an international association for research on early cinema. His research mainly concerns the period of the emergence of cinema and nineteenth-century visual culture, as well as the history of film theory. He currently leads a research project entitled Projecting Knowledge: The Magic Lantern as a Tool for Mediated Science Communication in the Netherlands, 1880–1940.

DANIELA LAZOROSKA is a political anthropologist with a particular interest in social change. Lazoroska's research has dealt with the interconnections between social change and agency, subjectivity, embodiment, gender and activism. Lazoroska was granted a PhD in anthropology from the University of Copenhagen for the thesis *Eating the Favela: The Taste of the Good Life in Contemporary Brazil* (2017), where they examined body culture and eating as avenues for acquiring agency for favela youth, and the vulnerability uncovered by their endeavours. Lazoroska has held postdoctoral positions at Lund and Malmö University, and is currently (2022) affiliated with Aoyama Gakuin University in Tokio.

MURRAY LEEDER is an Adjunct Professor in English, Film, and Theatre at the University of Manitoba. He holds a PhD in Cultural Mediations from Carleton University and taught film studies at Carleton 2009–13, and at the

University of Calgary 2014–18. His publications focus on horror, the supernatural and the ghostly in cinema. He is the author of *Halloween* (2013) and *The Modern Supernatural and the Beginnings of Cinema* (2017), and the editor of *Cinematic Ghosts* (2015) and *Refocus: The Films of William Castle* (2018).

ROGER LUCKHURST is Geoffrey Tillotson Chair of Nineteenth-Century Studies in the Department of English, Birkbeck College, University of London. His most recent book is *Gothic: An Illustrated History* (Thames & Hudson, 2021).

ÁLVARO MARTÍN SANZ is Professor of Film Studies at the University of Valladolid. He holds a PhD in media research from the Carlos III University of Madrid. Specialized in non-fiction cinema and memory studies, he has published more than thirty articles in academic journals and he has done research stays at the Sapienza University in Rome and at the Sorbonne University in Paris. He is also a filmmaker whose short films and documentaries have received over sixty awards and have been selected in more than four hundred festivals around the world.

CHRISTOPHER PITTARD is Senior Lecturer in English Literature and Director of the MA Victorian Gothic at the University of Portsmouth. He has published widely on Victorian popular culture, including the books *Purity and Contamination in Late Victorian Detective Fiction* (2011), *The Cambridge Companion to Sherlock Holmes* (2019) and *Literary Illusions: Performance Magic and Victorian Literature* (forthcoming 2022), and numerous articles in journals including *Victorian Periodicals Review, Studies in the Novel, Women: A Cultural Review, Clues* and *19: Interdisciplinary Studies in the Long Nineteenth Century.* He is a member of the advisory and editorial boards for *Victoriographies, Journal of Popular Culture* and the *Victorian Popular Fictions Journal.*

KATHARINA REIN was awarded a doctorate in Cultural History and Theory by the Humboldt-University of Berlin for her dissertation on stage magic in the late nineteenth century. For project, she also received the

Anniversary Prize for Young Researchers by the Buechner Publishing House. She currently works as a lecturer at the Arts and Media Department of the University of Potsdam, Germany. Previously, she worked at the International Research Institute for Cultural Techniques and Media Philosophy (IKKM) of the Bauhaus-University Weimar. She was a member of the international research project 'Les Arts Trompeurs. Machines, Magie, Médias' (Paris & Montréal, 2015–18). Rein is the author of *Gothic Cinema* (2021, forthcoming in English), *Techniken der Täuschung* (2020, forthcoming in English as *Techniques of Illusion*) and *Gestörter Film. Wes Cravens A 'Nightmare on Elm Street'* (2012) as well as the editor of *Illusions in Cultural Practice: Productive Deceptions* (2021). Her numerous academic essays have appeared in four different languages.

THIBAUT RIOULT is a scholar in magic studies. His doctoral thesis investigated the *Illusion of Supernatural and Illusionists during the Renaissance Period: Between Theories and Practices, Technical Conceptions and Social Representations* (Paris, ENS, 2018). He is assistant editor of *Arcana Naturae*, a new journal for the history of 'secret' sciences, and secretary of the French association Magie, Histoire et Collections (the world's oldest association of magic collectors, founded in 1937). He co-led a research seminar on the philosophy of magic (Paris, Collège International de Philosophie / ENS, 2015–18). He has written several research papers and book chapters on illusionism in various fields (performance studies, philosophy, history, media studies, aesthetics, etc.).

LEO RUICKBIE, BA (Hons), MA (Distinction), PhD (Lond), AKC, FRHistS, FRAI, is the author of six books on magic, witchcraft and the supernatural, most recently *Angels in the Trenches: Spiritualism, Superstition and the Supernatural during the First World War*. Actively involved in the parapsychological research community, he is a Council Member of the Society for Psychical Research and a Professional Member of the Parapsychological Association, as well as being a Fellow of both the Royal Historical Society and the Royal Anthropological Institute, and a Visiting Fellow at Northampton University (Exceptional Experiences and Consciousness Studies). In 2021, he was a major prize winner in the Bigelow Institute of Consciousness Studies essay competition on the question of life after death and in 2022 was invited to become one of the Institute's directors. He is also the editor of *The Magazine of the Society for Psychical Research*.

JENS SCHRÖTER, Prof. Dr, has been chair for media studies at the University of Bonn since 2015. Since April 2018, he has directed (together with Anja Stöffler, Mainz) the DFG-research project Van Gogh TV. Critical Edition, Multimedia-Documentation and Analysis of their Estate. Since October 2018 he has acted as a speaker of the research project (VW foundation; together with Prof. Dr Gabriele Gramelsberger, Dr Stefan Meretz, Dr Hanno Pahl and Dr Manuel Scholz-Wäckerle) Society after Money: A Simulation. He is the director of the VW-Main Grant *How is Artificial Intelligence Changing Science?*. In summer 2017, he was a senior fellow of the IFK Vienna, Austria, in winter 2018 at the IKKM Weimar; in summer 2020 a fellow of the DFG special research area 1015 'Muße' in Freiburg, Germany. His most recent publication is: *Medien und Ökonomie* (2019). Visit <www.medienkulturwissenschaft-bonn.de>, <www.theorie-der-medien.de>, and <www.fanhsiu-kadesch.de> for more information.

ROSWITHA SCHULLER is an independent researcher and visual artist. She is a part of Hanakam & Schuller artist duo based in Vienna, whose practice explores and redesigns the rules of the fine arts for particular contexts and purposes. In 2013, Schuller was a fellow of the Academy of the International Research Center for Cultural Studies of the University of Art and Design Linz. She holds a Dr phil. in art sociology and cultural studies from the University of Applied Arts Vienna. In 2012, she graduated with her thesis *Happy Ending Nature. The Role of the Arcadian in Sociocultural Space*. Schuller lectured at the Institute for Art and Architecture IKA at the Academy of Fine Arts Vienna (2019–20), held lectures at Duke University Department of Art, Art History and Visual Studies, Durham, USA (2019), NCCA, Moscow (2015) and ISEA International Symposium for Electronic Arts, Istanbul (2011), to name a few. Schuller's recent fields of research include cultural landscape studies, the Arcadian and art-based research. Her recent publications include: Hanakam & Schuller: *Trickster* (2016), and *The Emblematic Cabinet* (2020).

HANNAH SEGRAVE is a Curatorial Track PhD candidate in Baroque art history at the University of Delaware. A specialist on seventeenth-century Italian art and the Neapolitan painter-poet Salvator Rosa (1615–73) specifically, her research interests focus on issues of artistic identity, early modern art theory, materiality and technical art history, and witchcraft and magic. Her dissertation, *Conjuring Genius: Salvator Rosa and the Dark Arts of Witchcraft*, is an investigation of the artist's corpus of imagery of black magic, and its relationship to Rosa's creative and intellectual development, personal theory of picture-making and self-fashioning as an elite painter in seicento Florence and Rome. She has held numerous curatorial positions and fellowships at diverse institutions, including the Metropolitan Museum of Art, Harvard Art Museums, Cincinnati Art Museum and Virginia Museum of Fine Arts, and she was the curator of the 2015 exhibition *The Novel and the Bizarre: Salvator Rosa's Scenes of Witchcraft* at the Cleveland Museum of Art.

MATTHEW SOLOMON is Associate Professor in the Department of Film, Television, and Media at the University of Michigan. He is the author of *Disappearing Tricks: Silent Film, Houdini, and the New Magic of the Twentieth Century* (University of Illinois Press), winner of the 2011 Kraszna-Krausz award for best moving image book, and of a monograph on Chaplin's *The Gold Rush* for the BFI Film Classics series. He is also the editor of *Fantastic Voyages of the Cinematic Imagination: Georges Méliès's Trip to the Moon* (SUNY Press) and the author, most recently, of *Méliès' Footwear and Film Manufacturing in Second Industrial Revolution Paris* (University of Michigan Press), published open access through the Sustainable History Monogaph Pilot.

JAMY IAN SWISS [<www.jamyianswiss.com>] is a sleight-of-hand artist, corporate speaker and writer. He is the author of six books, contributor to books including co-authoring a chapter with Edward Tufte in *Visual Explanations* and to journals including the *Journal of Neuroscience*. He has lectured to magicians in thirteen countries, to academics and scientists about scepticism and critical thinking and to law enforcement professionals on con games, and consulted on casino game security. As a performer, he appeared on *The Today Show*, *The Late, Late Show*, *CBS 48 Hours* and *PBS Nova*, and in two feature-length documentaries, *An Honest Liar* and *Merchants of Doubt*.

FRÉDÉRIC TABET is Associate Professor in Film Studies at Toulouse 2 University in France. His research focuses on early media practices and their link to stage magic. He is the author of *Le Cinématographe des magiciens* (2018). In 2018 and 2020, he organized international conferences dedicated to stage magic's influence on genre and media.

PIERRE TAILLEFER is a French curator and art historian. His main area of interest is the early history of the conjuring arts and their iconography.

Tabet's and Taillefer's joint publications include: 'Influence de l'occulte sur les formes magiques: l'anti-spiritisme spectaculaire, des spectres d'Henri Robin au spiritisme abracadabrant de Georges Méliès.' *1895. Revue d'histoire du cinema* 76 (2015) and 'Les prestidigitateurs au casino ou les enjeux de l'illusion.' *Revue d'histoire du théâtre* (2017).

STEPHANIE WEBER obtained her doctoral degree in comparative literature at the University of Vienna, Austria in 2019. Her dissertation deals with the uncanny quality of freak characters and uncanny narrative strategies in post-modern literature. She is currently an independent scholar and a member of the work group Hautbilder/Skin Studies based at the Department of Social and Cultural Anthropology, University of Vienna. Her research interests are tattoos, body studies, popular culture, narratology and psychoanalysis.

MICHAEL WEDEL studied German literature, history and philosophy at the Free University Berlin and Film and Television Studies at the University of Amsterdam and obtained his PhD in 2005. From 2001 to 2005, he worked as a researcher and lecturer in Media Studies at the Konrad Wolf Film University of Babelsberg; from 2005 to 2009 as an assistant professor for the history and theory of media at the University of Amsterdam. Since 2009, he has been Professor of Media History in the Digital Age at the Film University Babelsberg and since 2015 Co-Director of the Cinepoetics – Center for Advanced Film Studies at the Free University Berlin (together with Hermann Kappelhoff). Since 2016, he has been a member of the founding directorate of The Brandenburg Centre for Media Studies (ZeM).

Index

Genre Fiction and Film Companions

Series Editor: Simon Bacon

The *Genre Fiction and Film Companions* provide accessible introductions to key texts within the most popular genres of our time. Written by leading scholars in the field, brief essays on individual texts offer innovative ways of understanding, interpreting and reading the topics in question. Invaluable for students, teachers and fans alike, these surveys offer new insights into the most important literary works, films, music, events and more within genre fiction and film.

We welcome proposals for edited collections on new genres and topics. Please contact baconetti@googlemail.com or oxford@peterlang.com.

Published Volumes

The Gothic
Edited by Simon Bacon

Cli-Fi
Edited by Axel Goodbody and Adeline Johns-Putra

Horror
Edited by Simon Bacon

Sci-Fi
Edited by Jack Fennell

Monsters
Edited by Simon Bacon

Transmedia Cultures: A Companion
Edited by Simon Bacon

Shirley Jackson
Edited by Kristopher Woofter

Toxic Cultures
Edited by Simon Bacon

Magic: A Companion
Edited by Katharina Rein